# The International Design Yearbook 1994

# The International Design Yearbook 1994

Editor **Ron Arad**  General Editor **Jeremy Myerson**  Assistant Editor **Jennifer Hudson**

**Laurence King**

Published 1994 by Laurence King Publishing
Copyright © 1994 Calmann & King Ltd and Abbeville Press, Inc.

A catalogue record for this book is available from the British Library.

ISBN 1 85669 048 2

Based on an original idea by Stuart Durant
Designed by Neville Brody and Giles Dunn for Neville Brody Studio, London
Printed in Singapore

Jeremy Myerson

# Foreword

There has been a growing and pervasive trend in recent years to argue that design is nothing without its context, to suggest that objects owe everything to the surrounding cultural, economic and social conditions which shape their form and define their content. Whether a chair, a light, a kettle or a camera, everyone strives to name the broader national characteristics, aesthetic movements or technological imperatives which help to pigeonhole the design. It is not just critics and academics who have sought to contextualize objects; designers too have been happy to jump on a bandwagon which legitimizes their work and makes it easier to discuss and promote.

In this climate of context above all else, what happens to the individualistic ideas of those designers whose objects owe almost nothing to broader trends and almost everything to personal invention and vision? Ron Arad could be said to be such a designer, and it is fitting that his guest selection for the ninth edition of *The International Design Yearbook* is underscored by his belief that what really matters are the objects and the individuals who create them, not the social or economic conditions in which they are created.

Arad could not care less about the bigger picture – the status of design cities or the credibility of design movements. He focuses on each individual design in a single-minded way to see what it says about the convictions of the person who has created it. This, then, is a book as much about people as it is about design – about their preoccupations and beliefs, and the way they express them through the artefacts they create.

Arad's selection is defined by his interest in fresh ways of seeing and making objects, and in methods which utilize new technologies and materials. The banal, the dully professional, the "safe" and competent are banished. What inspires Arad is the idea that somehow the individual is trying to break new ground, to communicate, to engage with the user, to say something fresh.

By divorcing the designs from contextual trends and assessing each object on its own merits, Arad avoids an over-emphasis on youth or on famous names. The mix of designers in the selection is a richly intriguing one, with an older generation of designers – represented by such names as Nanna Ditzel, Knud Holscher, Ettore Sottsass, Gaetano Pesce, Takenobu Igarashi, Kenneth Grange and Robert Heritage – rubbing shoulders with newer talent. Johanna Grawunder, Karim Rashid, Toby Russell, Casimir Reynders, Yasuyuki Hirai and others undoubtedly send a shot of freshness and vitality through international design; but the ability to innovate is by no means confined to the newer ranks, as Ditzel's furniture with flexible veneers or Holscher's seashell-styled spotlights demonstrate so clearly.

Only in one category – textiles – does Arad select designers within a more narrow and youthful age range. Here, though, his fascination with new techniques and materials perhaps informs his choice more forcefully than anywhere else. Helle Abild's use of computer scanners to develop repeat patterns from industrial components and Reiko Sudo's use of chemicals to burn fabric and create layered effects represent some of the most eye-catching work.

Such technological innovation in textile design is more than matched in other disciplines presented in this edition of the *Yearbook*. In tableware, for example, Gaetano Pesce's molten, deconstructed glass bowls reflect six new techniques in designing with glass – the results of his experiments for a French government agency. In furniture, Philippe Starck's extruded plastic shelving system for Kartell, *Booox*, presents the translucence of the material in a new way. In lighting, Tom Dixon's wobbling, shadow-casting *Spiral Uplighter* explores the kinetic dimension of the object. In product design, new techniques and materials abound – whether in the latest notebook computers and camcorders, or in the textured wall tiles of Masatoshi Sakaegi and semi-invisible titanium wire spectacle frames of Dissing and Weitling.

Arad's fascination with technical innovation is not in any way confined to new or advanced technologies, however, as is evident in his inclusion of graphic vases by Japan's Takenobu Igarashi which utilize the ancient metalworking techniques of Tsubame City, or the wicker furniture of Germany's Jan Armgardt which breathes new life into a traditional craft.

Behind Ron Arad's selection one can perhaps see a desire to highlight the poetic within the pragmatic artefacts of contemporary design, to look at the sheer volume of technology and production laid out before the guest editor and find the qualities of human thought and spirit at its heart. A central theme, not only of this book but of design over the past couple of years, has been the concern to find a way to humanize our ever-advancing technological age, to counterpoint the vast sweep of mass markets and mass production with a rediscovery of craft in conceiving and making the objects we use. Whether it takes new loops in advanced technology, such as flexible manufacturing systems, to achieve design with greater individuality, sensuousness, spirit, meaning and variation, or simply a revival of time-honoured techniques lost or abandoned in the modern era, it is hard to say. Both approaches are highlighted in this edition of *The International Design Yearbook.*

In a discipline such as furniture, where a strong element of craft making survives in the object, such a concern is less acute. In products, however, where multinational manufacturers face growing consumer apathy to anonymous, technical "black box" or "white box" design, such projects as Doug Patton's expressive hand-held remote controls or Marco Susani and Mario Trimarchi's new tools for the kitchen, based on old rituals and comfortable materials, have a special resonance in the search for a craft dimension to technological objects. The big manufacturers – Siemens, Toshiba, Philips and so on – are certainly trying to find a new direction, as prototype telephones, appliances and audio-visual equipment in the *Yearbook* demonstrate.

This search for a new humanizing design language in a sense overrides the increasingly meaningless debate about Modernism and Post-Modernism in international design. Arad sidesteps it altogether. He is attracted to the functional, and impatient with the decoratively useless. Yet he finds most of the conventionally accepted icons of "good design" – those pure lines devoid of ornament – boring and sterile. Only when objects are given a twist, such as Ursula Munch-Petersen's playful tableware for Royal Copenhagen, the impeccably functionalist Scandinavian manufacturer – do they qualify.

Many people, of course, are greatly attracted to the classic pioneer era of twentieth-century Modernism, and 1993 turned out to be a vintage year for classic modern reproductions – from Walter Gropius floor-coverings by Vorwerk to Frank Lloyd Wright's Johnson Wax furniture by Cassina. Arad passed them over, not because he thought such work was bad or without its place, but because he was making a selection of what was new in 1993, rather than a twentieth-century design selection; he believed that there was enough fresh talent and ideas around to justify their exclusion. One is reminded of a machine he built for a show at the Beaubourg in Paris in 1987. It was a monstrous metal compactor intended to crush all the Lloyd Wright, Breuer and Hoffmann chairs to make room for a new generation of furniture designers. Only when the classics were in miniature – such as those limited edition miniatures produced by Vitra and Woka – did Arad allow them into the book.

Harking back to the past is precisely the type of contextual trend which Arad does his best to escape. Nevertheless, it is impossible to totally ignore the fact that the period from which the designs in this book are drawn is rich in contextual change. International design has become accustomed to its own new world order. Bust followed boom. Environmental concerns made excessive style in production embarrassingly redundant. Functionality replaced the superficial go-faster stripes of style-addicted design in the 1980s. Arad's selection cannot help but reflect all of this is some way, however unconsciously, whether in the recycled materials of certain furniture or glassware pieces, the old newsprint bonded into new textiles, or poor materials such as Velcro strips or milk bottles incorporated into the latest light fittings. Lighting designs by King Miranda or Tejo Remy in particular reflect what has been called the "new modesty" in international design, a use of the old and the borrowed to create something new in an age of anxiety about the excesses of production.

Fears about the environment and the economic downturn have risen concurrently in design, spiralling into one another at different times. Ron Arad made his selection for this book just as the British and American economies were beginning to drag themselves slowly out of the recession, while the German, Italian, French and even Japanese economies were sliding into the industrial mire, accompanied by growing political instability and uncertainty. One can sense a certain anxiety in the way the industrial giants are looking again to the stylists to stimulate sales, just as they did in the early 1930s. Then Raymond Loewy and his peers came to the rescue, with the streamlined form to the fore. It is much harder to discern what single theme or style will constitute salvation for manufacturers this time around. There are certainly many objects in the *Yearbook* we would all aspire to own, but too many remain at prototype stage or in the realms of limited batch production, as manufacturers baulk at taking a gamble on their own future and continue to produce the type of design which sold in the recent past. Arad does not concern himself for a moment with the economic context, but it is there all the same. Even in those objects which reflect the triumph of individual will over materials and technologies (what three-dimensional design is really all about), there are economic questions in the background. When, following the personal tragedy of a car accident, Japanese designer Kazuo Kawasaki set out to create the perfect wheelchair, *Carna*, he had to overcome the high innovation costs attendant on a limited market. British designer-inventor James Dyson has chosen to take his championing of cyclonic technology in vacuum cleaners all the way by manufacturing and marketing his own *Dual Cyclone* product. Perhaps what really commends Ron Arad's selection is the way it says so much about the market pluralism of the age while refusing to play the contextual games of the design critic.

**Ron Arad**

# Introduction

**1.** Bookshelf *Bookworm* 1993
Sprung steel, fake books acting as brackets
Manufacturer: Ron Arad Associates

**2.** Chair *Transformer* 1982
PVC, unexpanded polystyrene beads
Air is removed by suction to provide a vacuum-packed chair that retains the shape of the sitter.
Manufacturer: One Off

**3.** *School Chair* 1988
Aluminium, rubber
Manufacturer: Vitra International, Switzerland

In my role of Guest Editor of *The International Design Yearbook* I was expected to reduce a mountain of slides that poured in from around the world to a book's worth of a selection that made some sense. This seemed an impossible task. I have no direction to point towards, nor do I have the urge to classify trends and fads, summing up the year's design in captions. I am deeply suspicious of people who do. I remember how in the mid 1980s *Face* magazine (and its satellites) promoted the use of matt black in the home as well as in the wardrobe, only to ridicule it as *passé* twelve issues later. Who are these people to take colour away and then give it back?

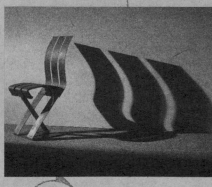

**4.** Carpet chair *Full House* 1987
Aluminium
An aluminium "carpet" winches up to become two chairs facing each other.
Manufacturer: One Off

**5.** *Well-Tempered Chair* 1987
Temper-rolled stainless steel
Manufacturer: Vitra International, Switzerland

I do not subscribe to any design religion. I have taken equal inspiration in my own work from things as engineered as a Prouvé chair or as expressive as a Pesce table. I am interested in objects and the individuals who create them, more than in the ever-changing social or economic climate that brought them about. I do not care if Milan is down, Barcelona is up, or if the Scandinavians have lost it forever or regained it. I cannot tell you on the basis of my selection about the state of international design today; I have never lived and worked in a different period, so I cannot really say. What I can say is that out of this year's crop of designs, I made a small personal selection of objects which for one reason or another attracted my attention. It is only in the strength of my own enthusiasm for individual ideas, shapes and processes that I could make any inclusion or omission. Oscar Wilde once wrote: "It is absurd to divide people into good or bad. People are either charming or tedious." I feel the same way about design – it either charms me or escapes me.

My initial instinct to deal with the task of selection was to publish each and every work that was submitted prior to the deadline, providing it met the criteria set down by the publisher for one of the different categories of the book. The allocated number of pages would then have been divided equally according to the number of knives and forks, cameras, clocks etc. Although the material sent in for selection was already "selected" to a great extent (companies chose to produce it, market it, individuals chose to make it, photograph and caption it), it could still be a record of what was happening in design in the past year. For publishing and production reasons my scheme proved impractical. So I reluctantly agreed to make the selection within the existing conventions of the book.

There are a few further points that should be made about this selection. First of all it represents a minority of a minority of the great mass of products that are manufactured around the world, and it should be seen in that context. For example, people refer to Richard Sapper's *Tizio* desk light as the best-selling light of all times. It is not. It is simply the best-selling light within the design community.

6

7

8

**6.** Chair *Big Easy Volume 1* 1988
Inital prototype for the *Rolling volume*. Weighted and balanced with sand
Manufacturer: One Off

**7.** Chair *Big Easy Volume 2* 1989
A hollow volume in black or stainless steel
Manufacturer: Ron Arad Associates

**8.** Chair *Rolling volume* 1989
A streamlined rocking chair weighted with lead
Manufacturer: Ron Arad Associates

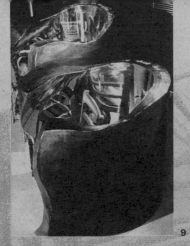

9

**9.** *Chair by its Cover* 1989–90
Highly reflective stainless steel
The curved mirror forms the armrests and reflects
endlessly changing distorted images of the chair.

**10.** *Tinker Chair* 1988
Mild steel, stainless steel

**11.** *Rover Chair* 1981
Rover car seat, tubular steel

**12.** Floor lamp, *Shadow of Time* 1986
Steel
The light projects a working clock face on to the
ceiling or wall.

**13.** Table lamp *Aerial Light* 1981
The aerial is multi-directional and extends to
100cm (39in). All functions are controlled by a
separate hand-held unit.
12v halogen bulb

10

11

12

13

When looking at the objects in my selection,
it is also important to bear in mind the fact that
they represent luxury. The world would be no
worse off if no new chairs were produced and
people had to make do with, say, the chairs in
the Thonet catalogue. The range there is wide
enough to meet all basic needs. Most new
designs are surplus to requirements and
therefore, though design objects do fulfil
a function, their main *raison d'être* is not purely
functional. Like music and fine art, they are there
to enrich our lives. The beauty of a car may be
best appreciated when there is no petrol in the
tank. This is not to say that the delight an object
gives is exclusively visual: comfort, performance,
wit, manufacturing ingenuity, economy or
richness of means can all be vital ingredients.

When we have such great market segmentation
and media fragmentation (it is difficult to imagine
a new "event" like the Beatles happening again,
when we no longer rely on the one radio or TV
station, but can tune in to many according to our
taste and culture), it is surprising when a newly
designed object becomes generic. This may
happen more in the products category, where
the technological race and giant market forces
act as catalysts and help to crystallize these
new generics.

I do not think there should be a moratorium
on ornament and decoration. However, in the
tableware category, I found myself more
interested in designers who create austere,
minimal objects.

When I came to look at the textiles category,
I was an outsider, a layman. I did not know the
names and had no background knowledge of
either the techniques or the history. I selected
purely on gut feeling, reacting to the patterns on
the page. It was interesting to be informed later
that the designers whose work I chose to feature
form a tightly knit group and belong to a narrow
age band.

14

15

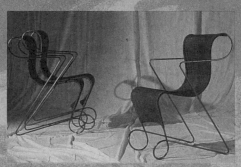

16

14. Rocking chair *Size 10* 1988
Stainless steel, mild steel
Part of the first *Volume* collection of 1988.

15. *Misfits* 1993
Manufacturer: Moroso, Italy

16. *Schizzo Chair* 1989
One chair that splits into two almost identical chairs.
Manufacturer: Vitra International, Switzerland

17. Chair *Zigo* 1993
Burnished steel rod, rattan
Manufacturer: Driade, Italy

18. Chair, *Heart and Industry* 1990
Mirror-polished steel
Manufacturer: Structure Design, Switzerland

17

18

**19**

**20**

**23**

**21**

**22**

After the selection meeting I was asked whether I was depressed by the exercise of sifting through an entire year's entries. The only depressing aspect was seeing a lot of misplaced energy put into ideas which are non-starters. Going through the entries was no different from walking through the Milan or Cologne Fair where you have to walk miles to find the few jewels. Not depressing, but to be expected.

## The jewels in this selection

The production technique behind Pietro Arosio's *Mirandolina* chair for Zanotta (page 54) involves taking a piece of pre-cut flat aluminium and bending and stamping it into a chair in one stroke. There is a charm in the simplicity, economy and limitations of this process which I, with my own bucket-and-spade metal workshop, appreciate. There is something optimistic about machine production – tooling reflects a belief in the design, it shows that someone is serious about it and is willing to take the risk of investing in it. Design is all about imposing one's will on materials, and the Zanotta metal-stamping machine is the culmination of this process.

Philippe Starck's *Booox* shelving system for Kartell in recycled translucent coloured plastic is totally industrial and yet completely poetic (page 72). Plastic pigeonhole-style shelving has a distinct heritage in the post-war Italian design scene through Kartell's work: Simon Fussel and Anna Castelli Ferrieri have produced memorable work in this area in the past. But somehow Starck manages to take a familiar object and completely reinvent it with a different feel, light and colour quality. It demands a certain touch to take a simple grid of shelving and create a totally new product. Starck's use of extrusions and components such as integral sprung hinges and translucent supports produces an entirely new look.

Gaetano Pesce's glass bowls made out of recycled bottles (pages 124, 146–7) – the result of his technical experiments for the French government agency CIRVA (Centre International de Recherche sur le Verre et les Arts plastiques) – fascinate me because they have not lost their past. Pesce has always been an outsider, and I find there is something romantic in his view of what designers do. This design is based on new technology and old materials. There could be a choir of people singing "This is not design" about Pesce's work. The products of his creativity more often than not result in amazingly beautiful objects. He is still taking risks. He has not been tamed over the years.

Gijs Bakker's perforated wallpaper (page 30) reveals and frames the previous wall surface. Bakker's current theme in furniture and furnishings is holes. In making a hole he takes something away, he reduces – but in that same process of reduction, he also reveals.

**Ron Arad Associates. Chalk Farm Studios, London**

**19.** One of seven calligraphic steel columns supporting expanded metal and PVC roof

**20.** Bridge/air conditioning duct connecting landscaped wooden floor of gallery with mezzanine office

**21.** Aerial view of PVC roof and steel east wall

**22.** Hollow wall with "negative" column supporting bridge and mezzanine

**23.** Cantilevered steps to mezzanine, welded to east steel wall

**24.** Soft PVC windows between calligraphic steel columns

**25.** Furniture display on steel bridge/air conditioning duct. Expanded steel and PVC roof

**26.** Close-up on junction of column, curved beams, patterned expanded metal and PVC roof and PVC soft windows

BOOKSHOP

**27**

**28**

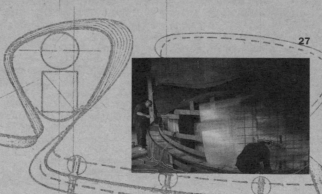

24

25

26

29

30

31

**Tel Aviv Opera House Foyer Architecture**

**27, 28.** Construction work on the Tel Aviv Opera House Foyer, January 1993

**29, 30, 31.** Construction work on the Tel Aviv Opera House Foyer

All architectural projects by Ron Arad and Alison Brooks, Ron Arad Associates Ltd.

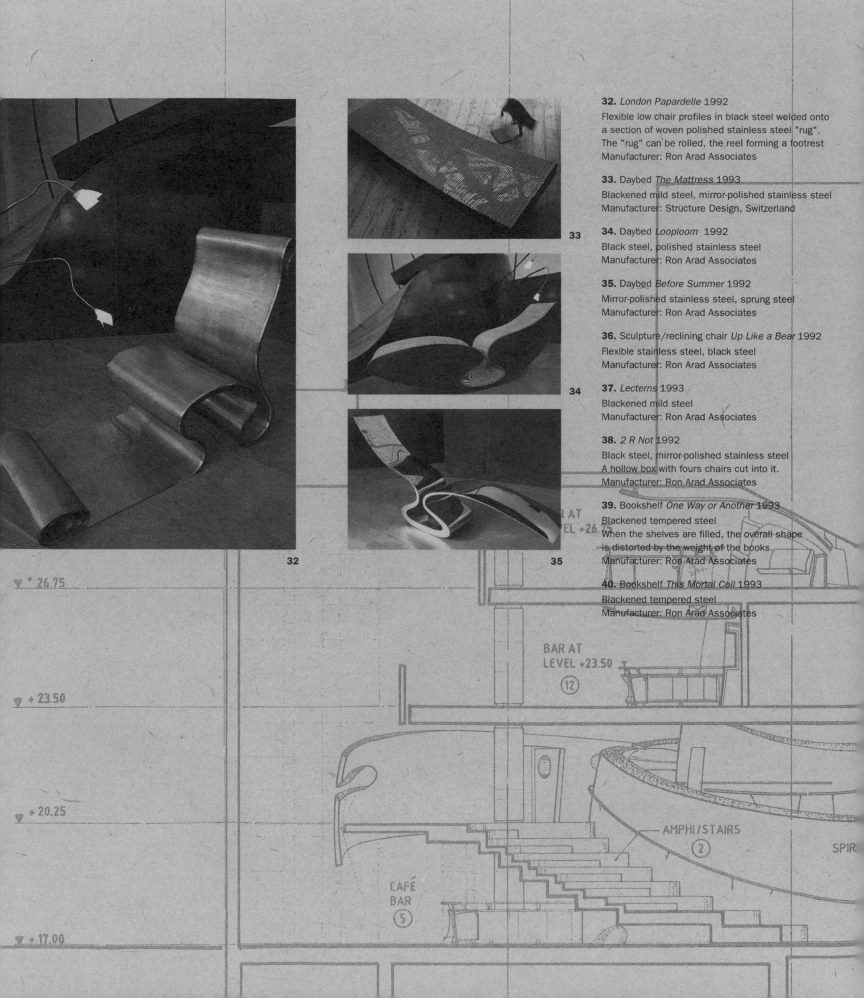

**32.** *London Papardelle* 1992
Flexible low chair profiles in black steel welded onto
a section of woven polished stainless steel "rug".
The "rug" can be rolled, the reel forming a footrest
Manufacturer: Ron Arad Associates

**33.** Daybed *The Mattress* 1993
Blackened mild steel, mirror-polished stainless steel
Manufacturer: Structure Design, Switzerland

**34.** Daybed *Looploom* 1992
Black steel, polished stainless steel
Manufacturer: Ron Arad Associates

**35.** Daybed *Before Summer* 1992
Mirror-polished stainless steel, sprung steel
Manufacturer: Ron Arad Associates

**36.** Sculpture/reclining chair *Up Like a Bear* 1992
Flexible stainless steel, black steel
Manufacturer: Ron Arad Associates

**37.** *Lecterns* 1993
Blackened mild steel
Manufacturer: Ron Arad Associates

**38.** *2 R Not* 1992
Black steel, mirror-polished stainless steel
A hollow box with fours chairs cut into it.
Manufacturer: Ron Arad Associates

**39.** Bookshelf *One Way or Another* 1993
Blackened tempered steel
When the shelves are filled, the overall shape
is distorted by the weight of the books.
Manufacturer: Ron Arad Associates

**40.** Bookshelf *This Mortal Coil* 1993
Blackened tempered steel
Manufacturer: Ron Arad Associates

32    33    34    35

36

37

38

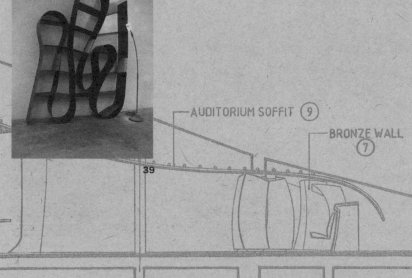

39

40

AUDITORIUM SOFFIT 9

BRONZE WALL
7

41

Denis Santachiara uses electronics and technology as other people use raw materials (pages 44, 46, 106–7, 194, 202). For example, he recently designed a rocking chair with a side-table attached: when the chair rocks, the table remains stable and parallel to the floor. It was an impossible image for which Santachiara found a solution. That sums him up. Ideas and inventions are everything, but the forms and shapes are often not the priority. It is almost as if he is saying: "It is not about creating pretty shapes. I don't want to upstage the idea with the pretty form."

Whereas other designers take the forms of furniture as their subject matter on which they play with variations, Marc Newson brings new shapes and forms to furniture. His *Event Horizon* table and *Felt Chair* (pages 22, 86) offer some interesting new thoughts on structure that have more to do with organic sources than with fifties nostalgia.

There is an experimental quality to the work of Yaacov Kaufman, so it is a nice surprise to see design research go into production (page 35). His experimental pieces have a different starting point to most furniture and the final products look like sketches yet to be developed.

Karim Rashid's work has a quality and flavour of the kind that I do not often see in either European or American magazines (pages 60, 100, 143, 174). He takes a phenomenological approach to designing, basing his work on the idea and experience of the object, not its physical presence. His is a family of objects whose form you cannot automatically classify as belonging to one school or another. The work is gentle and delicate, with small gestures and minimal effort. Yet it is also memorable, reflecting the strange motivations behind Rashid's clocks and chairs.

Ingo Maurer (pages 104–5) is probably the only designer who could get away with attaching bird wings to lightbulbs, touch dimmers to tin foil. The mass-manufactured industrial light looks as if it was just assembled *ad hoc* by an artist, and with that it is the light itself that matters – not the fitting.

Just as we thought that the clock was exhausted as a medium for new ideas, Andreas Dober has produced a genuinely new one (page 173): the figures themselves travel up and down on a continuous chain. This is an optimistic place to end my foreword – with a new designer, a brilliant new idea, a wonderful object and an endless chain of time.

**41.** *Up Like a Bear, Looploom, Looploop* and *London Papardelle*

**42.** *Strict Family Chairs* 1991
Polished stainless steel, black steel
Daybed, *Colour of a Running Dog* 1991
Mirror polished stainless steel, sprung steel strip

**43.** Detail of hollow wall with "negative" column cut-out, supporting bridge and mezzanine office.

42

# Furniture | 19

If furniture design provided the benchmark for radical creativity and commercial buoyancy in the 1980s, in the 1990s it has become the barometer for a growing conservatism and, in some parts of Europe at least, a crisis of confidence. In 1993 both the Cologne and Milan furniture fairs took place in a muted atmosphere: the German show opened just as the full costs of reunification were being realized and Europe's strongest economy was grinding into recession; the Milan *Fiera* began on the very day Italians voted in a national referendum for constitutional change.

Comfort, commercial viability and fitness for purpose have replaced the capacity to unsettle and shock as the chief *raison d'être* for new pieces. Function is back with a vengeance: tables fold, chairs stack, trolleys glide. Not all the practicality is entirely necessary, however. As Ron Arad remarked of one submitted design: "Two-seater sofas don't need to stack." The move towards environmentalism reflected in previous editions of *The International Design Yearbook* gathers pace in Arad's selection. The new desire to recycle materials and not just ideas is caught in a wide range of work. Kartell, for example, declared that it is "reconsidering its own history and starting to rewrite it" by reissuing its classic Gino Colombini wastepaper bins in recycled plastics. Even a designer so closely identified with the design excesses of the 1980s as Philippe Starck pronounced: "We have everything we need and too much we don't need. We're entering a more moral market where people like me, whose responsibility is to produce, must ask themselves about the legitimacy of their work."

In this moral market, constrained by economics and changing social attitudes, vacuous stylistic trends in furniture have less of a place. This does not worry Ron Arad, who makes the distinction in his selection between designers who refashion the generic idea of a chair, those who invent new forms, those who play clever games of dissection and deconstruction, and those who combine different aspects of all three strategies. What interests Arad is genuinely innovative furniture design which reflects new ways of both seeing and making objects. Even in a climate of political and commercial uncertainty, or perhaps expressly because of it, many designers are rising to the occasion to create pieces which incorporate new concepts, techniques and materials. It is not just the younger designers, such as Karim Rashid, Marc Newson or Jane Atfield, who are in the vanguard of change; such established figures as Vico Magistretti, Nanna Ditzel and Shigeru Uchida show a capacity for fresh thinking. When Arad saw Zanotta's *Mirandolina* chair by Pietro Arosio (who is hardly a newcomer), its economy of production and form – stamped from a single sheet of extruded aluminium – provided a high point in the selection process.

Detail: **Luigi Baroli** Screen *Cartoons*

**1. Tejo Remy** *Chest of drawers*
Limited batch production
Each drawer is part of a new block of maplewood.
A band keeps the chest together.
Variable dimensions
Manufacturer: Droog Design, The Netherlands

2

**Marc Newson**

Many furniture designers in Ron Arad's selection – Robert Wettstein or Stefan Werwerka, for example – play with the generic idea of the chair. They stand back from the object and treat it as subject matter, as a sculptor would look at the human body. But Australian designer Marc Newson goes a stage further in that he creates entirely new shapes. The energy and invention that has made Newson such a familiar name on the international design circuit is present in his latest designs for Cappellini.

Newson worked with Ron Arad in London and for a long time in Japan for the manufacturer Idée. Both phases of his career were influential in helping him to develop and transcend the organic shapes of the 1950s which he so evidently admires. But perhaps more important was his original training as a jewellery designer: the detailing and craftsmanship in each Newson piece has marked him out as a rare talent. (See also page 86.)

**2. Marc Newson** *Felt Chair*
Reinforced fibreglass, anodized aluminium
H 86cm (33⅞ in)  W 67cm (26⅜ in)  D 106cm (41¾ in)
Manufacturer: Cappellini, Italy

**3**

**3. François Bauchet** *Chair*
Resin, metal
H 90cm/78cm (35½ in/30¾ in)
W 43cm/38cm (16⅞ in/15in)
D 45cm (17¾ in)
Manufacturer: Néotù, France

**4. Stefan Wewerka** Bench *Long Chair*
Beechwood
H 75cm (29½ in)
Seat H 45cm (17¾ in)  L 111cm (43⅜ in)
D 26cm (10¼ in)
Manufacturer: Källemo, Sweden

**5. Richard Hutten** *Table-on-table-chair*
Beechwood, beech plywood
Limited batch production
H 71cm (28in)  W 60cm (23½ in)
D 60cm (23½ in)
Manufacturer: Droog Design, The Netherlands

**4**

**5**

**6. Robert Wettstein** Armchair *Lukretia*
Wood, paper. Limited batch production
H 200cm (78in)  W 58cm (22⅞ in)  D 70cm (27½ in)
Manufacturer: Structure Design, Switzerland

**7. Robert Wettstein** Chair *Balthasar*
Wood, paper. Limited batch production
H 92cm (36⅛ in)  W 38cm (15in)  D 53cm (20⅞ in)
Manufacturer: Structure Design, Switzerland

**8. Robert Wettstein** Chair *Pilot 2*
Wood, paper
H 92cm (36⅛ in)  W 38cm (15in)  D 45cm (17¾ in)
Manufacturer: Artipresent-Autentics, Germany

**9. Robert Wettstein and Stanislaus Kutac** Chair *Aeros*
Hard plastic, gymnastic ball. Prototype
H 85cm (33½ in)  Di 65cm (25⅝ in)
Manufacturer: Structure Design, Switzerland

6

7

8

9

**10. Tejo Remy** Chair *Rag*
Limited batch production
The rags are held together by steel strips.
H 110cm (43⅜ in) W 60cm (23½ in) D 60cm (23½ in)
Manufacturer: Droog Design, The Netherlands

**11. Gaetano Pesce** *Seaweed Chair*
Polyurethane, fabric
H 76cm (30in) W 109cm (43in) D 86cm (34in)

**12. Gaetano Pesce** *Seaweed Chair*
Polyurethane, fabric
H 80cm (31½ in) W 111cm (44in) D 89cm (35in)

11

12

**14**

13

**13. Shin Takamatsu** *Chair*
Leather. Limited batch production
H 110cm (43⅜ in)  W 46cm (18⅛ in)  D 81cm (31⅞ in)
Manufacturer: Flores Design Edition, Germany

**14. Jane Atfield** *Chair and stool*
Recycled industrial felt. One-off
Chair: H 63cm (24⅞ in)  W 80cm (31½ in)  D 80cm (31½ in)
Stool: H 31.5cm (12⅜ in)  W 40cm (15¾ in)  D 55cm (21¾ in)
Manufacturer: Royal College of Art, UK

**15. Jane Atfield** *R.C.P. Chair*
Recycled plastic. Prototype
H 85cm (33½ in)  W 56cm (22in)  D 50cm (19⅝ in)
Manufacturer: Royal College of Art, UK

**Jane Atfield**

Not many designers can claim to have created a furniture piece solely from the industrial felt used to line the insides of British army tanks, but Royal College of Art graduate Jane Atfield is a London-based furniture designer who gets her inspiration from utilizing unusual recycled materials. Her felt chair and stool derive from a visit to a Nottinghamshire felt factory where she discovered a soft recycled felt made up to a Ministry of Defence specification to act as a sound barrier inside tanks. The manufacturer sponsored her to create felt furniture with a raw, inherent structure showing how the pieces are made. "I wanted to get away from the idea of chairs with traditional wooden frames, covered with foam and fabric," she says. "The felt has wonderfully tactile properties."

In another project, Atfield, who studied architecture before attending the RCA, visited an American furniture manufacturer, Yem & Hart in St Louis, which is experimenting with making recyled plastic sheets from shampoo and detergent bottles which are shredded and heat-pressured. Atfield's *R.C.P. Chair* explores the unusual visual effects created by recycling plastics in this way. It is a material, she says, which can be worked with conventional woodworking tools. Jane Atfield is continuing to work with Yem & Hart on "green" furniture concepts, as well as undertaking more conventional projects for such clients as Habitat. The materials in her work may be recycled, but her ideas are as original as any around today.

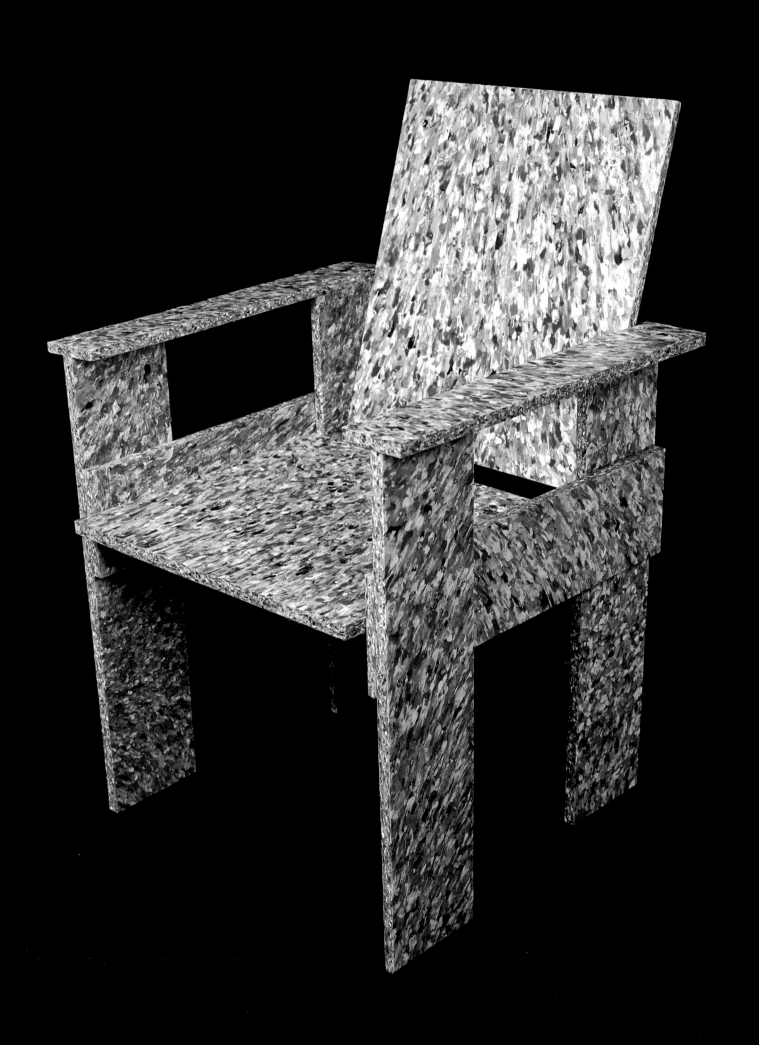

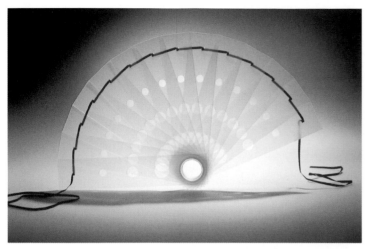

16

**16. Gijs Bakker** *Fan*
Polypropylene
H 20cm (7⅞ in)  W 4cm (1½ in)  D 1.5cm (⅝ in)
Manufacturer: Droog Design, The Netherlands

**17. Gijs Bakker** Candlestick *Vertical Holes*
Stainless steel
H 25cm (9⅞ in)  W 2.5cm (1in)  D 2.5cm (1in)
Manufacturer: Droog Design, The Netherlands

**18. Gijs Bakker** Wallpaper *Peep show*
The holes in the wallpaper reveal the layer beneath.
Manufacturer: Droog Design, The Netherlands

**19. Gijs Bakker** *Chair with holes*
Maplewood. Limited batch production
H 47cm (18½ in)  W 44cm (17¼ in)  D 44cm (17¼ in)
Manufacturer: Droog Design, The Netherlands

17

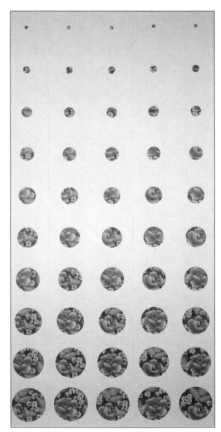

18

**Gijs Bakker**

Dutch artist and designer Gijs Bakker has prepared a new collection of pieces based on the use of holes in artefacts. Behind this chair and the associated furnishings lies the idea of retaining a sense of the material space invaded by the object; in the case of the perforated wallpaper, for example, it is still possible to see the wall which Bakker's paper covers.

Bakker is one of the most fluent and inventive talents on the European avant-garde scene. He trained in the late 1950s as a jewellery designer at what is now the Rietveld Academy before developing a multi-faceted career embracing industrial design, technology and art. He now combines a freelance design practice with the post of head of the furniture department at the Eindhoven Academy of Industrial Design.

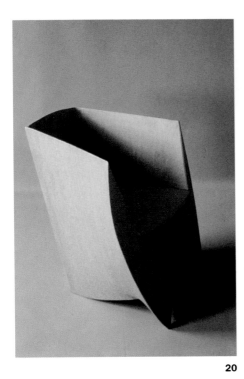

**20. Jan Armgardt** *Resting chair*
Plywood, laminated paper
Prototype
H 75cm (29½ in)  W 35cm – 57cm (13¾ in – 22⅜ in)
D 65cm (25⅜ in)

**21. Jan Armgardt** Chair and stool *Reader's Place* and *Stay*
Iron, laminated paper. Prototype
*Reader's Place*:
H 90cm (35½ in)  W 87cm (34¼ in)  D 75cm (29½ in)
*Stay*:
H 60cm (23½ in)  W 30cm (11⅞ in)  D 60cm (23½ in)

**22. Laslo Conek** Chair *On Horseback*
Plywood. Prototype
H 97cm (38¼ in)  W 50cm (19⅝ in)  D 59cm (23in)

**23. Jan Armgardt** Chair *JA43G*
Iron wire, boomdoor. Prototype
H 95cm (37½ in)  W 30cm – 45cm (11⅞ in – 17¾ in)
D 56cm (22in)
Manufacturer: Katz-Flechtmöbel, Germany

**24. Jan Armgardt** Sofa *JA33G*
Iron, boomdoor
H 75cm (29½ in)  W 100cm (39½ in)  D 75cm (29½ in)
Manufacturer: Katz-Möbelkollektion, Germany

**25. Jan Armgardt** Chair *JA46G*
Iron, boomdoor
H 128cm (50⅜ in)  W 43cm (16⅞ in)  D 40cm (15¾ in)
Manufacturer: Katz-Flechtmöbel, Germany

**20**     **21**

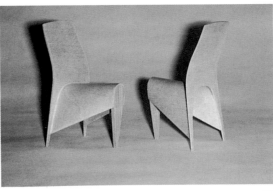

**22**

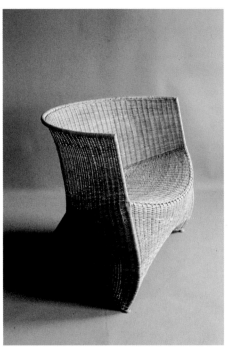

**23** **24** **25**

### Jan Armgardt

High-design furniture made of wicker represents a growing trend. Ron Arad was not alone when he launched a wicker stacking chair for Driade at the Milan Fair in 1993: many other leading designers also produced wickerwork pieces, so giving the material a new creative lease of life. Cynics will say that this trend reflects a need to economize in production and use low-cost labour, rather than any aesthetic concern. But, in some hands, wicker furniture can be expressed with great sensitivity and subtlety.

Jan Armgardt is a German furniture designer whose delicate pieces for Katz-Möbelkollektion show the potential of wicker in its best light. His ideas are both experimental and charming, in an entirely natural way. Armgardt trained first as a cabinet-maker before establishing his own design studio at Bensheim in 1974. Since then he has worked for manufacturers all over Europe, from Wittmann in Austria to De Padove in Italy and Baumann in France. Apart from his wicker pieces, the selection also features formal exercises with plywood and laminated paper, again reflecting a concern to achieve plasticity in his designs.

**26. Andrea Branzi** Chair and stool *Niccola*
Stainless steel, polyurethane, cowhide
Chair: H 100cm (39½ in)  seat H 44cm (17¼ in)
W 58cm (22⅞ in)  D 88cm (34⅝ in)
Stool: H 40cm (15¾ in)  W 39cm (15⅜ in)  D 46cm (18⅛ in)
Manufacturer: Zanotta, Italy

**27. Andrea Branzi** Chair *Altera*
Steel, cast iron, polyurethane foam
H 78cm (30¾ in)  seat H 46.5cm (18⅜ in)
W 59cm (23in)  D 56cm (22in)
Manufacturer: Zanotta, Italy

26

27

### Andrea Branzi

Over the past couple of years, as Milan has struggled to reassert its creative supremacy in international furniture design, few designers have enjoyed a higher profile than Andrea Branzi. His radical credentials with Studio Alchimia and Memphis, cultural directorship of the Domus Academy, large body of published theory, and active association with respected manufacturers combined to make him a leading figure in the campaign to prove that Italian design has not run out of steam.

Branzi's response at the 1993 Milan Fair was to do what he does best: play miniature architectural games. He enjoys the process of dissecting and deconstructing the chair, adding a new twist here and there but never straying too far from the functional basis of the object. His *Revers* chair for Cassina takes a folded beechwood strip and sends it soaring upwards from the feet to form the back and arms (see page 36). His *Altera* upholstered chair for Zanotta pirouettes from a circular steel-frame base, in Branzi's own words, "like a ballet dancer on one leg", while his *Niccola* easy chair for the same manufacturer is another essay in teasingly subtle deconstruction with seat distanced from back. All these stylistic exercises reflect Branzi's interest in the idea of the universal chair, equally suitable for home, office or restaurant.

**28**

**29**

**28. Yaacov Kaufman** *Chair*
Plywood, steel. Prototype
H 71cm (28in)  W 60cm (23½ in)  D 60cm (23½ in)

**29. Yaacov Kaufman** Stool *Atus*
Beechwood, steel, nylon. Limited batch production
H 65cm (25⅝ in)  W 43cm (17⅞ in)  D 100cm (39½ in)

**30. Yaacov Kaufman** Chair *Hinged Zig-Zag*
Beechwood, spring steel. Limited batch production
H 90cm (35½ in)  W 25cm (9⅞ in)  D 38cm (15in)

**31. Yaacov Kaufman** Chair *Ergo-nom-Chic*
Beechwood, steel, rubber. Limited batch production
H 90cm (35½ in)  W 80cm (31½ in)  D 38cm (15in)

**30**

**31**

## Yaacov Kaufman

Successful commissions for Italian companies such as Arflex, Tecno and Seccose have brought Israeli designer Yaacov Kaufman to the attention of the international design community. Kaufman, who teaches at the Bezalel Academy of Art and Design in Jerusalem, says the lack of an export-orientated furniture industry in Israel led him to look overseas for industrial and furniture design work. "If I'd been a fashion designer, things would have been different," he says, "because Israel has a large fashion industry."

Kaufman may lack some of the outlandish conceptual power of his compatriot Ron Arad, but none of the wit and ingenuity. The pieces shown here were developed over the past three years as part of a series of studies which reflect Kaufman's interest in the potential of interlocking steel rod. Some pieces, such as the *Hinged Zig-Zag* chair, have been batch-produced; others simply remain design exercises. Kaufman studied sculpture before he became a designer, but today says: "I can live without art. But I can't live without industrial design."

**32. Andrea Branzi** Chair *Revers*
Aluminium, beechwood
H 75cm (29½ in)  W 58cm (22⅞ in)  D 51cm (20⅛ in)
Manufacturer: Cassina, Italy

**33. David Palterer** Chair *Sedotta*
Ashwood, leather
H 79cm (31in)  W 57cm (22⅜ in)  D 60cm (23½ in)
Manufacturer: Acerbis, Italy

**34. Perry King and Santiago Miranda** Chair *DeTriana*
Beechwood
H 85cm (33½ in)  W 61cm (24in)  D 61cm (24in)
Manufacturer: Atelier International, USA

**32**

**33**

**34**

**King Miranda**

Rodrigo DeTriana was the sailor in the crow's nest who first spied land and alerted the crew when Columbus discovered the Americas and proved that the world was not flat in 1492. The Milan studio of King Miranda turned to DeTriana for inspiration when it designed a new beechwood chair for Atelier International. This distinctively crafted piece has an "eye" in its cutout back.

Englishman Perry King and his Spanish partner Santiago Miranda, no strangers to *The International Design Yearbook*, have long made a practice of using legend, myth and poetry, often in direct conjuction with new technologies. The *DeTriana* chair is offered in a range of wood finishes plus aniline stains in vibrant colours. There is an appropriate sense of irony – captured by the chair – in Atelier International, now part of the giant Steelcase furniture group and a symbol of design in the New World, looking back to mainland Europe, and a Spaniard in particular, for design ideas.

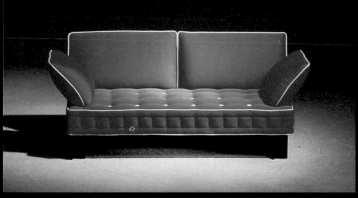

36

**35. Toni Cordero** Armchair *Faia*
Metal, silk, velvet
H 110cm (43¾ in)  W 90cm (35½ in)  D 88cm (34⅝ in)
Manufacturer: Sawaya & Moroni, Italy

**36. Matteo Thun** Sofa/bed/chaise *Materassi*
H 79cm (31in)  seat H 40cm (15¾ in)
W 188cm (74in)  D 86cm (33⅞ in)
Manufacturer: Franz Wittmann, Germany

**37**

**38**                                         **39**

**37. David Kawecki** Table and chair *Puzzle*
Birch plywood
Table: W 61cm (24in)  Di 50.8cm (20in)
Chair: H 82.5cm (32½ in)  W 75cm (29½ in)  D 61cm (24in)
Manufacturer: Néotù, USA

**38. Maurizio Peregalli** Chair *Poltroncina*
Steel, MDF
H 68cm (26¾ in)  seat H 47cm (18½ in)
W 54cm (21¼ in)  D 43cm (16⅞ in)
Manufacturer: Noto - Zeus, Italy

**39. Maurizio Peregalli** Chair *Comoda*
Steel, MDF
H 84cm (33in)  seat H 48cm (18⅞ in)
W 54.5cm (21½ in)  D 47cm (18½ in)
Manufacturer: Noto - Zeus, Italy

**40**

**40. Constantin Boym** *Searstyle furniture*
Prefabricated parts from the Sears catalogue, oak, upholstery. Prototype
Dining chair: H 84cm (33in)  W 38cm (15in)  D 74cm (29⅛ in)
Lounge chair: H 76cm (30in)  W 46cm (18⅛ in)  D 74cm (29⅛ in)
Stool: H 38cm (15in)  W 46cm (18⅛ in)  D 46cm (18⅛ in)
Sofa: H 82cm (32¼ in)  W 138cm (54⅜ in)  D 90cm (35½ in)
Manufacturer: Boym Design Studio, USA

## Constantin Boym

When US President Franklin D. Roosevelt was asked which American book he would put into the hands of every Russian should such an opportunity arise, he allegedly replied: the Sears catalogue. This Searstyle furniture, designed by a Russian emigré now based in New York, takes the familiar, derided vernacular design language of Sears and attempts to reinstate it into contemporary design expression.

Moscow-born Constantin Boym is a designer, writer and teacher at Parsons School of Design. He staged a one-man show entitled "Searstyle" in New York in a bid to "bring the language of Sears – symbolic of America, yet relegated into kitsch – back into design discourse". His pieces use ready-made furniture parts from the Sears catalogue, placed in a new context and combined with specially designed wooden supports. They explore the cultural heritage of Sears, which was at one time a symbol of the practical and dependable goods produced by the US capitalist system.

**41**

**41. Erik Krogh** *Chair*
Compressed elmwood. Prototype
H 75cm (29½ in)  W 60cm (23½ in)  D 46cm (18⅛ in)
Manufacturer: Institute of Technology, Denmark

**42. Hans Jakobsen** *VIA Spring Chair*
Polyester, artificial rubber, steel
H 76cm (30in)  W 67cm (26⅜ in)  D 65cm (25⅝ in)
Manufacturer: Via, USA

43

**43. Denis Santachiara** Sofabed *Trans*
Manufacturer: Campeggi, Italy

**44. Yaacov Kaufman** Armchair *Virgola*
Metal, moulded polyurethane
H 76cm (30in)  W 73cm (28¾ in)  D 70cm (27½ in)
Manufacturer: Arflex, Italy

45

46

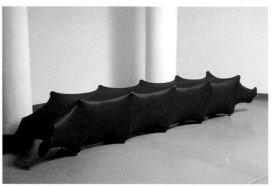

47

48

49

**45. Denis Santachiara** Child's chair *Pzza di Toyama*

**46. Martin Szekely** Stool *Bobine*
Bronze, walnut
H 43cm (16⅞ in)  Di 30cm (11⅞ in)
Manufacturer: Néotù, France

**47. Philip McNally** *Bench*
Tubular steel, Lycra. Prototype
H 50cm (19⅝ in)  L 325cm (126¾ in)  D 50cm (19⅝ in)
Manufacturer: Royal College of Art, UK

**48. Andrew Gillmore** *Bench*
Steel tube. Prototype
The knitted covers are by Karina Holmes.
H 50cm (19⅝ in)  W 300cm (118⅛ in)  D 50cm (19⅝ in)
Manufacturer: Royal College of Art, UK

**49. Maurizio Peregalli** Stool *Golia*
Steel tube, heartwood or leather
H 80cm/71cm (31½ in/28in)  Di 41cm (16⅛ in)
Manufacturer: Noto - Zeus, Italy

**52**

**50**

**51**

**50. Erik Krogh** *Bench*
Compressed ashwood, steel. Limited batch production
H 84.5cm (33⅜ in) L 189cm (74⅜ in) D 72cm (28⅜ in)
Manufacturer: Institute of Technology, Denmark

**51. Uwe Wagner** Bench and table *Casino container set*
Aluminium, spring steel, wickerwork, MDF
Bench: H 45cm (17¾ in) L 200cm (78¾ in) D 36cm (14⅛ in)
Table: H 72cm (28⅜ in) L 210cm (82⅝ in) D 68cm (26¾ in)
Manufacturer: Pentagon, Germany

**52. Pepe Cortes** Bench *Gracia*
Metal, laminated iroko
H 78cm (30¾ in) L 180cm (70⅝ in) D 57cm (22⅜ in)
Manufacturer: Punt Mobles, Spain

**53. Casimir Reynders** Cupboard/bench *Loden Meubel*
Wood, lead. Limited batch production
H 30cm (11⅞ in) L 300cm (118⅛ in) D 60cm (23½ in)
Manufacturer: Casimir Reynders, Belgium

**53**

**54**

**55**

**56**

**57**

**58**

**59**

**60**

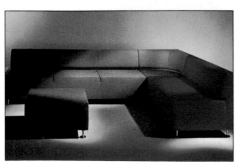

**61**

**62**

**54. Paolo Piva** Three-seater sofa *Living*
H 89cm (35in)  W 225cm (88⅝ in)
D 85cm (33½ in)
Manufacturer: Wittmann, Austria

**55. Sottsass Associati** Chair *Selim*
Steel, polyurethane
With arms: H 68cm (26¾ in)
Seat H 38cm (15in)  W 84cm (33in)
D 69cm (27⅛ in)
Without arms: H 69cm (27⅞ in)
Seat H 37cm (14½ in)  W 56cm (22in)
D 73cm (28¾ in)
Manufacturer: Cassina, Italy

**56. Mathias Hoffmann** Sofa *Ibello*
Metal, polyester
H 74cm (29⅛ in)  W 235cm (91⅝ in)
D 108cm (42½ in)
Manufacturer: Perobell, Spain

**57. Jasper Morrison** *Three Sofa Regular*
Manufacturer: Cappellini, Italy

**58. Matthew Hilton** Day bed *Miller*
Wood, polyurethane foam
H 48cm (18⅞ in)  W 214cm (84¼ in)
D 83cm (32¾ in)
Manufacturer: Idée Co., Japan

**59. James Irvine** Sofabed *Zzofa*
Metal, polyurethane foam, lacquered anti-
scratch and anodized aluminium
H 83cm (32¾ in)   seat H 40cm (15¾ in)
W 201cm (79⅛ in)  D 95cm (37½ in)
(Open) H 40cm (15¾ in)
W 201cm (79⅛ in)  D 126cm (49⅝ in)
Manufacturer: Cappellini, Italy

**60. Olivier Gagnere** Sofa *Pémane*
Oak, bronze, velvet
Limited batch production
H 110cm (43½ in)  W 205cm (80¾ in)
D 105cm (41⅜ in)
Manufacturer: Néotù, France

**61. Jasper Morrison** *Three Sofa System*
Wood, aluminium, polyurethane foam
Sofas: H 72cm (28⅜ in)
W 210cm/140cm (82⅝ in/55⅛ in)
D 70cm (27½ in)
Corner element: H 72cm (28⅜ in)
W 70cm (27½ in)  D 70cm (27½ in)
Pouffe: H 42cm (16½ in)
W 70cm (27½ in)  D 70cm (27½ in)
Manufacturer: Cappellini, Italy

**62. Harri Korhonen** *C.D. Sofa*
Moulded aluminium, beechwood
H 75cm (30in)  W 137cm (54in)
D 78cm (30¾ in)
Manufacturer: Inno, Finland

**63**

**63. Bang Design (David Granger)** *The Piggly Wiggly range*
Plywood, foam, wool, hoop pine. Limited batch production
Chair: H 83cm (32¾ in)  W 60cm (23½ in)  D 70cm (27½ in)
Manufacturer: Anibou, Australia

**65**

**66**

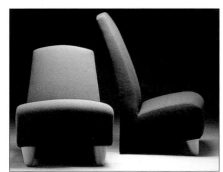

**64. Massimo Iosa Ghini** *Armchair and sofa*
Metal, resin, wool, Dacron, polyurethane
Sofa: H 80cm (31½ in)  seat H 43.5cm (17⅛ in)
W 130cm (51⅛ in)  D 67cm (26⅜ in)
Armchair: H 80cm (31½ in)  seat H 43.5cm (17⅛ in)
W 72.5cm (28½ in)  D 67cm (26⅜ in)
Manufacturer: Renault Italia, Italy

**65. Bang Design (David Granger)** *The Piggly Wiggly range*
Plywood, foam, wool, hoop pine. Limited batch production
Sofa: H 83cm (32¾ in)  W 145cm (57⅛ in)  D 70cm (27½ in)
Manufacturer: Anibou, Australia

**66. Bang Design (Bryan Marshall)** Chairs *Long Quick* and *Short Quick*
Plywood, foam, wool, hoop pine. Limited batch production
*Long Quick*: H 100cm (39½ in)  W 60cm (23½ in)  D 70cm (27½ in)
*Short Quick*: H 75cm (29½ in)  W 60cm (23½ in)  D 65cm (25⅝ in)
*Short Quick* (twin back): H 75cm (29½ in)  W 120cm (47¼ in)
D 65cm (25⅝ in)
Manufacturer: Anibou, Australia

**67. Pietro Arosio** Chair *Mirandolina*
Stove-enamelled aluminium alloy
H 84cm (33in)  seat H 46cm (18⅛ in)
W with arms 48cm (18⅞ in)  without arms 40cm (15¾ in)
D 53cm (20⅞ in)
Manufacturer: Zanotta, Italy

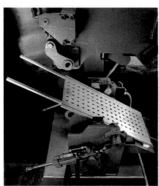

## Pietro Arosio

Take a flat, thin sheet of extruded aluminium. Cut to desired length and create legs. Punch decorative holes to make the chair weigh less and look lighter. Bend and shape the single piece to give the chair its form. Provide paint finish.

The *Mirandolina* chair, suitable for indoor and outdoor use, is a miracle of economical production and delicate design in four short steps. Designed by Pietro Arosio and manufactured by Zanotta, it is a compact aluminium stacking chair, light yet solid. Arosio, who has been in practice as a designer since 1972, has made a point of using new technologies to create spare forms throughout his career. Although it may look simple, however, the *Mirandolina* requires extruded aluminium just 40cm in width; only one firm in Italy was able to supply Zanotta with the material.

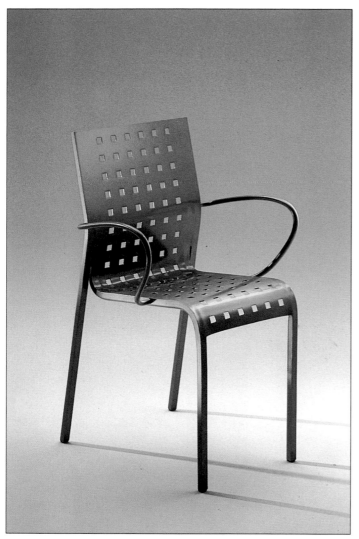 

67

**68. Marco Ferreri** *Less is More*
Beechwood, Softwood
Chair: H 75cm (29½ in)
Seat H 45cm (17¾ in)  W 47cm (18½ in)  D 40.5cm (16in)
Stool: H 45cm (17¾ in)  W 40cm (15¾ in)  D 35cm (13¾ in)
Table: H 72cm (28⅜ in)  W 200cm/160cm/80cm (78¾ in/63in/31½ in)
D 80cm (31½ in)
Manufacturer: Nemo, Italy

**69. Thomas Bley** *Folding chair*
Refined steel, maple
H 80cm (31½ in)  W 40cm (15¾ in)  D (folded) 2.5cm (1in)
Manufacturer: Pentagon, Germany

**70. Lievore y Asociados** Chair *Radical*
Veneered plywood
H 84cm (33in)  W 38.5cm (15⅛ in)  D 50cm (19⅝ in)
Manufacturer: Andreu World, Spain

**71. Axel Kufus** Chair *Stöck*
Birchwood, linoleum
The chair comes packaged in kit form.
H 85cm (33½ in)  W 41cm (16⅛ in)  D 46cm (18½ in)
Manufacturer: Atoll Möbelideen, Germany

**70**

**71**

**68**

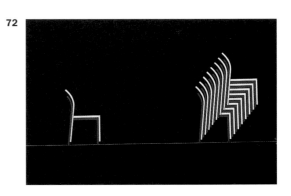

**72**

**73**

**72. Komplot Design (Boris Berlin and Poul Christiansen)** *One Chair*
Laminated and solid beechwood. Prototype
H 80cm (31½ in)  W 44cm (17¼ in)  D 48cm (18¾ in)
Manufacturer: Komplot Design, Denmark

**73. Andrée Putman** Chair *Sangles*
Ashwood, cotton
H 84cm (33in)  W 56cm (22in)  D 59cm (23in)
Manufacturer: Ecart Design, France

**74**

**74. William Petrie** *Stacking chair*
Cast aluminium, steel tube. Prototype
H 72cm (28⅜ in)  seat H 44cm (17¼ in)
W 55cm (21¾ in)  D 36cm (14⅛ in)
Manufacturer: Royal College of Art, UK

**75. Jack Woolley** *EMW Chair*
Aluminium. Limited batch production
H 80cm (31½ in)  W 50cm (19⅝ in)
Manufacturer: Chairwork, UK

**76. Vico Magistretti** Chair *Mauna-Kea*
Aluminium tube, die-cast aluminium, thermoplastic polymer
H 77cm (30⅜ in)  W 58cm (22⅞ in)  D 54cm (21¼ in)
Manufacturer: Kartell, Italy

**75**

**76**

### Vico Magistretti

Nobody at the 1993 Milan Furniture Fair signalled the seachange starting to take place in the Italian furniture industry more expressively than Kartell. The scenario is as follows: out goes the decadent image-making, the pursuit of visual exuberance for its own sake; in comes the search for quality, defined as much in terms of function and materials as in aesthetic appeal. Kartell's manifesto for change called for more emphasis in Italian design on fitness for purpose and on the environmental problems of industrial production. It is a serious issue: Kartell has been part of an industry bandwagon which has been successfully producing an endless stream of glossy design novelties for more than a decade. How do you turn that wagon around and send it in a different direction?

The answer provided by Kartell at the *Fiera* did not just lie in the recycled plastics reissue of its classic Gino Colombini wastepaper bins or in the radiant, anthropomorphic plastic elements of Philippe Starck's *Booox* bookcase (see page 72). Vico Magistretti's *Mauna-Kea* chairs suggested an utter concentration on utilitarian production. They are prosaic in appearance, and altogether familiar and functional in construction – with aluminium tube frame, die-cast aluminium seat support, and mass-market polymer seat and backrest. There is also a very wide choice of colour combinations, again reflecting a move away from the imposition of a narrow style from on high. Magistretti even eschewed that decadent designer art – drawing. Instead it is understood that he simply went to the Kartell factory and experimented with bending the materials to create the *Mauna-Kea* chair.

Furniture designed on the basis of fastidious social observation is the keynote of Yasuyuki Hirai, a Japanese product designer trained at the Kyoto University of the Arts and the Royal College of Art in London. His café-style stacking chairs are part of a system of "relaxation" furniture developed while Hirai was studying at the RCA. Before developing the range, the designer monitored social behaviour during coffee breaks in offices in Britain, Holland, Germany and Sweden using a time-lapse automatic camera. He discovered that people want to lean on furniture and remain half-standing as much as sit on it, so he designed forms to suit. The base, with a cutaway portion to facilitate stacking, resembles a Pacman of video arcade games in an ironic reference to Japanese technology.

In the past Hirai has collaborated with Japanese designer Toshiyuki Kita to develop new furniture. Now his latest range is being put into production by one of Japan's largest furniture producers, the Osaka-based firm Kokuyo, which employs Hirai as a design manager.

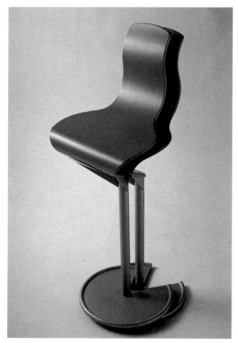  

77

**77. Yasuyuki Hirai** *High Chair*
Laminated wood, steel tube, cast aluminium
H 93cm (36⅝ in)  seat H 65cm (25⅝ in)
W 35cm (13¾ in)  D 35cm (13¾ in)
Manufacturer: Royal College of Art, UK

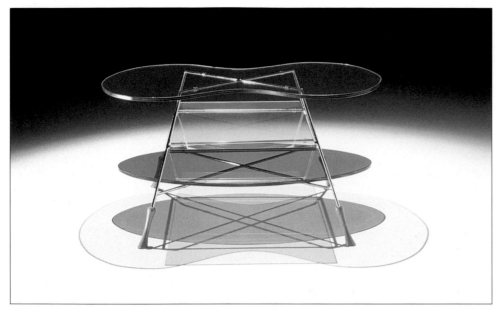

**78. Karim Rashid** Coffee table *Aura*
½in glass, steel rod, redwood
H 45cm (17¾ in)  W 48cm (18¾ in)  L 85cm (33½ in)
Manufacturer: North Studio, Canada

**79. Karim Rashid** Chair *Arp Series*
Elastic webbing, plywood, steel
H 75cm (29½ in)  W 45cm (17¾ in)  D 52cm (20½ in)
Manufacturer: Area Group, Canada

## Karim Rashid

The organic forms of the Swiss–French sculptor Jean Arp are reflected in the *Arp* chair series by Karim Rashid, the much-travelled young Canadian designer who has studied under Ettore Sottsass and Gaetano Pesce. Rashid's aim was to design a stacking chair that was as lightweight as possible with a spring in the seat. He developed a cantilevered plywood arch to achieve the necessary spring and tight stacking relationship. The project began as a self-generated design which was then taken up by a manufacturer.

Cairo-born Karim Rashid is the brother of architect Hani Rashid and they have jointly exhibited their work. Karim Rashid worked for eight years as an industrial designer in Toronto before moving to New York in January 1993 in a bid to gain more international exposure. Today he combines practice with an assistant professorship in industrial design at the Pratt Institute. The *Arp* chair series reflects what Rashid describes as "my phenomological approach to design – I'm thinking about the experience, not the object".

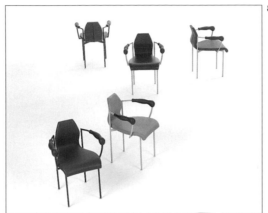

81

80

82

**80. Pascal Mourgue** Chair *Lolita*
Metal, beechwood veneer
H 77cm (30⅜ in)  W 44cm (17¼ in)  D 45cm (17¾ in)
Manufacturer: Artelano, France

**81. Marie-Christine Dorner** Stacking chair and armchair
*Fantome*
Leather, polyurethane, metal
The seat comes away from the frame, and the seats and
frames stack separately.
H 75cm (29½ in)  W 45cm (17¾ in)
(armchair) 57cm (22⅜ in)  D 51cm (20⅛ in)
Manufacturer: Montis, Holland

**82. James Irvine** Chair *Carugo*
Dyed beechwood
H 74cm (29⅛ in)  seat H 43.5cm (17⅛ in)
W 51cm (20⅛ in)  D 44cm (17¼ in)
Manufacturer: Cappellini, Italy

83

## Nanna Ditzel

Nanna Ditzel belongs to the generation of Danish furniture designers who laid the foundations for the international success of Scandinavian Modernism. She trained under Kaare Klint at the Royal Academy in Copenhagen, and many of her pieces from the 1950s are today regarded as classics. But unlike some of her Danish peers who have become stuck in a blonde beechwood timewarp, she has managed to imbue her work with a contemporary freshness and win new audiences. Her recent gold medal at the Hokkaido International Furniture Design Competition in Japan is evidence of the continuing relevance and resonance of her ideas.

Ditzel's *Fan Chair* results from her work with flexible veneers. She wanted to create a chair that was as light as possible, in aesthetic terms as well as in weight. The frame of the chair is made of solid ash, with the U-shaped bow which forms the rear legs bent from compressed ash. The seat and back are made from laminated veneer.

Elegance and symmetry have always been a focus of Ditzel's work. Her *Folding Stool*, made of laminated veneer and solid maple with brass fittings, is designed so that when the two leaves of the seat are folded together in a vertical position, the legs also go together. The *Folding Stool* is a prototype, one in a series for a new range of garden furniture. After nearly 50 years producing beautiful furniture for interiors, Nanna Ditzel says that the garden is the environment that really interests her now.

85

86

87

**85. Gerard van den Berg** Armchair *Longa*
Metal, cold foam, wood. Limited batch production
H 88cm (34⅝ in)  W 88cm (34⅝ in)  D 95cm (37½ in)

**86. Negrello and Scagnellato** Chair *Ergodeko*
Steel, foam, fabric, plastic
H 98cm – 108cm (38⅝ in – 42½ in)  W 62cm (24⅜ in)
D 55cm – 63cm (21¾ in – 24⅞ in)
Manufacturer: Deko Collezioni, Italy

**87. Wulf Schneider** Chair *Drehstuhl S 740*
Latex, leather, foam, spring steel. Prototype
H 85cm – 92cm (33½ in – 36⅛ in)  W 62cm (24⅜ in)  D 62cm (24⅜ in)
Manufacturer: Thonet, Germany

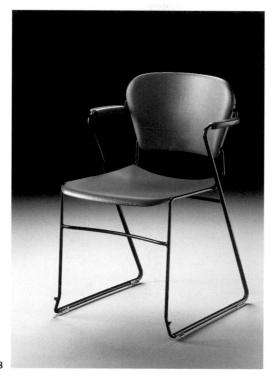

88

90

89

91

**88. Charles Perry** Armchair *Perry*
Steel wire, steel tube, injection-moulded polypropylene
H 82.5cm (32½ in)  W 57.5cm (22¾ in)  D 54.5cm (21½ in)
Manufacturer: KI, USA

**89. Josep Mora** Chair *Egoa*
Ashwood, steel
H 83cm (32¾ in)  W 51cm (20⅛ in)  D 53cm (20⅞ in)
Manufacturer: Stua, Spain

**90. Tzachi Gal** *Chair*
Metal, wood
H 87cm (34¼ in)  W 47cm (18½ in)  D 50cm (19⅝ in)
Manufacturer: Neto Furniture Design, Israel

**91. Thomas König and Matthias König** Chair, armchair and stool *Chuck I – III*
Steel tube, beechwood
Chair and armchair:
H 81cm (31⅞ in)  W 45cm (17¾ in)  D 51cm (20⅛ in)
Stool: H 111.5cm (43⅞ in)  W 37cm (14½ in)  D 44cm (17¼ in)
Manufacturer: D-Tec Industriedesign, Germany

**92**

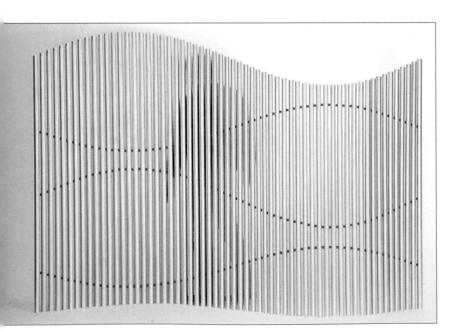

**93**

**92. Cheryl and Paul Ruine** *Dancing Mummy Screen*
Raw steel, brass, stretch fabric. Limited batch production
H 213.5cm (84in)  W 127cm (50in)  D 68.5cm (27in)
Manufacturer: Ruine Design Associates, USA

**93. Glendon Good** Screen *Poseidon*
Aluminium
H 185.5cm (73in)  W 152.4cm (60in)
Manufacturer: Néotù, USA

**94. Luigi Baroli** Screen *Cartoons*
Corrugated cardboard, aluminium, PVC
H 170cm (66⅞ in)  W 40cm – 400cm (15¾ in – 156in)
D 3cm (1⅛ in)  Di 40cm (15¾ in)
Manufacturer: Baleri Italia, Italy

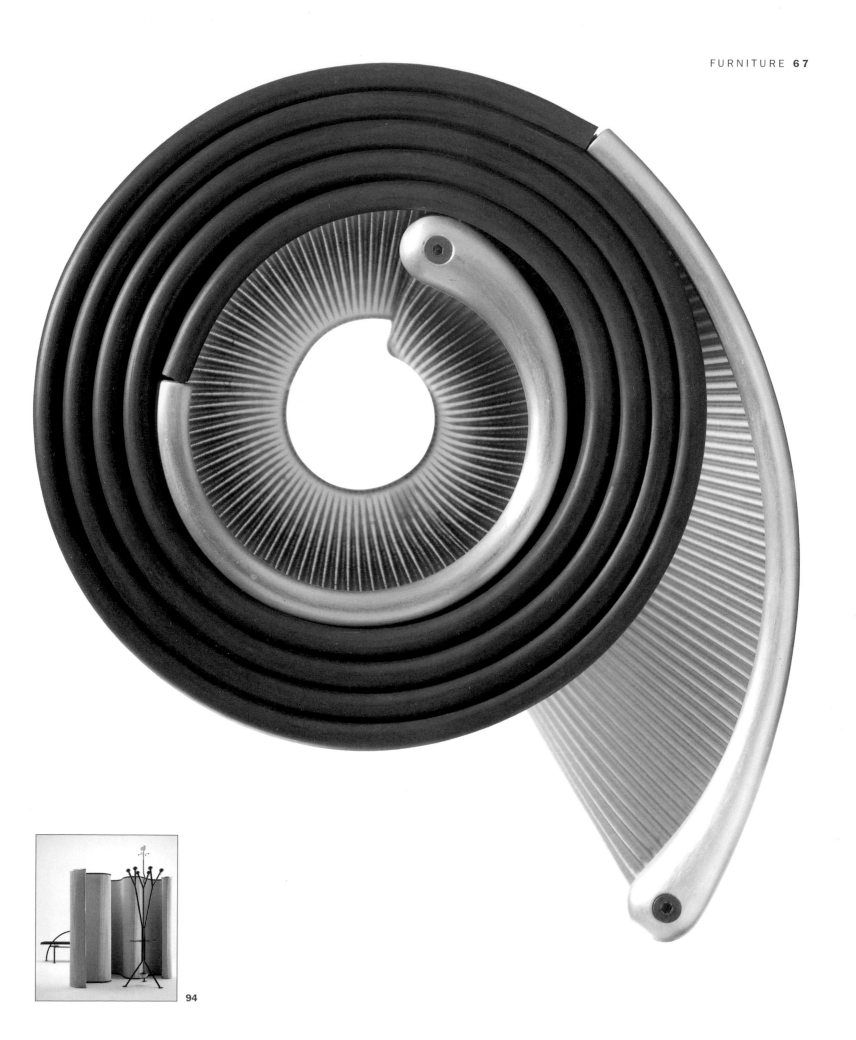

**94**

97

96

98

pages 68–9  **95. Juli Capella and Quim Larrea** Shelves *Greca*
Wood, marble
H 146cm – 164cm (57½ in – 64⅝ in)  W 16cm (6½ in)  D 18cm (7⅛ in)
Manufacturer: Chueca, Spain

**96. Gaetan Coolen** Shelves *Zigzag*
Cherrywood, Triplex
H 205cm (80¾ in)  W 120cm (47¼ in)  D 30cm (11⅞ in)
Manufacturer: Gaetan Coolen, Belgium

**97. Masanori Umeda** Glass cabinet *Memories of Pets*
Glass, aluminium. Limited batch production
H 140cm (55⅛ in)  W 45cm (17¾ in)  D 48cm (18⅞ in)
Manufacturer: Nihon Sheet Glass Co., Japan

**98. Jan Konings and Jurgen Bey** *Bookcase*
Maplewood, paper, linen
The bookcase expands as books are added.
H 220cm (85⅞ in)  W variable  D 21cm (8¼ in)
Manufacturer: Droog Design, The Netherlands

99

100

101

102

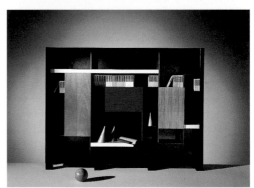

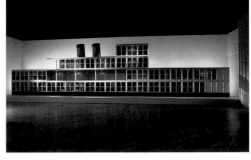

103

**99. Konstantin Grcic** Shelves *Bric*
Folded aluminium sheet, anodized silver, plywood
H 113cm/59cm (44½ in/23in)
W 27cm (10½ in)  D 27cm (10½ in)
Manufacturer: SCP, UK

**100. Alberto Lievore** Shelving system *Cavanagh*
Beechwood, veneered boards
H 250cm/220cm (98¾ in/85⅞ in)
W 50cm/35cm (19⅝ in/13¾ in)  D 35cm (13¾ in)
Manufacturer: Divano, Spain

**101. Shiro Kuramata** *Bookshelf*
Wood
H 250cm (97½ in)  W 250cm (97½ in)  D 40cm (15¾ in)
Manufacturer: Cappellini, Italy

**102. Andrea Branzi** Cabinets/shelving units *York*
Manufacturer: Acerbis International, Italy

**103. Luca Meda** Shelving system *Piroscafo*
Wood, steel
H and W variable  D 50cm (19⅝ in)
Manufacturer: Molteni & Co., Italy

**104. Kurt Thut** Cupboard *Faltvorhang-Schrank*
Polyethylene, MDF, aluminium
H 184cm (72⅜ in)  W 139cm (54¾ in)  D 40cm (15¾ in)
Manufacturer: W. Thut, Switzerland

**105. Parallel Design (Ali Tayar)** *Shelves*
Fibreboard, aluminium
H 122cm (48in)  L 274.3cm (108in)
Manufacturer: Néotù, USA

**106. Kristian Gavoille** Bookcase *Don Redade*
Sycamore, walnut. Limited batch production
H 200cm (78¾ in)  L 57.5cm (22⅝ in)  D 26.5cm (10⅜ in)
Manufacturer: Néotù, France

**104**

**105**

**107. Philippe Starck** Shelves *Booox*
Extruded and injection-moulded thermoplastic polymer
H, W and D variable
Manufacturer: Kartell, Italy

**107**

**106**

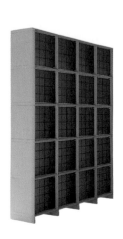

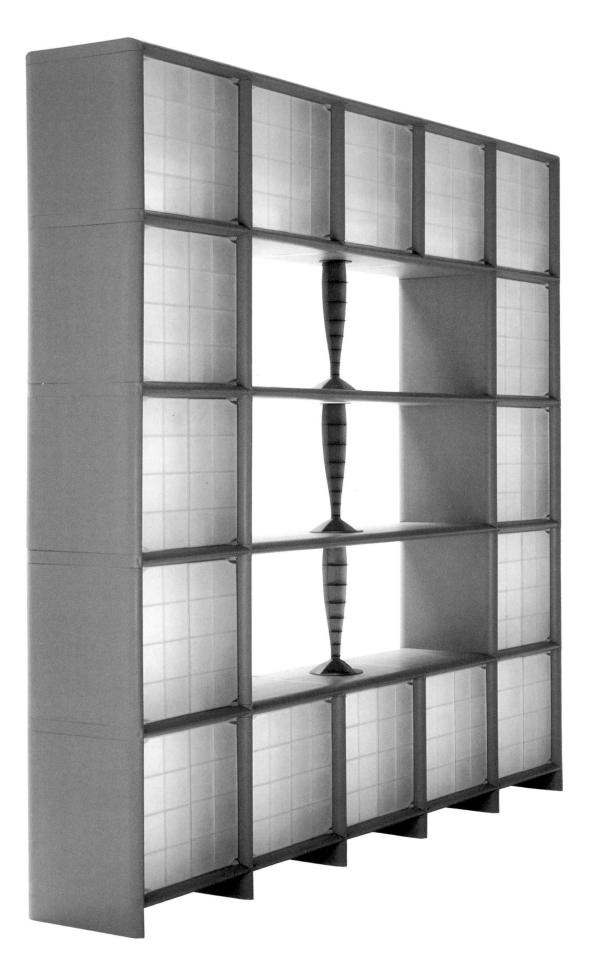

## Philippe Starck

Throughout his career the ubiquitous Philippe Starck has constantly redefined himself as a designer. Now he is undergoing a fresh and perhaps more far-reaching metamorphosis following his announcement that he plans to give up interior design schemes to spend more time on industrial design and architecture projects.
A strategically important design consultancy with Thomson, the French-owned electronics group, is one of the reasons why the world's most fashionable designer wants to switch down a gear. Another is Starck's environment-conscious belief that the game is up in industrial production. As he was quoted in the catalogue for his 1993 one-man show at the Design Museum in London: "The old style – the nineteenth century and twentieth century love affair with materials – is finished. It's obsolete. We can't go on and on digging and burning materials out of the ground just to spoil ourselves."

In that respect, his views chime with those of Kartell, the Italian company which commissioned him to create the modular, injection-moulded plastic shelving system entitled *Booox*. Complete with glowing, translucen accessories – a lamp, statue, silhouette and pair of doors – the system made an impact at the Milan Fair, confirming Starck to be far more than a mere stylist. Even at his most sober, Starck has the form-making capacity to leave almost all other designers standing.The Design Museum show asked the question: is Starck a designer?
On the evidence of *Booox* and on Starck's incredible inventiveness in successive editions of *The International Design Yearbook*, the answer is yes, arguably the finest of his generation.

**108. Zeev Aram** 1963 Shelving, *Dino Mk II*
Re-edited by **Jasper Morrison** in 1993
Beechwood, MDF
H (adjustable) 110cm (43⅜ in) or 206cm (81⅛ in)  W 90cm (35½ in)
D 33cm (13in)
Manufacturer: Aram Designs, UK

**109. Jan Konings** Wardrobe
Aluminium, cotton
H 200cm (78¾ in)  W 50cm (19⅝ in)  D 50cm (19⅝ in)
Manufacturer: Droog Design, The Netherlands

**110. Formfürsorge** Storage space *Bandit*
Steel, wood, rubber bands
H 205cm (80¾ in)  W 55cm (21¾ in)  D 34cm (13⅜ in)
Manufacturer: Formfürsorge, Germany

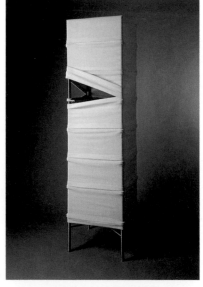

109

110

108

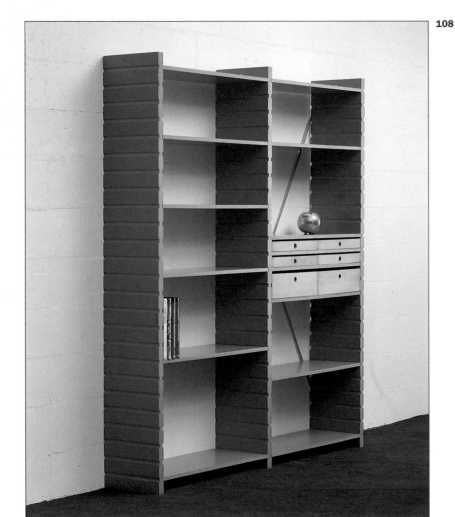

### Zeev Aram/Jasper Morrison

The *Dino* adjustable shelving system neatly bridges two generations of furniture designers in London. Originally designed in 1963 by Zeev Aram, it has been re-edited 30 years later by Jasper Morrison. Both Aram and Morrison are important today, for different reasons. Aram has become a tireless and influential patron of young designers; Morrison has become the champion of the new pared-down, unpretentious, utilitarian English look that numerous international manufacturers, Cappellini and Vitra among them, so clearly admire.

The story goes that Aram wanted Jasper Morrison to design a new piece for his contract furniture outlet Aram Designs. But, in an understated act of homage, Morrison instead chose to revisit one of Aram's own pieces. *Dino Mk II* is made of solid beech and medium-density fibreboard; it comes in two heights and characteristically manages to convey a personality while conforming to Morrison's belief that ornament is not only a crime but a hanging offence.

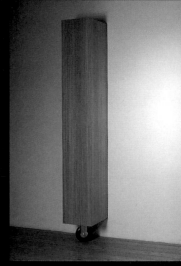

## Casimir Reynders

Belgium has always been the poor relation in comparison with Holland when it comes to discussion of design in the Benelux countries. With the notable exception of modern pioneer Henry van de Velde, Belgian furniture design has had something of an inferiority complex. At the 1993 Cologne and Milan shows, however, there was evidence that young Belgian designers are beginning to make a strong showing, with wit, boldness and invention to the fore. This piece by Casimir Reynders is typical of the new Belgian wave. Entitled *Je m'appelle Anna*, it is a cupboard with a twist: the cupboard door is fixed to the wall and the cupboard itself swings outwards to open.

111

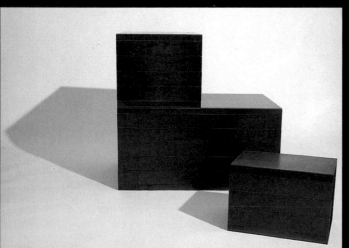

**111. Casimir Reynders** Cupboard *Je m'appelle Anna*
Oak, Bubinga or pearwood
Limited batch production
H 190cm (74⅞ in)  W 30cm (11⅞ in)  D 40cm (15¾ in)
Manufacturer: Casimir Reynders, Belgium

**112. Uwe Wagner, Reinhard Müller and Meyer Voggenreiter** *Graphic cabinet*
Steel, wood, magnet
Three modules:
H 27cm (10½ in)  W 39cm (15⅜ in)  D 27cm (10½ in)
H 34cm (13⅜ in)  W 39cm (15⅜ in)  D 53cm (20⅞ in)
H 41cm (16⅛ in)  W 78cm (30¾ in)  D 53cm (20⅞ in)
Manufacturer: Pentagon, Germany

112

**113**

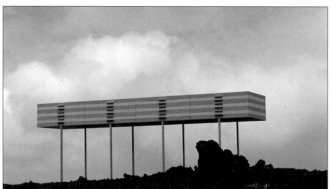

**114**

**113. Shigeru Uchida** Chest of drawers *Vertical*
Steel, birch plywood. Prototype
H 160cm/129cm (63in/47¼ in)  W 28cm (11in)  D 28cm (11in)
Manufacturer: Chairs, Japan

**114. Shigeru Uchida** Chest of drawers *Horizontal*
Steel, birch plywood. Prototype
H 100cm (39½ in)  W 270cm (106⅜ in)  D 60cm (23½ in)
Manufacturer: Chairs, Japan

**115. Rod and Alison Wales** *Cabinet with nine drawers*
Fumed and natural English oak, gold leaf, paint. One-off
H 164cm (64⅝ in)  W 42cm (16½ in)  D 32cm (12½ in)
Manufacturer: Wales and Wales, UK

**116. Rod and Alison Wales** *Cabinet with ten drawers*
Ebonized and natural English oak. One-off
H 142cm (55⅜ in)  W 52cm (10½ in)  D 38cm (15in)
H 161.5cm (63⅝ in)  W 38cm (15in)  D 35cm (13¾ in)
Manufacturer: Wales and Wales, UK

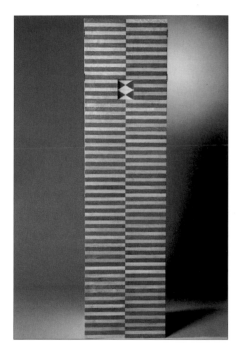  

115                                                                                      116

### Shigeru Uchida/Wales and Wales

*Horizontal + Vertical* was the title of an exhibition held in Tokyo in 1992 by Japanese designer Shigeru Uchida with Hideo Mori. In the show, Uchida returned to his familiar theme of exploring the relationship between free-standing objects and their environment. He placed striped chests of drawers – each stripe is a drawer – on slender supports in an installation which he described as "creating a framework that transcends experience".

Uchida's vertical pieces, which have since been manufactured by Chairs of Tokyo, find an echo in recent work by British designer-makers Wales and Wales. This is ironic in that Japanese free-standing furniture has little or no history before 1945 whereas Wales and Wales are working within a well-established heritage of free-standing English furniture design and have been described as belonging to the twentieth-century tradition of Lutyens.

Rod and Alison Wales work from a converted farm building in East Sussex and have developed a reputation for timeless, intelligent design, often commissioned by architects. They created outdoor seating for the Canary Wharf development in London Docklands, in a bid to reflect the traditions of London's open spaces and parks, and sculptural chess chairs for the Broadgate complex just a few miles away. Their cabinets, which share an affinity with Shigeru Uchida's designs, are made of natural, ebonized and fumed English oak.

**117**

**117. Simon de Boer** Bookcase *Von Arragon*
MDF. Limited batch production
H 180cm (70⅝ in)  W 20cm – 40cm (7⅞ in – 15¾ in)  D 35cm (13¾ in)
Manufacturer: Meubels en daavomheen, The Netherlands

**118. Bang Design (Bryan Marshall)** Shelves *Swerve*
Hoop-pine plywood, timber. Prototype
H 170cm (66⅞ in)  W 110cm (43⅜ in)  D 73cm (28¾ in)
Manufacturer: Bang Design, Australia

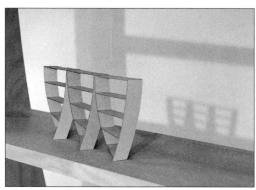

**118**

### Bang Design

The image of swaying people balancing water buckets on their shoulders provided the inspiration for the precarious balance and motion evident in the *Swerve* shelf unit produced by Bang Design. Australian designers Bryan Marshall and David Granger set up Bang Design in Sydney in 1989 to develop prototypes to be made by manufacturers under licence. Their approach is to take standard household objects and add irony, humour and freshness without taking the design to the point where it loses its simplicity and elegance. The *Swerve* shelf unit, made of hoop-pine plywood and timber sections, reflects this philosophy. The dynamism of the original idea to create "walking shelves" is still there, but it is also plainly a functional shelf unit which can be used as a single display case or in combination to create room dividers.

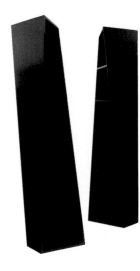

**119. Joachim Eckhardt** Desk *Gebogener Tisch*
Elmwood, steel
H 76cm (30in) L 325cm (126¾in)  D 38cm (15in)
Manufacturer: X99, Germany

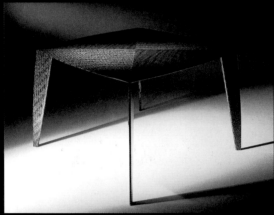

120

## Masayuki Kurokawa

Japanese architect Masayuki Kurokawa has designed furniture in the past – including a small coffee table and metal chair – but *Table 1992* is the first of his pieces to go beyond prototype stage into mass production. A thick Italian veneer called "Tabu" covers irregular strips of bonded wood. The polyurethane paint finish gives the table a solid, metallic appearance, but the timber surface also provides warmth and irregularity. Much of the elegance of the design comes from its subtly curved lines.

The combination of hard and soft is a recurrent feature of Kurokawa's work. The black rubber GOM ashtray – designed 20 years ago and now in the permanent collection at MOMA in New York – remains his best-selling product. "Working between hard and soft is the most important thing in furniture design for me," he says. "I like to make something hard have a soft shape – and make something in soft materials have a solid form, like boyish girls." But despite the forays into furniture, architecture still accounts for 70 per cent of Kurokawa's work. "Even if I design a product or piece of furniture I think of it as part of architecture. A chair is a small house. A house is a small city."

**120. Masayuki Kurokawa** *Table 1992*
Wood, polyurethane. One-off
H 70cm (27½ in)  W 110cm (43⅜ in)  D 110cm (43⅜ in)

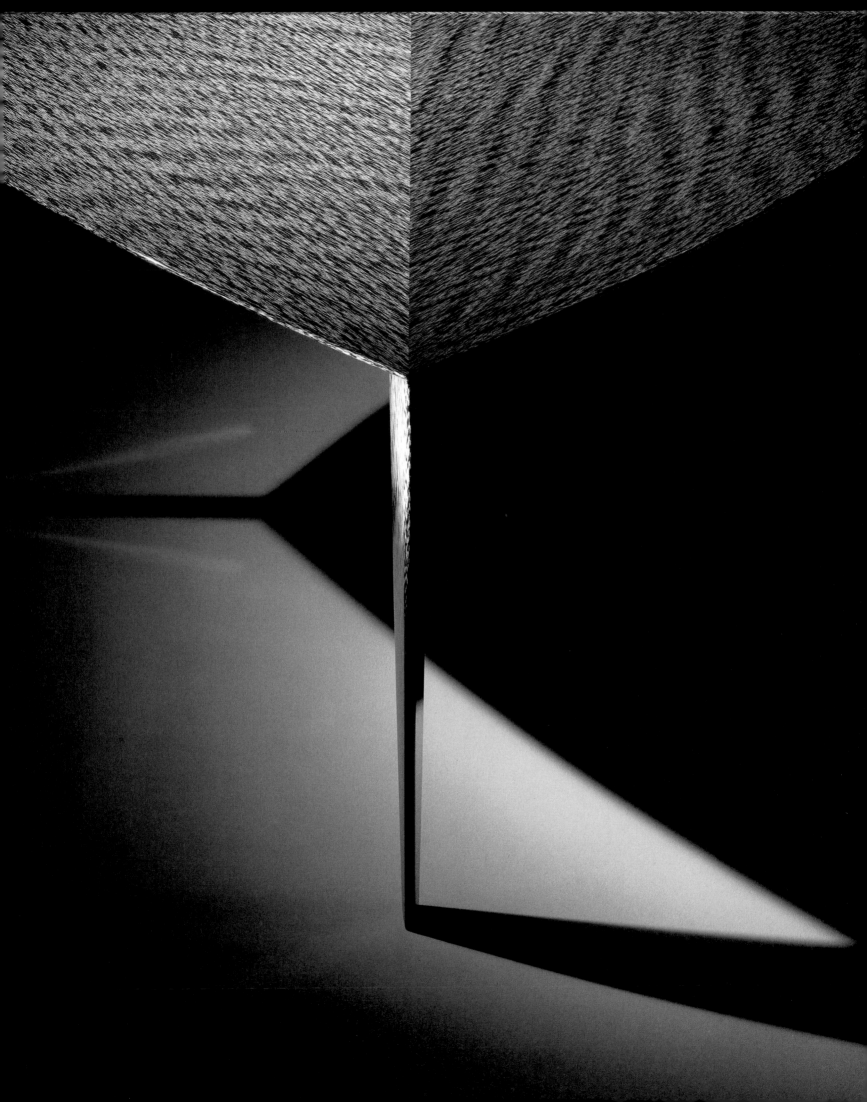

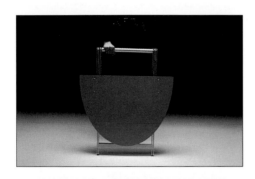

**121**

**122**

**121. Celina Clarke and Simon Christopher** Folding table *Amazing Larry*
Aluminium, MDF. Limited batch production
H 72cm (28⅜ in)  W 75cm (29½ in)  L 110cm (43⅜ in)
Manufacturer: Ism Objects, Australia

**122. Bryce Sanders** Table *Ajas*
Plywood, aluminium
H 74cm (29in)  W 170.5cm (67in)  D 89cm (35in)
Manufacturer: Néotù, USA

**123. Donato d'Urbino and Paolo Lomazzi (DDL Studio)** Collapsible table *Clap*
Metal, laminate
H 71cm (28in)  Di 60cm (23½ in)
Manufacturer: Zerodisegno Divisione Quattrocchio, Italy

**124. Christopher Connell** Side table *Ledge*
Recycled ABS plastic. Prototype
H 72cm (28⅜ in)  W 40cm (15¾ in)  L 120cm (47¼ in)
Manufacturer: MAP, Australia

**125. Donato d'Urbino and Paolo Lomazzi (DDL Studio)** Table *Tabù*
Aluminium
H 55cm (21¾ in) or 75cm (29½ in)  Di 45cm (17¾ in)
Manufacturer: Zerodisegno Divisione Quattrocchio, Italy

**126. Hiroshi Awatsuji** Table *Egg*
Acrylic
H 70cm (27½ in)  W 110cm (43⅜ in)  L 110cm (43⅜ in)
Manufacturer: Design House AWA, Japan

**127. Hauke Murken** Folding table *Last Minute*
Birch plywood
H 73cm (28¾ in)  W 76cm (30in)  D 81cm (31⅞ in)
Manufacturer: Moormann, Germany

123

124

125

127

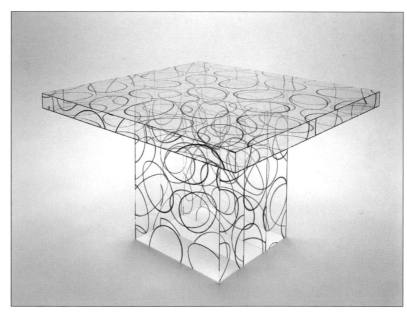
126

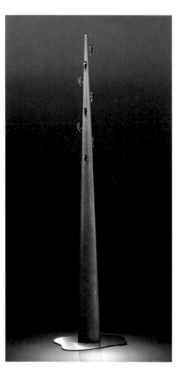

**129** **130**

**131**

**129. Maurizio Pierino** Coat rack

**130. Pol International** Coat rack *Barcelona*
H 180cm (70⅝ in)  Di 45cm (17¾ in)
Manufacturer: Pol International Design Co., Belgium

**131. Susan Frank and David Frisch** Occasional table *Hat Box*
Sand-blasted steel, maple plywood. Limited batch production
H 75cm (29½ in)  Di 42.5cm (16¾ in)
Manufacturer: Palazzetti, USA

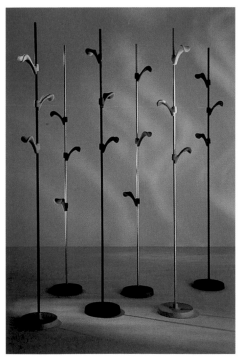 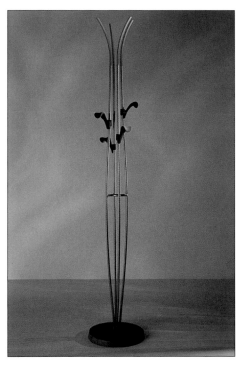 

**132**                                        **133**

**132. Prospero Rasulo** Coat rack *Albera*

Chromium-plated steel tube, rubber
H 215cm/185cm (84⅝ in/72⅞ in)  Di 40cm/20cm (15¾ in/7⅞ in)
Manufacturer: B.R.F., Italy

**133. Piero de Martini** Coat rack *Viz*

Cherrywood, oak
H 174cm (68½ in)  W 43cm (16⅞ in)  D 43cm (16⅞ in)
Manufacturer: Morphos (Acerbis International), Italy

Despite the absence of *Euroluce* in 1993, which has now become a biennial event, the sense of adventure and innovation that has surrounded lighting design for the past decade showed little sign of diminishing. In the combination of new technologies and sculptural freedom, the light fitting presents creative opportunities which designers continue to find irresistible. As many have pointed out, there is also the sense that no matter how far you push the boundaries, lighting remains a functional object whereas much avant-garde furniture quickly becomes useless to sit on or relax with.

# Lighting | 91

Lighting is not just about creating industrial sculpture, however. There is also the question of the quality of light itself created by the luminaire. That made selecting the best designs of the year a more difficult task for Ron Arad, who proved highly resistant to the visual clichés inherent in low-voltage wire systems and spiky post-Modern fittings. Arad admires the clever new idea that is both witty and functional. That is why he so enjoys Denis Santachiara's lights, which hold fruit or project sheep on to the wall for insomniacs to count at night.

Arad's selection also reflects what German design manager Matthias Dietz describes as the "new modesty" in design. Rich effects are achieved using poor materials, found objects even. There are lights incorporating wine bottles (by Stephan Doesinger) and milk bottles (Tejo Remy); lights made of fabric and Velcro (King Miranda's *Senyera* system for the Barcelona Olimpiada Cultural); even lights made using paper images photocopied on to overhead projector foils (Matthias Dietz's *Copy Edition* collection) or comprising fluorescent tubes only half removed from their packaging (Ron Arad for Belux). This is lighting reduced to its bare essentials, devoid of all decorative or production excess – a design counterpoint to the energy-saving technology being developed by light source manufacturers.

There is still room for the beautiful or quirky statement – most notably in work by Ingo Maurer or Tom Dixon or in the new Nemo *Home Stars* collection – but here too there is an economy of form, a precision in the poetic. Arad's selection avoids the more violent, extreme forms of lighting sculpture showcased in previous editions of *The International Design Yearbook*. It prefers instead to concentrate on the scope for genuine ideas-based innovation that the nature of light itself intrinsically provides.

Detail: **Tejo Remy** *Milk Bottle Lamp*

**1.** Detail from
**Stephan Doesinger** Floor lamp *Mind-Ignit*
(See page 109)

2

**2. Masayuki Kurokawa** Suspension lamp *Lavinia*
Aluminium alloy, painted steel, polycarbonate
100w mini krypton bulb
H 27.2cm (10⅜ in)  W 66cm (25¾ in)  D 56cm (22in)
Manufacturer: Yamagiwa Corporation, Japan

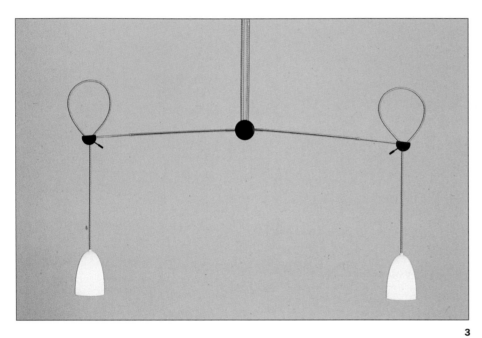

3

## Nemo

Visitors to the 1993 Milan Furniture Fair were not expecting to see a new lighting collection, given the absence of *Euroluce* and the strict instructions that furniture exhibitors should not display light fittings. As a habitual absentee from the *Fiera* site, Cassina was able to play host in the casual spendour of its Via Turati showroom to the new *Home Stars* light collection from Nemo, which is part of the Cassina group.

The creative force behind Nemo is Carlo Forcolini, no stranger to design innovation in Milan through his work for Alias and Artemide. Forcolini's aim is to create light fittings for the home which "fuse function and invention" and "make discipline and imagination work together". Each light in the new collection is named after a different star in the galaxy.

*Home Stars* features a lot of Forcolini's own designs, plus work by Vico Magistretti. What really caught Ron Arad's eye, however, was an idea by Laura Agnoletto and Marzio Rusconi: *Sharatan*, available in single and double versions, is an adjustable suspended lamp for dining rooms or desks, with wound spiral flex in stainless steel and diffusers in opal blown glass. Its discreet minimal form has a graceful presence. (Sharatan, incidentally, is a blue-white star which is 44 light years from Earth.) Another Nemo light is more overtly playful: Ilaria Gibertini's small, surreal-looking *Virgo* table lamp in cast aluminium and polypropylene is named after a star 50 million light years from the Milky Way and traditionally associated with spring, love and fertility. Not suprisingly Nemo is promoting it as a lover's lamp.

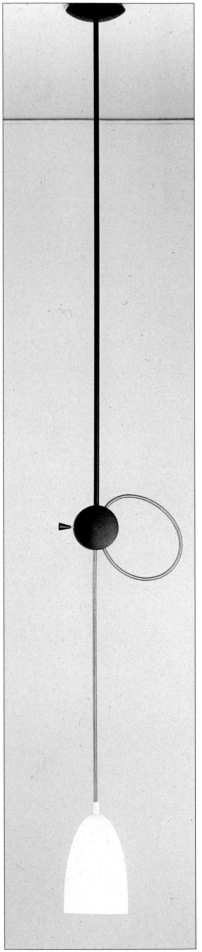

4

**3. Laura Agnoletto and Marzio Rusconi** Suspension light *Sharatan 2*

Steel, stainless steel, opal blown glass
100w 220/240v bulb
W 116cm – 190cm (45⅝ in –74in)  L 127cm  – 192cm (49⅝ in – 74⅞ in)
Manufacturer: Nemo, Italy

**4. Laura Agnoletto and Marzio Rusconi** Suspension light *Sharatan*

Stainless steel, opal blown glass
100w 220/240v bulb
W 12cm (4¾ in)  L 127cm – 192cm (49⅝ in – 74⅞ in)
Manufacturer: Nemo, Italy

**5**

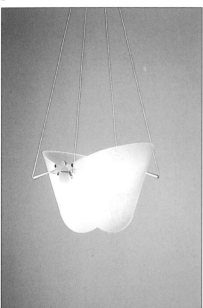

**6**

**7**

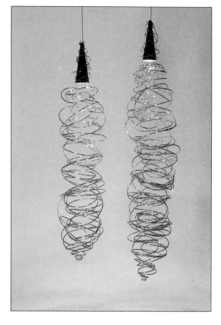

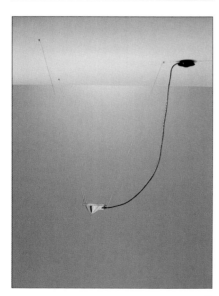

**8**

**9**

**5. Michele de Lucchi** Suspension lamp *Si Gira*
Silver, painted metal, plastic
Limited batch production. 2 max 100w bulbs
H max 150cm (58⅝ in)  W 52cm (20½ in)  L 36cm (14⅛ in)
Manufacturer: Classicon, Germany

**6. Michele de Lucchi** Suspension lamp *Luna*
Murano glass. Limited batch production
100w bulb
W 12cm (4¾ in)  Di 36cm (14⅛ in)
Manufacturer: Av Mazzega, Italy

**7. Lyn Godley** Suspension light *Cyclone Chandelier*
Aluminium, chrome-plated steel. 50w 12v bulb
H 134.6cm (53in) or 167.6cm (66in)  Di 33cm (13in)
Manufacturer: Néotù, USA

**8. Lluis Clotet** Ceiling lamp *Castor*
Varnished cast bronze, Pyrex glass
Max 150w halogen bulb
H 6.5cm (2½ in)  L 18cm (7⅛ in)  D 12cm (4¾ in)
Manufacturer: Bd. Ediciones de Diseño, Spain

**9. Christian Steiner** Suspension light *IX*
Ceramic, aluminium. Two to six 220v bulbs
H variable  W 60cm – 120cm (23½ in – 47¼ in)
D 60cm – 120cm (23½ in – 47¼ in)
Manufacturer: Vest Leuchten, Austria

**10. Philippe Starck** Suspension light *Light Lite*
Plastic. Max 23w electronic fluorescent bulb
H 600cm (234in)  Height of light 24cm (9⅜ in)  Di 43cm (16⅞ in)
Manufacturer: Flos, Italy

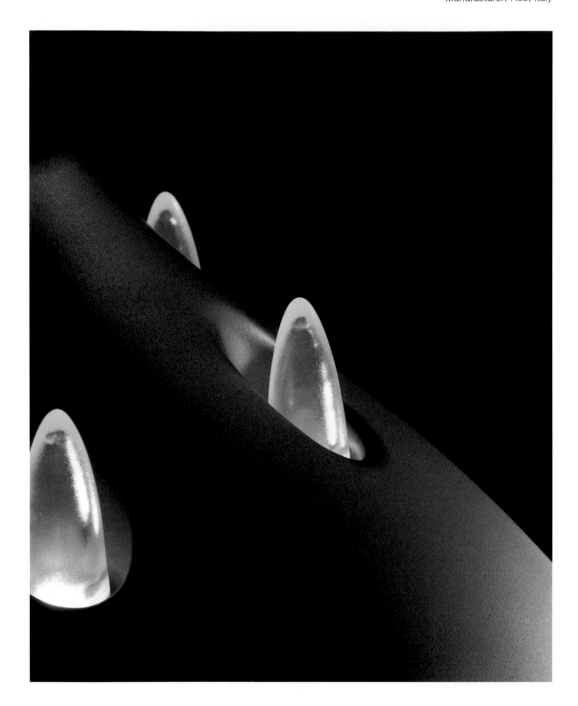

## Philippe Starck

While Philippe Starck's *Miss Sissi* table lamp for Flos rapidly assumes classic status and appears in design museum mail order catalogues, the same combination of designer and manufacturer has produced another engagingly decorative new light – one with an appropriately environment-conscious angle.

*Light Lite* is an energy-saving luminaire with reflector made from two vacuum-formed plastic sheet shells put through a special serigraph process to achieve the metallic colour finish. Coloured inserts which give the light its characteristic anthropomorphic image are made of injection-moulded plastic. *Light Lite* can work either as a ceiling light or as a wall light, hung from a hook. It is said that Starck's buildings often look like giant light fittings, but his lights are always true to themselves.

11                    12                    13                    14

**11. Roberto Pamio** Table lamp *Lucerna*
Chromed metal, glass
60w 220v bulb
H 42cm (16½ in)  W 19cm (7½ in)  D 19cm (7½ in)
Manufacturer: Leucos, Italy

**12. Karim Rashid** *Dulcinea*
Hand-blown glass, nickel or brass
Limited batch production
75w halogen bulb
H 45cm (18in)  Di 23cm (9in)
Manufacturer: North Studio, Canada

**13. Vico Magistretti** Table lamp *Tacita*
Metal. 60w bulb
H 40cm (15¾ in)  Di 28cm (11in)
Manufacturer: Candle, Italy

**14. Kish Munshi** *Electric Candle*
Acrylic, aluminium. 6v bulb. Limited batch production
The bulb is powered by rechargeable battery cells kept inside the base.
H 21cm (8¼ in)  Di 20cm (7⅞ in)
Manufacturer: Sunsha Comm. & Marketing, India

**15. Alessandro Mendini** Table lamp *Antares*
Crystal, metal. 35w 12v halogen dimmer
H 81cm (31⅞ in)  Di 16cm (6½ in)
Manufacturer: Venini, Italy

**16. Marcel Wanders** Table lamp *Set up Shades*
Ready-made from five existing lampshades.
H 66cm (25¾ in)  W 20cm (7⅞ in)  D 20cm (7⅞ in)
Manufacturer: Droog Design, The Netherlands

**17. Jan Tesar** Table lamp *Smile*
Steel, iron. 25w bulb
H 46cm (18⅛ in)  W 19cm (7½ in)  D 22cm (8⅝ in)
Manufacturer: Idée Co., Japan

**18. Jan Tesar** Floor lamp *L'Amant*
Steel, iron. 110w bulb
H 173cm (68⅛ in)
W 42cm (16½ in)  D 46cm (18⅛ in)
Manufacturer: Idée Co., Japan

15                        16

17

### Jan Tesar

Nobody articulates the pure abstract sculpture of the light fitting more clearly than Paris-based designer Jan Tesar. His *L'Amant* floor lamp and *Smile* table lamp, both for Idée Co. of Japan, reflect his background and training as a sculptor and stone cutter.

Tesar's use of paper, wood and stone in lamps shows what the commentator Jean Leymarie has described as "a respect for material, talent for creating vital and autonomous shapes in space, which are sensitive to the touch, and are spiritualised by the light". It is in the use of light to bring his pure sculpture alive that Tesar makes the leap from art to industrial design with his vision uncompromised.

18

19

21

20

**David D'Imperio**

Many designers are drawn to the challenge of the light fitting because as an object it is seen to offer more artistic and poetic scope than, say, a piece of furniture. Miami-based designer David D'Imperio certainly believes this to be the case: "Lighting is a relatively new field in the scheme of things and it offers a lot more opportunities," he says. "It enables you to work more sculpturally yet the finished product still tends to be functional. When you attempt similar ideas in furniture, the finished product tends to be unusable."

D'Imperio trained as a graphic designer but he now batch-produces both furniture and lighting pieces, selling his work through galleries in New York and Los Angeles. His *Patella* and *Cygnet* low-voltage halogen lights shown here reflect his concern to produce sculptural objects with a lightness and purity of touch.

**19. David D'Imperio** Table lamp with dimmer *Patella*
Wood, brass, plastic. Limited batch production
H 38cm (15in)  Di 6.3cm (2½ in)
Manufacturer: David D'Imperio, USA

**20. David D'Imperio** Table lamp *Cygnet*
Wood, brass, plastic. Limited batch production
20w 12v halogen bulb
H 23cm (9in)  W 9cm (3½ in)  L 31cm (12in)
Manufacturer: David D'Imperio, USA

**21. Mario Barbaglia and Marco Colombo**
Table lamp *Tabla*
Technopolymers. 50w 12v halogen bulb
H 36cm (14¼ in)
L of arm 93.5cm (37in)  Di 12cm (4¼ in)
Manufacturer: Italiana Luce, Italy

**22. Ilaria Gibertini** Table lamp *Virgo*
Cast aluminium, polypropylene
20w 12v halogen bulb
H 27.2cm (10⅜ in)  W 10cm (4in)  D 6.7cm (2½ in)
Manufacturer: Nemo, Italy

**23. Hikaru Mori** Table lamp *Iota*
Heat resistant opal polycarbonate,
heat resistant plastic material
20w 12v halogen bulb
H 31cm (12¼ in)  W 11.5cm (4½ in)  D 11cm (4⅜ in)
Manufacturer: Nemo, Italy

**24. Pol International Design** Desk lamp *Ned-land*
Neoprene, aluminium. 60w 220v halogen bulb
Manufacturer: Pol International Design, Belgium

22

23

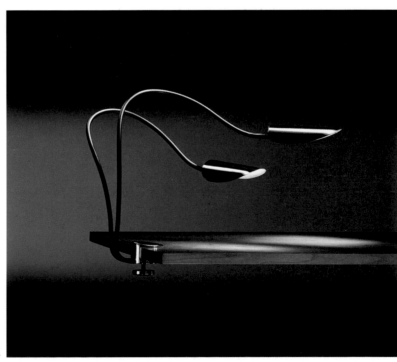

24

25

### Ingo Maurer

Ingo Maurer's gift for the unexpected and the exquisite has made the Munich-based lighting designer a regular feature in successive editions of *The International Design Yearbook*. Nobody else quite achieves the daring and sensitivity of his approach. In his latest work, which develops the idea of attaching angel's wings to what look like ordinary lightbulbs (they are in fact 24-volt versions), he flirts with kitsch but somehow remains in the realms of the poetic. That enduring sense of artistic danger is what recommends Maurer to Ron Arad. Together they exhibit their work every year in Milan: the combination of Arad's powerful metal sculptures and Maurer's delicate, feathered light structures makes for compelling viewing.

Maurer's use of normal-sized lightbulbs is, incidentally, a scaling down of an earlier idea. He first came to the attention of many in Europe with his pop art-inspired *Bulb Bulb* range of 1980 – giant lightbulbs masquerading as colourful plastic floor lamps.

**25. Ingo Maurer** *Birds, Birds, Birds*
Metal, plastic, glass
Max of 24 15w 24v non-halogen bulbs
H 200cm (78¾ in)  W 120cm (47¼ in)
Manufacturer: Ingo Maurer, Germany

**26. Ingo Maurer** *Lucellino*
Glass, brass, plastic, dove feathers
The light has an electronic
transformer-sensor-dimmer.
50w 24v non-halogen bulb
Wall version:
H 30cm (11⅞ in)  Di 8cm (3⅛ in)
Table version:
H 43cm (16⅞ in)  Di 15cm (6in)
Manufacturer: Ingo Maurer, Germany

**27. Ingo Maurer** *Oh Mai Ma*
Silver-plated paper. Prototype
Manufacturer: Ingo Maurer, Germany

26

28

### Perry King and Santiago Miranda

In conjunction with the 1992 Barcelona Olympics, the Olimpiada Cultural commissioned five key objects for the home: a sofa, bed, chair, table and light system. Perry King and Santiago Miranda of King Miranda Associates in Milan were invited to design the lighting for the Casa de Barcelona. The result: a low-voltage halogen lighting system called *Senyera* (the name of the Catalan flag), which has subsequently been developed by Flos/Arteluce.

*Senyera* is light fitting as flag – or flag as light fitting. It is made predominantly of fabric and Velcro. The idea is that the light unfolds like a fabric banner after purchase. It has a low-voltage electric current running through Velcro strips at the edges of the panel. Each lamp is a plane of light, which can be fixed in place anywhere in a room by Velcro feet. By putting up lamps in different combinations, you can create large vertical or horizontal screens of light capable of being suspended in the middle of a space. "It is a form of light architecture," explains Santiago Miranda. "It is very tactile, soft and flexible, more like a piece of clothing than a normal light fitting. It also required very little tooling to manufacture." By using poor materials with a little imagination, King and Miranda have created a system rich in potential and visual effect.

29

30

**31**

### Denis Santachiara

The objects and interiors of Denis Santachiara never fail to engage. He is one of the most inventive, intriguing and humorous talents at work in Milan. He is not interested simply in creating a prettier shape; what drives his designs is the power of the idea, often given a twist. Sometimes his ideas race ahead of their execution and the forms do not live up to the originality of the concept, but lighting is one area in which he manages to strike a balance between his ideas and their realization. His *Sedux* fitting combines wall light with fruit holder, while his *Notturno Italiano* night-light projects a continuous and infinite procession of sheep on to the wall. Santachiara's *Artificial Fire* light is perhaps the most inventive: a wind-blown fabric simulates flame. He is currently working on the Museum of Magic in Paris. Few commissions could be better suited to his skills and temperament.

**32**

**33**

**34**

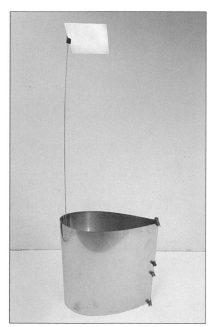

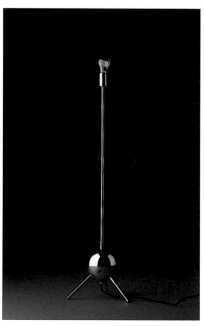

36                                    37                                    38

**35. Hannu Kähönen** *Bow*

Carbon fibre. Prototype
The light fits between the floor and ceiling or between two walls and is held in
place by its own tension.
H 270cm/250cm/180cm (105⅜ in/97⅝ in/70⅛ in)

**36. Thomas Eisl** *Floor lamp*

Stainless steel, aluminium, wood. One-off
A narrow beam spotlight is bounced off an adjustable reflector.
H 250cm (97⅝ in)  W 85cm (33½ in)  D 35cm (13¾ in)

**37. Thomas Eisl** *Floor lamp*

Rubber, aluminium
100w 12v bulb. One-off
H 215cm (83⅞ in)  W 125cm (48¾ in)  D 30cm (11⅞ in)

**38. Stephan Doesinger** Floor lamp *Mind-Ignit*

Brass. One-off
There are sand-blasted messages and quotations on the lightbulb.
60w 220v bulb
H 110cm (43⅜ in)  Di 32cm (12½ in)
Manufacturer: Doesinger/Doesinger, Austria

39

## Wolfgang Karolinsky

Wolfgang Karolinsky must be one of Europe's most unusual lighting designers and entrepreneurs. A former music student who financed his studies by working in a Vienna flea market selling Art Nouveau and Jugendstil lamps, he set up Woka to manufacture faithful hand-finished reproductions of classic lights of the *Wiener Werkstätte* by Hoffman, Loos and Wagner. Woka is an amalgam of Karolinsky's name.

Respect for design history has not blinded Karolinsky to the future, however. Money earned from the historical reproductions has financed a bold and sometimes controversial new Woka "art collection" of contemporary designs. Karolinsky dubs them the "antiques of tomorrow". *Snodo*, shown here, is his own design: an anodized aluminium fitting, which like many of the zoomorphic ideas in the collection (including Walter Schoegner's spider-like *Mimi* light), threatens to take on a life of its own.

**39. Wolfgang Karolinsky** *Snodo*
Anodized aluminium. 50w 12v bulb
*Snodo 1:* H 41cm (16⅛in)  W 9cm – 42cm
(3½ in – 16½ in)
*Snodo 6:* H 40cm (15¾ in)  W 10cm – 40cm
(4in – 15¾ in)
*Snodo 7:* H 45cm (17¾ in)  W 30cm – 90cm
(11⅞ in – 35½ in)  D 10cm (4in)
Manufacturer: Woka Lamps Vienna, Austria

**40. Tom Dixon** Floor lamp *Spiral Uplighter*
Bright steel. Limited batch production
12v halogen dichroic bulb
H 150cm (58⅝ in)  W 50cm (19⅝ in)
D 40cm (15¾ in)
Manufacturer: Space, UK

## Tom Dixon

"The things I make tend to evolve rather than start as a concrete idea," says London-based designer Tom Dixon, whose crudely imaginative, welded "salvage furniture" of the 1980s has now given way to more sophisticated shapes in metal. His *Spiral Uplighter* evolved from a spiral door handle via a spiral sculpture to test the idea on a bigger scale. Dixon is a recent convert to lighting objects, having hitherto concentrated on furniture. "There's more scope to do something kitsch or naive in lighting because lights are easier to sell. People have to renew their lights," he maintains.

The *Spiral Uplighter* is made from 3mm-thick malleable bright steel pulled or scrolled on a vice until the desired coil is achieved. A small low-voltage dichroic bulb in the base throws light up through the coiled steel. Dixon says he is most interested in the "kinetic aspect" of the uplighter: if you gently push the light, it will wobble, and a moving shadow of the coil will be reflected on the ceiling. At a time when, aesthetically, so many low-voltage fittings betray little other than technical sterility, this design combines new technology with a striking decorative presence.

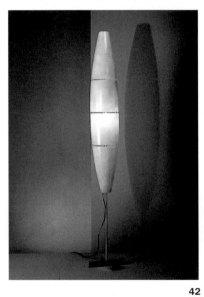

41                    42                    43                    44

**41. Rodolfo Dordoni** Floor lamp *Blossoms Terra*
Murano glass, metal
H 165cm  – 195cm (64⅜ in – 76⅞ in)
Di 53cm (20⅞ in)
Manufacturer: Foscarini Murano, Italy

**42. Joseph Forakis** Floor lamp *Havana Terra*
Polyethylene, metal
H 170cm (66⅞ in)  Di 30cm (11⅞ in)
Manufacturer: Foscarini Murano, Italy

**43. Bernhard Dessecker**  Floor lamp *Swingading*
Steel, plastic, glass, translucent plastic
50w 12v bulbs in lamp and 15w 12v bulb
in base. With a 55w 12v electronic transformer.
H 190cm (74⅞ in)

**44. Josep Aregall** Floor lamp *Alta Costura*
Metal, glass. Two 30w bulbs
H 260cm (102⅜ in)  L 50cm (19⅝ in)
Manufacturer: Metalarte, Spain

**45. Tejo Remy** *Milk Bottle Lamp*
Twelve sand-blasted milk bottles, oven lamps
W 36cm (14⅛ in)  L 300cm (117in)
D 27cm (10½ in)
Manufacturer: Droog Design, The Netherlands

45

**46. Knud Holscher** Spotlight *Quinta*
Die-cast aluminium
Manufacturer: Erco Leuchten, Germany

### Knud Holscher/Robert Heritage

Spotlights belong to a technical sector of lighting which has traditionally left the designer with little individual scope for expression. But new ranges from design-aware manufacturers Concord and Erco show how a distinct personality can be projected even in high-performance lighting systems. Danish designer **Knud Holscher**, a former assistant of Arne Jacobsen, designed the *Quinta* range for Erco; British designer **Robert Heritage**, a former professor of furniture at the Royal College of Art, developed the *Control Spots* for Concord (see page 116). Both systems are made of die-cast aluminium. Both designers are distinguished practitioners who began their careers in the 1950s.

*Quinta* is a range of track-mounted spotlights and floodlights which enables the accurate setting of rotation and tilt angles for light beams. It draws its aesthetic from a humanist Scandinavian approach to Modernism. As Holscher explains: "I'm not a dyed-in-the-wool functionalist. On the *Quinta* spotlights, there are lines which are not strictly needed but they are there as part of an expression to make the product better understood." Concord's *Control Spot* is a range of accent and projection fittings with a wide array of specialist attachments such as a framing head and gel holder to achieve particular effects. Heritage is better known for his furniture than lighting designs, but he enjoys the challenge of lighting. "Furniture is a craft industry, there is still quite a lot of hand-finishing needed," he says. "But with lighting you can control it more and the end product comes off the machine as you designed it."

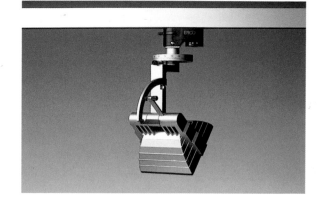

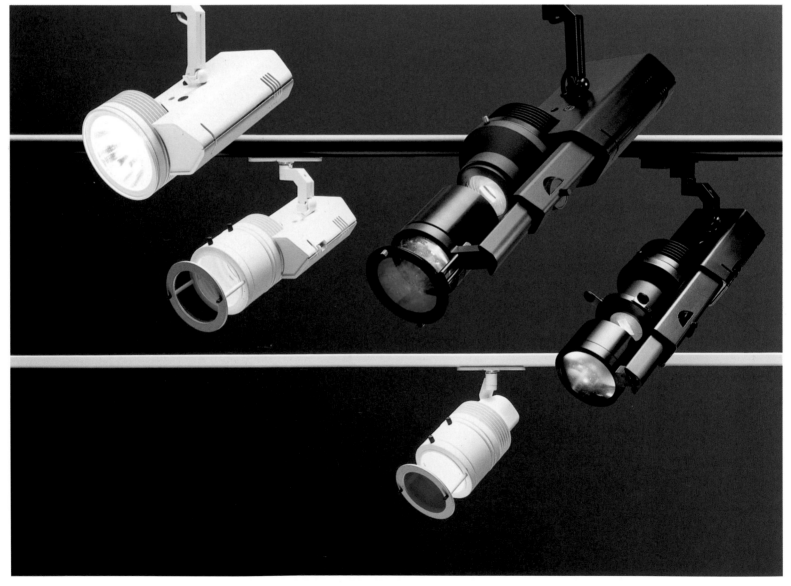

48

49

50

**47. Robert Heritage** Spotlight *Control Spot*
Die-cast aluminium
Manufacturer: Concord Lighting, UK

**48. Shigeaki Asahara** Spotlight *Chivicco SX92*
Die-cast aluminium casting. 35w 12v dichroic bulb
H 7.4cm (3in)  Di 4.2cm (1⅝ in)
Manufacturer: Siom, Japan

**49. Shigeaki Asahara** Spotlight *Chivicco SX91*
Die-cast aluminium casting. 35w 12v dichroic bulb
H 7.4cm (3in)  Di 4.2cm (1⅝ in)
Manufacturer: Siom, Japan

**50. Shigeaki Asahara** Pin spot lamp *Chivicco SX93*
Die-cast aluminium casting. 35w 12v dichroic bulb
H 13cm (5⅛ in)  Di 4.2cm (1⅝ in)
Manufacturer: Siom, Japan

**Stephan Doesinger**

The found object in lighting
has a growing heritage. Ever
since Achille and Pier
Giacomo Castiglioni used a
fishing rod, bandsaw and car
headlight to create the
industrial-looking *Toio*
uplighter for Flos in 1962,
designers have been combing
their workshops and
backyards to find readymades
to diffuse and direct light.
Bottles have a long history
as bases for first candles
and then electric lamps,
but this year the humble wine
and milk bottle both enter
*The International Design
Yearbook* in their own right
as luminaires.

Stephan Doesinger's *Prost*
lighting system uses a
standard double-litre Austrian
wine bottle as a translucent
lampshade with typography
sand-blasted on to the glass.
"The basic idea is to fill the
bottle with light, not wine,"
says Doesinger, who is an
industrial design student at
Linz in Austria. "I wanted to
use a banal product, a cheap,
expendable object to cover
the light, in order to transmit
messages and quotations.
The bottle is exchangeable;
the quality of light is most
important."

Doesinger, who has worked
with Alessandro Mendini in
Milan, created the *Prost* light
installations for exhibitions in
Linz and Vienna. In a similar
exercise, **Tejo Remy** of Droog
Design used milk bottles to
create a dramatic light (see
page 113).

51

**51. Stephan Doesinger** Lighting system *Prost*
Standard wine bottles

52

53

54

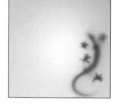

55

**52. Matthias Dietz** *Copy Edition*
Zinc sheet, acrylic glass
Limited batch production.
Lampshades produced on
the photocopier by a variety
of designers:
**53. Hironen**
**54. Ben Bleibe**
**55. Formfürsorge**
**56. James Irvine**
**57. Pedro Silva Dias**
**58. Hideo Mori**
**59. Stiletto**
**60. Konstantin Grcic**
40w bulb
H 30cm (11¾ in)
W 30cm (11¾ in)
D 12cm (4¾ in)
Manufacturer: Dietz Design
Management, Germany

56

57

58

59

60

## Copy Edition

Some of the best lighting ideas are also the simplest. *Copy Edition* is a collection of a hundred designs by artists and designers all over the world assembled by Matthias Dietz of Dietz Design Management in Frankfurt. He was instructed by a German client, Thomas Schulte Designmanufaktur, to develop a new range of lights featuring leading design names for launch at the Ambiente trade show in Frankfurt in February 1993. There was very little time so Dietz simply took an existing wall-lamp design by Metamoderne of Hanover – a simple white acrylic square shade fixed with a bulldog clip – and wrote to more than a hundred designers requesting a surface pattern on a single A3 sheet of paper. These poured in from far and wide. Dietz then used a colour photocopier to print the images on to overhead projection foils. These were laminated on to the translucent sheets with transparent adhesive tape, and shades mounted on to the light with the clip.

The result is a collection of decorative lights which can be changed daily. People can even create their own designs using a photocopier machine with foils, says Dietz. "The theoretical point about this project is that it eliminates the division between arts and crafts and industrial manufacture," he explains. "*Copy Edition* is like the bare bones of lighting, what you would see on an x-ray. It reflects the new modesty in design for production."

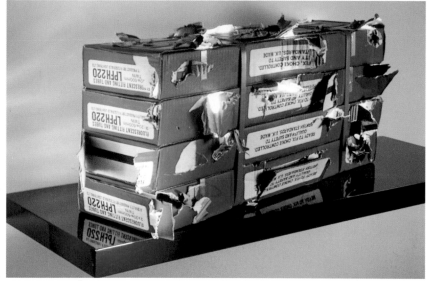

**61**

**62**

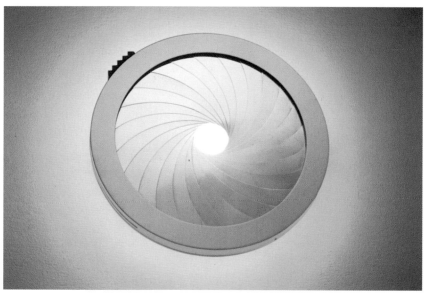

**63**

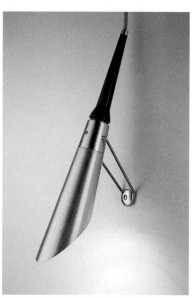

**64**

### Belux

When Swiss lighting manufacturer Belux invited 14 leading European designers to create a wall light for its *Private Light* collection, the ideas ranged from the practical to the abstract. Some lights could be made; others represented ironic commentaries on the nature of light. Dietz Design Management of Frankfurt worked with Belux to develop the *Private Light* concept into an exhibition.

**Andrea Branzi's** windmill-style *Luce*, **Hannes Wettstein's** conical *Lucifer* and **Paolo Pallucco's** circular-vortex *Shelter from the Storm* all reflect the creative preoccupations of their authors while remaining true to the artifice of wall-light design. Ron Arad's entry – *Boxes* – goes a stage further than anyone else in deconstructing the wall light and divorcing the core idea from the world of lighting production. Arad simply purchased a pack of fluorescent tubes, opened the end, connected a wire and plug, and ripped the cardboard to reveal the light. The packs were placed on a simple shelf to become a wall light; Arad explains that the more light you want, the more cardboard you rip. As the tubes are cold cathode, there is no danger of *Boxes* catching fire.

**61. Ron Arad** Wall lamp from the *Private Light* collection *Boxes*
Cardboard boxes, fluorescent tubes. Prototype
W 54cm (21¼ in)  L 53cm (21¼ in)
D 18cm (7⅛ in)
Manufacturer: Belux, Switzerland

**62. Andrea Branzi** Wall lamp from the *Private Light* collection *Luce*
Carton. Prototype. 100w halogen bulb
W 27cm (10½ in)  L 60cm (23½ in)
D 17cm (6⅝ in)
Manufacturer: Belux, Switzerland

**63. Paolo Pallucco** Wall lamp from the *Private Light* collection *Shelter from the Storm*
Aluminium, iron. Two 13w bulbs
H 6cm (2⅜ in)  Di 25cm (9⅞ in)
Manufacturer: Belux, Switzerland

**64. Hannes Wettstein** Wall lamp from the *Private Light* collection *Lucifer*
Wood, aluminium. Prototype. 60w bulb
L 45cm (17¾ in)  Di 7cm (2¾ in)
Manufacturer: Belux, Switzerland

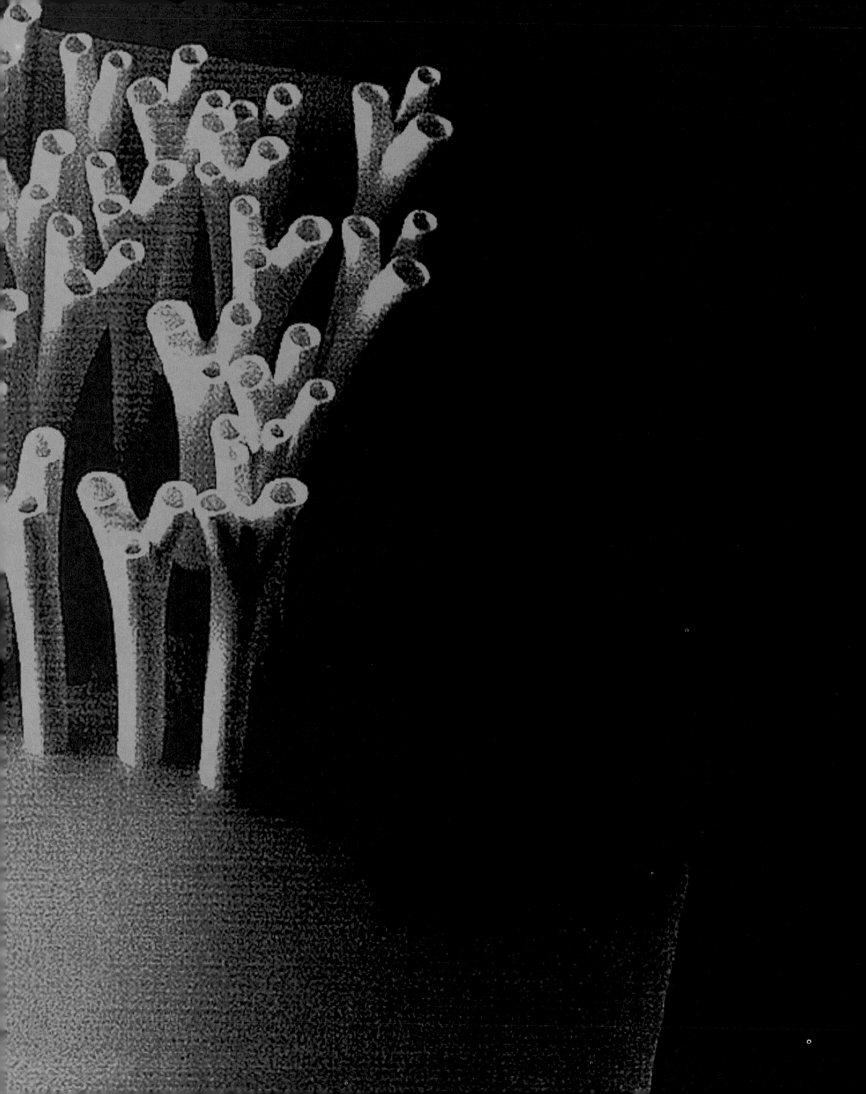

Detail: **Makoto Komatsu** *Vase*

Tableware reflects the most fundamental cultural rituals of our society in that the way we eat and entertain and the objects we put on our table say a lot about social and economic progress. It also reveals much about the technology of the age, and the industrial processes and materials that are available. This year's tableware designs show both a growing trend towards informality and simplicity in dining, and a growing fascination among designers with technical innovation.

# Tableware | 123

As a category, tableware has often divided guest editors of *The International Design Yearbook* between those who opt for pieces with ornate richness and pattern, and those drawn to starkly sculptural forms which do not require any decoration at all to work as objects. Ron Arad's selection shows that he is firmly in the latter camp. He believes that decoration and surface pattern often get in the way of the intrinsic design idea that gives the artefact its reason to exist. He also finds raw materials seductive in themselves, especially glass. "I think it is very difficult to blow ugly glass," he commented, while pondering over his selection. "This is the case even more so than with ceramics or plastics which also have seductive qualities."

Arad is not interested in fashion, often the watchword in tableware; he is interested in functional invention. Phillipe Starck's teapot for Alessi was chosen not simply because it is an exercise in style (which it is) but because it was designed to be deliberately unstable so that the slight motion helps the tea to brew. The presence of work by Takenobu Igarashi and Toby Russell – one designer working with Japanese traditional craft metalworkers to create objects of pure conviction, the other experimenting with origami techniques to score and fold pewter – reveals Arad's interest in the effects that handworking with metal can achieve. There are, of course, strong echoes of this in his own work. But, above all else, it was a series of experimental glass pieces by Gaetano Pesce for the CIRVA research institute in Marseilles that captured Arad's imagination. These explore six radical new techniques and suggest new directions for design. "I like the way Pesce uses objects wholesale as raw material," Arad explained. "The object is recycled with the memory of what it was before. When you look at the glass bowls, you can see the process – you can even feel the heat."

As in furniture and lighting, Arad prefers the bold, even anarchic new idea or technique which is not quite resolved in execution, over and above the competent, professional-looking, uncritical piece which does not break any new ground in either thinking or making. He finds a lot of the Scandinavian functionalist-inspired tableware boring, even though it is devoid of decoration and suggests "good Euro-modern design" in the accepted sense. However, Arad finds room in his selection for Ursula Munch-Petersen's colourful and playful *Ursula* tableware range for Royal Copenhagen – Modernist with a refreshing twist.

**1. Gaetano Pesce** Bowl *Red Blue*
Glass. Limited batch production
H 16cm (6½ in)  W 58cm (22⅞ in)  D 60cm (23½ in)

1

3

**2. Masayuki Kurokawa** Vase *Arc*
Brass
Left to right: H 15cm (6in)  Di 21cm (8¼ in)
H 35cm (13¾ in)  Di 9.5cm (3¾ in)
H 23.5cm (9¼ in)  Di 15cm (6in)
Manufacturer: Takenaka Works Co., Japan

**3. Kristian Gavoille** *Vase*
Bronze
H 22cm (8⅝ in)  Di 16cm (6½ in)
Manufacturer: Néotù, France

**4. Mario Bellini** Vase *Alzata*
Blown glass
H 26cm (10¼ in)  Di 45cm (17¾ in)
Manufacturer: Venini, Italy

**5. Mario Bellini** Vase *Veronese*
Blown glass
H 44cm (17¼ in)  Di 28cm (11in)
Manufacturer: Venini, Italy

**6. Christopher Williams** Vase *Button*
8% lead glass. Limited batch production
H 17cm (6⅝ in)  W 4cm – 7cm (1½ in – 2¾ in)  D 4cm (1½ in)
Manufacturer: The Glasshouse, UK

**7. David Palterer** Vase *Botticelli*
Crystal
H 40cm (16in)  W 27cm (10½ in)  D 27cm (10½ in)
Manufacturer: Driade, Italy

**8. David Palterer** Vases *Bellini* and *Boulbon*
Transparent crystal
*Bellini*: H 35cm (13¾ in)  Di 16cm (6½ in)
*Boulbon*: H 26cm (10¼ in)  L 7cm (2¾ in)  D 7cm (2¾ in)
Manufacturer: Driade, Italy

4

5

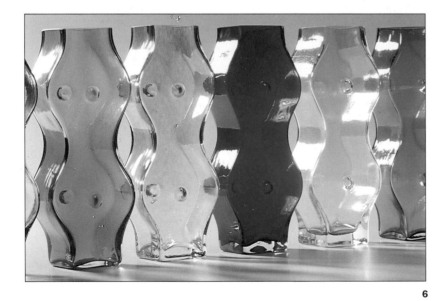

6

7

8

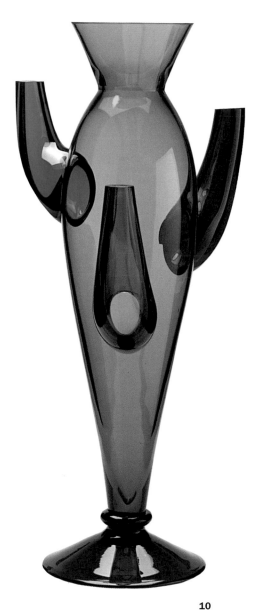

9

10

11

**9. David Palterer** *Vase No. 226*
Glass, potassium. Limited batch production
H 55cm (21¾ in)  Di 15cm (6in)
Manufacturer: Alterego, The Netherlands

**10. David Palterer** *Vase No. 227*
Glass, potassium. Limited batch production
H 47cm (18⅜ in)  Di 15cm (6in)
Manufacturer: Alterego, The Netherlands

**11. David Palterer** *Centrepiece No. 412*
Glass, potassium. Limited batch production
H 47cm (18⅜ in)  Di 20cm (7⅞ in)
Manufacturer: Alterego, The Netherlands

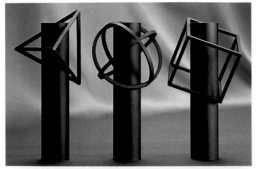

**12**

**13**

**12. Takenobu Igarashi** Vase *Kaze*

Iron, tin alloy
Left to right:
H 26.5cm (10⅜ in)  W 13.9cm (5⅜ in)  D 9.7cm (3¾ in)
H 24.1cm (9¾ in)  W 13cm (5⅛ in)  D 13cm (5⅛ in)
H 25cm (9⅞ in)  W 14cm (5½ in)  D 17.5cm (6⅞ in)
Manufacturer: Yamada Shomei Lighting Co., YMD Division, Japan

**13. Takenobu Igarashi** Vase *Fuji*

High-zinc
H 20cm (7⅞ in)  W 22.5cm (8⅞ in)  D 5cm (2in)
Manufacturer: Yamada Shomei Lighting Co., Japan

## Takenobu Igarashi

New pieces by Japanese designer Takenobu Igarashi are the result of his collaboration over the past couple of years with a group of local craft metalworkers in Tsubame City, Niigata Prefecture, far away from the Igarashi Studio's Tokyo base. These craftsmen use traditional techniques which have been a feature of the locality for 350 years.

Igarashi is well known in the west for his colourful, exuberant compositions, both graphic and in three dimensions, but his latest work takes a more simple, monochromatic turn. Igarashi says he wants to refine his ideas to the point at which they express an elegant simplicity without becoming dull. Characteristically, his vases play with graphic elements. The *Kaze* vase features tin alloy squares, circles and triangles on a standard iron base. The *Fuji* vase, named after Mount Fuji, is composed of straight lines with a softening curve at the peak to add a "touch of spirituality" to a high-zinc metallic finish. Igarashi's starkly formed stainless steel cutlery, meanwhile, utilizes hand skills requiring 30 different steps to make a spoon (see pages 138–9).

The entire collection is being distributed by the Yamada Shomei Lighting Co. – the first time it has undertaken such a project – in Japan and America. Already it is selling successfully. The Guggenheim Museum in New York has shown particular interest in the *Kaze* vase. Igarashi, who studied at the University of California, has always enjoyed a strong following in America.

**14. Makoto Komatsu** *Vase*
Porcelain, polycarbonate. Prototype
H 15cm (6in)  W 50cm (20⅛ in)  D 50cm (20⅛ in)
Manufacturer: Product M., Japan

**15. Masafumi Sekine** *Plate*
Brass. One-off
H 8cm (3⅛ in)  W 45cm (17¾ in)  D 45cm (17¾ in)

**16. Masafumi Sekine** Plate *Compote*
Brass. One-off
H 9cm (3½ in)  Di 46cm (18⅛ in)

15

16

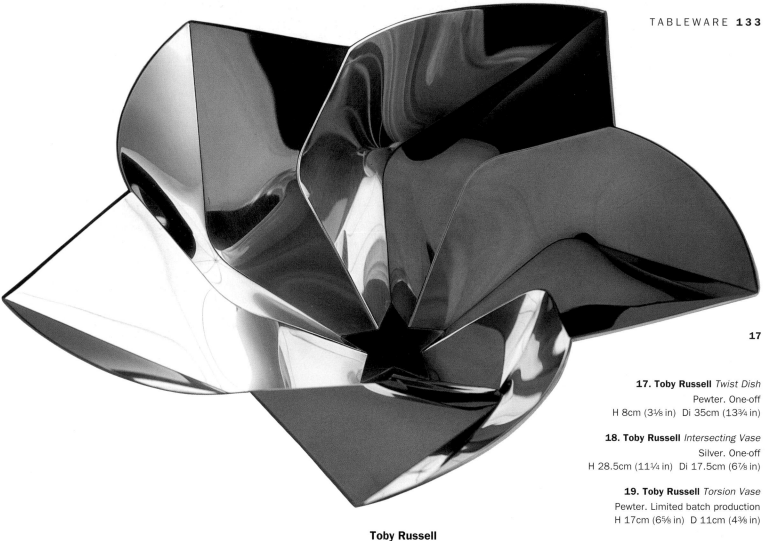

**17**

**17. Toby Russell** *Twist Dish*
Pewter. One-off
H 8cm (3⅛ in)  Di 35cm (13¾ in)

**18. Toby Russell** *Intersecting Vase*
Silver. One-off
H 28.5cm (11¼ in)  Di 17.5cm (6⅞ in)

**19. Toby Russell** *Torsion Vase*
Pewter. Limited batch production
H 17cm (6⅝ in)  D 11cm (4⅜ in)

## Toby Russell

Toby Russell is a British designer-maker who
works mainly in pewter and silver. A graduate
of Camberwell School of Art and Design in
London, his main concern in recent years has
been to find new ways to manipulate metal
into vessel shapes without falling back on the
time-honoured techniques. His principal
technique is graphic: scoring and folding a
metal sheet in the manner of origami to create
a vase or dish. He works in pewter because
it is a solid but soft, handworkable material
which creates a highly reflective surface.

Russell explains that his aim is to "twist, curve
and distort my work in a controlled rhythmic
fashion, through which the highly polished
surfaces provide a transformed vision of the
environment with the main emphasis on fluid
form." Graphic techniques also inform his
silver work. His *Intersecting Vase* in silver was
developed using card forms. "I don't do a lot
of drawing, I work with card to develop the
shapes," says Russell, who claims that his
work has two main allegiances: first,
architectural awareness of Modernism; and
second, the plasticity of organic form. He adds
that coastal formations, desert landscapes
and the reflective qualities of water have also
been strong influences.

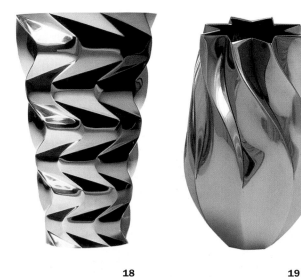

**18**                    **19**

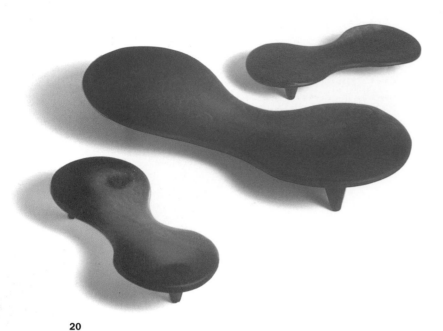

**20**

**20. Marc Newson** Dish *Progetto 9230*
Murano glass
H 6.8cm (2¾ in)  W 49cm (19¼ in)  D 22cm (8⅝ in)
H 3.8cm (1½ in)  W 30cm (11¾ in)  D 13.2cm (5⅛ in)
Manufacturer: Cappellini, Italy

**21. Masatoshi Sakaegi** Tableware *Compact II*
Porcelain
Mug: H 8.5cm (3⅜ in)  W 11.5cm (4½ in)  D 8cm (3⅛ in)
Tea cup: H 6.4cm (2½ in)  W 11.5cm (4½ in)  D 8cm (3⅛ in)
Sugar bowl: H 7.8cm (3½ in)  W 10cm (4in)  D 7.7cm (3⅛ in)
Plate: H 2.2cm (⅞ in)  W 17.5cm (6⅞ in)  D 14.5cm (5¾ in)
Manufacturer: Sakaegi Design Studio, Japan

**22. Kish Munshi** Cup and saucer
Ceramic. Prototype
*Cup*: H 7cm (2¾ in)  Di 9.5cm (3¾ in)
*Saucer*: H 2.5cm (1in)  Di 15cm (6in)
Manufacturer: Sunsha Comm. & Marketing, India

**23. Monica Guggisberg and Philip Baldwin** *Sand-blasted bowl and plate*
5% lead half crystal glass, Kugler colour. Limited batch production
*Bowl*: H 11.6cm (4½ in)  Di 24.5cm (9⅝ in)
*Plate*: H 4cm (1½ in)  Di 37cm (14½ in)
Manufacturer: Verrerie de Nonfoux, Switzerland

**21**

**22**

**23**

## Ursula Munch-Petersen

Few companies reflect developments in Scandinavian design more closely than Royal Copenhagen, which has become the largest decorative arts producer in the region following a series of acquisitions in recent years. Silversmith Georg Jensen, Holmegaard Glassworks and Bing & Grondahl have all come under the Royal Copenhagen banner, as the Danish manufacturing giant develops an integrated portfolio of tableware products in porcelain, silver and glass.

Under Royal Copenhagen design director Karsten Ravn, many new ideas have been explored and, in some cases, the sterile grip of functionalism relaxed. Export markets have expanded, especially in Japan where Danish design continues to have a special cachet. Ceramicist Ursula Munch-Petersen's *Ursula* dinner set, made of faience, reflects the tradition of the cheerful use of colour in Scandinavian Modernist design in the vibrancy of its glazes. In their playful informality, Ursula's shapes also point to new directions, however: an oval dinner plate, for example, and a zoomorphic jug contribute to a sense of freshness and individuality.

**24. Ursula Munch-Petersen** Dinner set *Ursula*
Faience
Large jug: H 16cm (6½ in)  W 10.5cm (4½ in)  L 15.5cm (6⅛ in)
Medium jug: H 12.5cm (5in)  W 8.5cm (3⅜ in)  L 12.5cm (5in)
Small jug: H 10cm (4in)  W 7.2cm (2⅞ in)  L 10.5cm (4½ in)
Small bowl: H 5cm (2in)  W 6.4cm (2½ in)  L 8.5cm (3⅜ in)
Cup: H 6.7cm (2⅝ in)  Di 8.5cm (3⅜ in)
Plate: H 2.3cm (⅞ in)  W 13cm (5⅛ in)  L 17.8cm (7in)
Manufacturer: Royal Copenhagen, Denmark

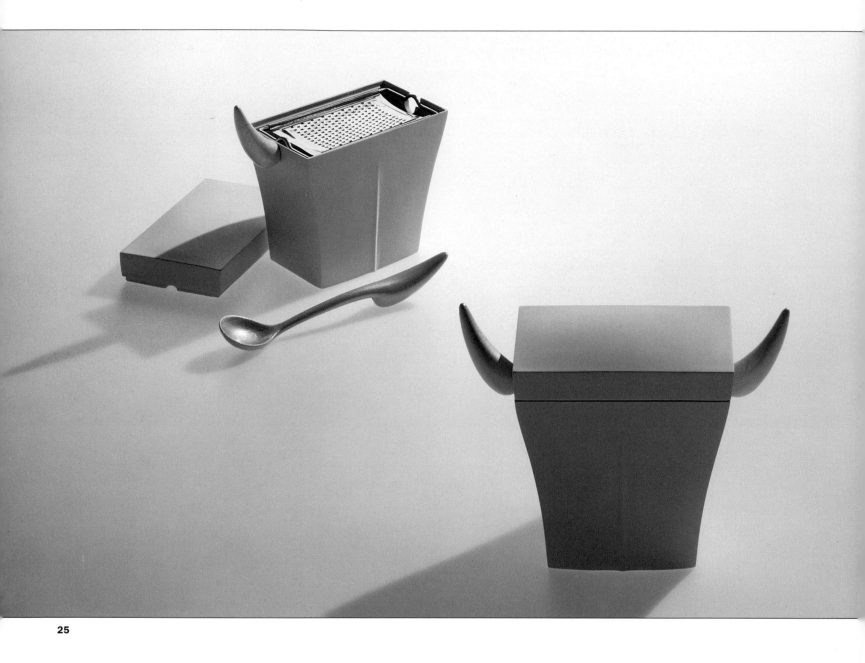

25

**25. Philippe Starck** Container/grater for Parmesan cheese *Mister Meumeu*
ABS polyamide, stainless steel
H 13.5cm (5⅜ in)  W 20.5cm (8⅛ in)  D 8.5cm (3⅜ in)
Manufacturer: Alessi, Italy

**26. Philippe Starck** Knife *Jojo Long Legs*
Bakelite, stainless steel
L 29.5cm (11⅝ in)
Manufacturer: OWO, France

**27. Philippe Starck** Teapot *Ti Tang* and milk jug/sugar bowl *Su-Mi Tang*
Porcelain, aluminium, stainless steel
Teapot: H 22cm (8⅝ in)  W 18cm (7⅛ in)  D 14cm (5½ in)
Milk jug/sugar bowl: H 14cm (5½ in)  Di 7.5cm (3in)
Manufacturer: Alessi, Italy

**26**

**27**

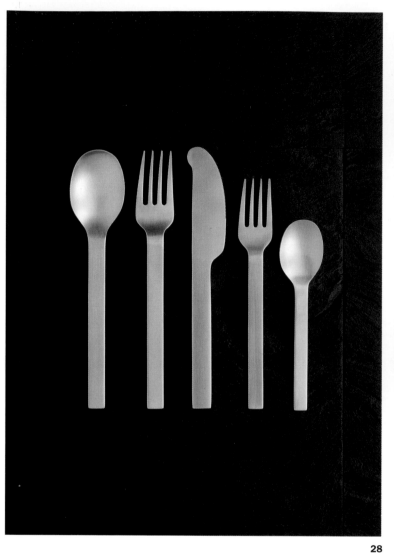

28

29

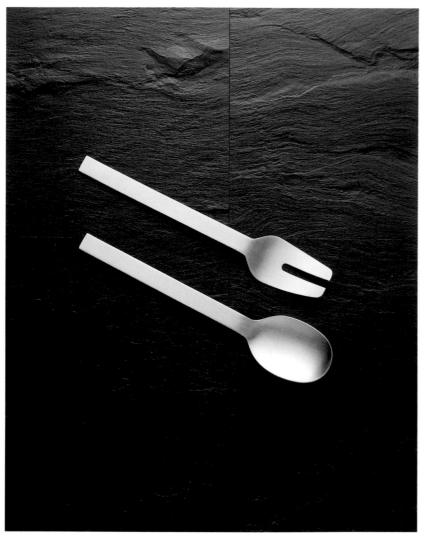

**28. Takenobu Igarashi** Cutlery *Basic Series 5-piece set*
Stainless steel. Left to right:
W 1.3cm – 4.2cm (½ in – 1⅝ in)  L 19.5cm (7¾ in)
W 1.3cm – 2.9cm (½ in – 1⅛ in)  L 19.5cm (7¾ in)
W 1.4cm – 2.3cm (½ in – ⅞ in)  L 19.5cm (7¾ in)
W 1.2cm – 2.5cm (⅜ in – 1in)  L 17.5cm (6⅞ in)
W 1cm – 3.3cm (⅜ in – 1⅜ in)  L 14.5cm (5¾ in)
Manufacturer: Yamada Shomei Lighting Co., YMD Division, Japan

**29. Takenobu Igarashi** *Baby's spoon and fork*
Stainless steel
L 13cm (5⅛ in)
Manufacturer: Yamada Shomei Lighting Co., YMD Division, Japan

**30. Takenobu Igarashi** Cutlery *Basic Series service fork/spoon*
Stainless steel
Spoon: W 1.5cm – 3.1cm (⅝ in – 1⅛ in)  L 27cm (10½ in)
Fork: W 1.5cm (⅝ in)  L 27cm (10½ in)
Manufacturer: Yamada Shomei Lighting Co., YMD Division, Japan

## Anna Castelli Ferrieri

Anna Castelli Ferrieri and Sambonet are two of the most evocative names in post-war Italian design. Architect, town planner and industrial designer Castelli Ferrieri made her name as a leading figure in the Italian period of *riconstruzione,* and as the art director of Kartell between 1976 and 1987. Sambonet is a maker of fine tableware and kitchenware owned by the Sambonet family who were originally goldsmiths and silversmiths. They came from France to Vercelli, between Milan and Turin, in the mid-nineteenth century: the first Sambonet hallmark was stamped on a piece of silverware in 1859. When Roberto Sambonet joined the firm in the early 1950s, having studied under Alvar Aalto, he introduced more pure, streamlined forms utilizing stainless steel.

That sculptural Modernist legacy lives on in Sambonet today. Anna Castelli Ferrieri's new *Hannah* cutlery range has a slim, tapering sculptural intensity. The collection is made in thick, solid steel using a pioneering cold-coining process. A clue to its aim to appeal internationally can be seen in the circular and shallow spoon shape: this is the tradition of English-speaking countries, as opposed to a longer and deeper cup with which Italians are more familiar.

**32**

**31. Anna Castelli Ferrieri** Cutlery *Hannah*
Stainless steel
Table spoon: L 20.5cm (8⅛ in)  W 5.3cm (2⅛ in)
Teaspoon: L 13.5cm (5⅜ in)  W 3.5cm (1⅜ in)
Dessert spoon: L 17.5cm (6⅞ in)  W 4.6cm (1⅞ in)
Service spoon: L 22.5cm (8⅞ in)  W 5.8cm (2¼ in)
Dessert fork: L 17.5cm (6⅞ in)  W 2.1cm (⅞ in)
Table fork: L 20.5cm (8⅛ in)  W 2.4cm (1in)
Service fork: L 22.5cm (8⅞ in)  W 2.6cm (1⅛ in)
Dessert knife: L 20.2cm (8in)  W 1.5cm (⅝ in)
Table knife: L 23.3cm (9⅛ in)  W 1.7cm (¾ in)
Manufacturer: Sambonet, Italy

**32. Robert le Héros** Cutlery from the *Corail des Jardins* range
Nickel-plated silver
Left to right:
L 22cm (8⅝ in)  L 19cm (7½ in)  L 18.5cm (7¼ in)  L 13cm (5⅛ in)
Manufacturer: Objets Pompadour, France

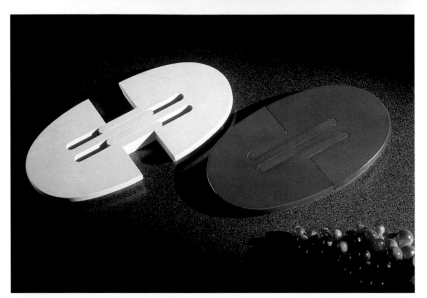

## Jorge Pensi

Argentinian-born Jorge Pensi's prolific work in furniture and lighting has made him a familiar figure on the design circuit in Barcelona, the city which has been his home since 1977. He specializes in using simple, organic forms to create design of considered elegance and quality.

His *Soko* tableware range for Barcino Disseny, a small company requiring a low-cost range which could be made with only modest investment, is his first foray into tableware. Manufactured in wood, cast aluminium, steel and glass, it has all the hallmarks of Pensi's refined, restrained style. The designer, whose *Toledo* café chair for Amat is one of the best-selling models around, would now like to design more tableware – perhaps for a larger factory with more advanced technology. "I always get asked to design chairs," he remarks. "People just don't think of me in the context of other objects."

**33. Jorge Pensi** Tableware range *Soko*
Beechwood, mahogany, aluminium
Fruit bowl: H 17cm (6⅝ in)  Di 40cm (15¾ in)
Trivet: H 2.5cm (1in)  W 19cm – 28cm
(7½ in – 11in)  D 18cm (7⅛ in)
Tray: H 2.5cm (1in)  W 66cm (26in)
D 29cm (11⅜ in)
Manufacturer: Barcino Disseny, Spain

**34. André Ricard** Salt cellar *Salero*
Glass, aluminium
H 11.5cm (4½ in)  W 5.5cm (2⅛ in)
D 3.5cm (1⅜ in)
Manufacturer: Nani Marquina, Spain

**35. Karim Rashid** Pepper grinder *Abaxial*
Birchwood, nickel-plated steel
H 25cm (10in)
Manufacturer: North Studio, Canada

34

35

**36. Michele de Lucchi** Saucepans *Gourmet*
Stainless steel, thermoplastic resin
Casserole: H 10cm (4in)  Di 18cm (7⅛ in)
Deep casserole: H 16cm (6½ in)  Di 20cm (7⅞ in)
Shallow casserole: H 9cm (3½ in)  Di 27cm (10½ in)
Skillet: H 4cm (1½ in)  Di 20cm (7⅞ in)
Manufacturer: Sambonet, Italy

**37. Louis Lara** *Salt and pepper shaker and pepper mill*
Aluminium
Salt and pepper shaker: H 9.4cm (3¾ in)
Di 4.2cm (1⅝ in)
Pepper mill: H 18.3cm (7⅛ in)  Di 6.2cm (2⅜ in)
Manufacturer: Lara Designs, USA

**38. Bang Design (Bryan Marshall)** Range of household
products *Bang Products*
Cast and spun aluminium. Limited batch production
Ashtray: H 2.8cm (1⅛ in)  Di 14.5cm (5¾ in)
Salt and pepper shakers: H 6cm (2⅜ in)
Di 6cm (2⅜ in)
Coaster: H 1.2cm (⅜ in)  Di 8.8cm (3½ in)
Manufacturer: Bang Design, Australia

**39. Kazuo Kawasaki** Chopping board and knife *Cellaria*
Stainless steel, polypropylene
Chopping board: H 1.5cm (⅝ in)
W 30cm (11⅞ in)  D 23cm (9in)
Knife: W 4cm (1½ in)  L 26cm (10¼ in)
Manufacturer: Takefu Knife Village, Japan

36

37

38

39

**40**

**40. Alberto Meda** Food warmer *Kalura*
Copper
When the thermopile within the plate
is powered from the mains for five minutes,
the plate will remain at 70°c
for three hours.
H 5cm (2in)  Di 40cm (15¾ in)
Manufacturer: Domodinamica, Italy

**41. Smart Design** Corkscrew *Good Turn*
ABS
H 20.3cm (8in)  W 7.5cm (3in)
D 5cm (2in)
Manufacturer: Oxo International, USA

**42. Monica Guggisberg and Philip Baldwin**
*Bottles*
5% lead half crystal glass, Kugler colour.
Limited batch production
H 49cm (19¼ in)  Di 9.5cm (3¾ in)
Manufacturer: Verrerie de Nonfoux,
Switzerland

## Smart Design

Since its creation in 1990, New York housewares company
Oxo International has worked with US consultancy Smart
Design on a range of products it describes as representing
"universal design". The aim is to create artefacts which are
aesthetically pleasing, comfortable to use and modestly
priced, explains John Farber of Oxo: "Tools that everyone
can use and everyone can buy."

The *Good Turn* corkscrew reflects that philosophy. Made of
ABS plastics, it works on the principle of the wings spreading
pressure across the hand so that pulling out the corkscrew
is made easier. The product also has a playful visual image
with wings spread out; the designers cannot make up their
minds whether it looks like a Ghanaian fertility doll, a flying
nun or an angel in white. Oxo now plans to move out of the
home and launch a range of products for the garden.

**41**

43

44

## Gaetano Pesce

The international reputation enjoyed by Gaetano Pesce is due in no small part to his polemical furniture pieces which explore the potential of innovative new materials. Although he is an Italian, Pesce has always worked outside the mainstream of Italian design, even its avant-garde wing, dividing his time between Manhattan and Strasbourg. Pesce's lumpen seats and asymmetrical bookshelves have in the past reflected a personal artistic statement that owes little to his native design culture. His latest piece of pure research – experimenting with glass techniques – does, however, have echoes in his boyhood when he watched Venetian glassblowers on the island of Murano. Pesce's new glass pieces are the result of an invitation from CIRVA (Centre International de Recherche sur le Verre et les Arts plastiques) to research new ways to work with glass. This glass workshop in Marseilles, sponsored by the French government, wanted Pesce to use his experience with other materials, notably plastics, to suggest new directions for glass.

Pesce developed a series of glass bowls based on six techniques. These formed the subject of a CIRVA exhibition. The first process, entitled *Mistral*, entails doing with molten glass what an airbrush does with paint. A compressed air jet is used to blow fine sand through a flame hot enough to melt it into beads which then impact on the surface of a mould. The second process, *Plage*, involves baking sand within a mould with or without the addition of glass beads and oxides to provide colour and pattern. *Joliette*, meanwhile, entails thermoforming glass beads to create spontaneous works that have a pointillistic pictorial quality. *Vieux Port* takes ribbons of glass and moulds them together to create vibrant pieces. In a fifth process, *Pastis* (named after a favourite French aperitif), old bottles, either whole or broken, are salvaged and sandwiched between panes of glass to suggest the environmental process of de-materialization in a humorous way. Pesce also updates, in a sixth process, the *pâté de verre* technique using lost-wax moulds to enable the formation of more intricate designs.

The bold way in which these pieces deconstruct and reinvent the material takes tableware design beyond formal order into the realms of chance and even chaos. Yet this pure research is of great interest to manufacturers and confirms Pesce's position as a leading theorist in new design. The *Mistral* technique in particular is regarded as having industrial potential – one manufacturer wants to use it to make perfume bottles.

45

**Gaetano Pesce**

**43.** Bowl *Vert Bouteille*
Glass. Limited batch edition
H 17cm (6⅝ in)  W 65cm (25⅝ in)  D 60cm (23½ in)

**44.** Bowl *Octobre*
Glass. Limited batch production
H 19cm (7½ in)  W 80cm (31½ in)  D 72cm (28⅜ in)

**45.** Bowl *Noir Bouteille*
Glass. Limited batch edition
H 18cm (7⅛ in)  W 70cm (27½ in)  D 65cm (25⅝ in)

**46**. Bowl *Petit Bouteille*
Glass. Limited batch edition
H 10cm (4in)  W 35cm (13¾ in)  D 32cm (12½ in)

46

Detail: **Yoshiki Hishinuma** *Tape Knit*

Nowhere are Ron Arad's main criteria for inclusion in *The International Design Yearbook* – freshness, boldness and invention using new techniques and materials – more clearly expressed than in the textiles category. Out of the range of designs submitted from around the world, he has chosen in an unprecedented way to focus on the work of just five textile designers. Four of them are Japanese: Yoshiki Hishinuma and Koji Hamai, who cross effortlessly from fabrics to fashion, controlling the whole design process; Reiko Sudo, who follows in the hand-weaving tradition of Junichi Arai; and the Maki Design Studio, run by sisters Kaori and Chiaki Maki, which has a workshop producing designs in natural silk in India. The only non-Japanese designer to be selected was Helle Abild, a Danish designer based in New York, whose witty, innovative computer-based portfolio was the only work which Arad regarded as on a par with the technical and creative brilliance of the Japanese.

# Textiles | 149

In many ways it is a fascinating selection because Arad has been unknowingly drawn to the work of designers representative of a new generation in textiles. All are young, in their late twenties to late thirties, and this is surely more than coincidence. The dominant Japanese designers of recent years – Junichi Arai, Hiroshi Awatsuji and Eiji Miyamoto – are no longer interested in working for commerce and industry and have become pure artists. Meanwhile the next generation, heavily influenced by these designers, has started to make its mark.

Japanese textile design fascinates the West because of the way in which the essence of Kimono culture, with its high standard of technique, sense of colour and civilizing influence, continues to be incorporated into the making of modern clothes and interiors by modern means. Japanese tradition coexists with new technologies and designs, even though Kimono culture has been slowly disappearing as Japanese society has become progressively westernized since 1945.

This disappearance of a craft-weaving industry in Japan led the Maki sisters to establish a workshop in New Delhi to achieve the pure, hand-spun techniques that characterize their highly textured designs. Other designers, meanwhile, interpret textile traditions on a more abstract level. Above all, Arad's selection reflects a group of designers for whom the glossy perfection of surface pattern has become less important than showing a deeper textural personality. Though the computer is in use as a design tool, there is great concern to produce work which symbolizes the human spirit. As Reiko Sudo says of her ragged, montage-style *Cracked Cloth* series, "Today everything is perfect, symmetrical and clean, but in these fragile things we can feel more spirit. I really want to create that effect."

**1. Koji Hamai** *Bits of polyester 4*
Polyester. Prototype. W 100cm (39½ in)
L 200cm (78¾ in)

**2. Koji Hamai** *Crinkled 6*
Polyester. Prototype. W 50cm (19⅝ in)
L 150cm (59in)

1

## Koji Hamai

Koji Hamai abhors the artificial boundaries between the fashion and textile designer. He refuses to be pigeonholed as one or the other. In fact he only accepts the title "material designer" as his fabrics are used not only in fashion and interiors but also in stage and costume design, and in advertising, graphics and posters. He graduated from the same fashion school as Yoshiki Hishinuma, winning several awards as a student, and he has always been in the limelight as a designer. He worked in Eiji Miyamoto's textile design studio for two years and spent five years with Issey Miyake before establishing himself as an independent designer.

Hamai's *Crinkled* series, recently exhibited in Japan, is the most adventurous of his new work. The 100 per cent polyester is made up into costume and then heavily pleated. What will it be used for? Not just fashion, says Hamai. "There were many theatre and costume designers at my exhibition, and graphic designers who are interested in it for album covers."

Hamai believes that his fabrics can cross disciplines – he is currently interested in using the materials he has designed in commercial interiors, not just for curtains and furnishings but as floor- and wall-coverings. "Even in this age of industrial design," he says, "I do not want to lose the feeling of the hand-made. A complex high-tech design can be copied in 20 minutes on the computer, but a computer cannot replicate the human spirit."

**Koji Hamai**

**3.** *Bits of polyester 3*
Polyester. Prototype. W 100cm (39½ in)
L 100cm (39½ in)

**4.** *Bits of polyester 5*
Polyester. Prototype. W 100cm (39½ in)
L 100cm (39½ in)

**5.** *Bits of polyester 1*
Polyester. Prototype. W 100cm (39½ in)
L 100cm (39½ in)

**6.** *Bits of polyester 2*
Polyester. Prototype. W 100cm (39½ in)
L 100cm (39½ in)

**7.** *Crinkled 1*
Polyester. Prototype. W 50cm (19⅝ in)
L 150cm (59in)

**8.** *Crinkled 2*
Polyester. Prototype. W 50cm (19⅝ in)
L 150cm (59in)

**9.** *Crinkled and Crinkled 3*
Polyester. Prototype. W 50cm (19⅝ in)
L 150cm (59in)

**10.** *Crinkled 4*
Polyester. Prototype. W 50cm (19⅝ in)
L 150cm (59in)

**11.** *Crinkled 5*
Polyester. Prototype. W 50cm (19⅝ in)
L 150cm (59in)

**12.** *Crinkled 7*
Polyester. Prototype. W 100cm (39½ in)
L 100cm (39½ in)

3

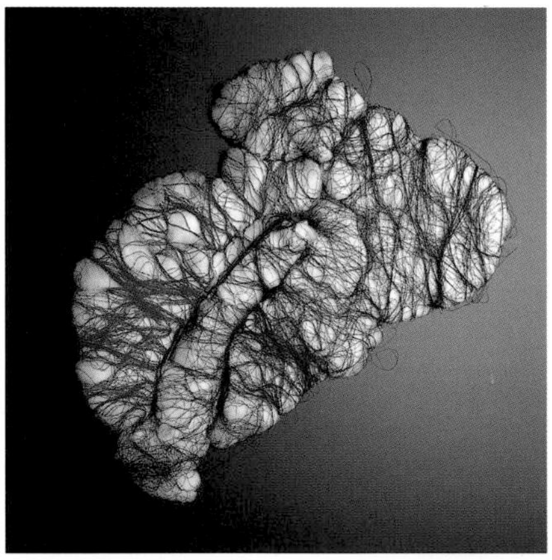

4

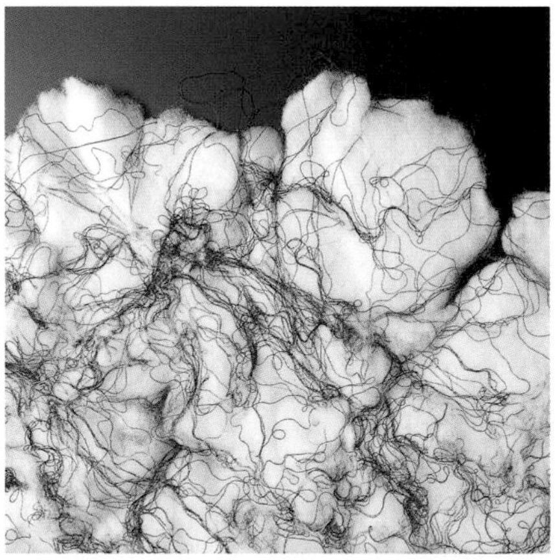

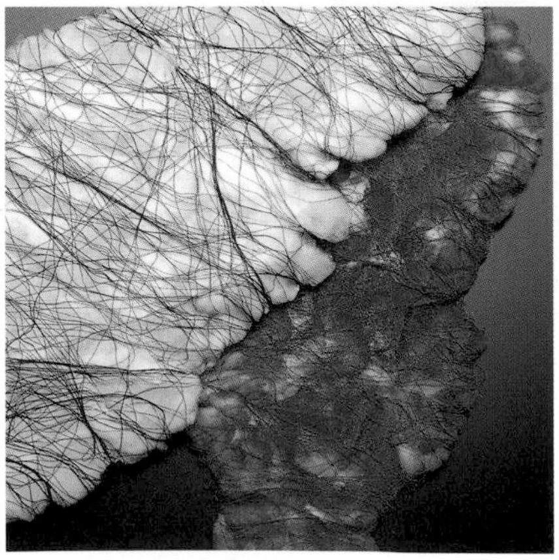

5

6

7

8

9

10

11

12

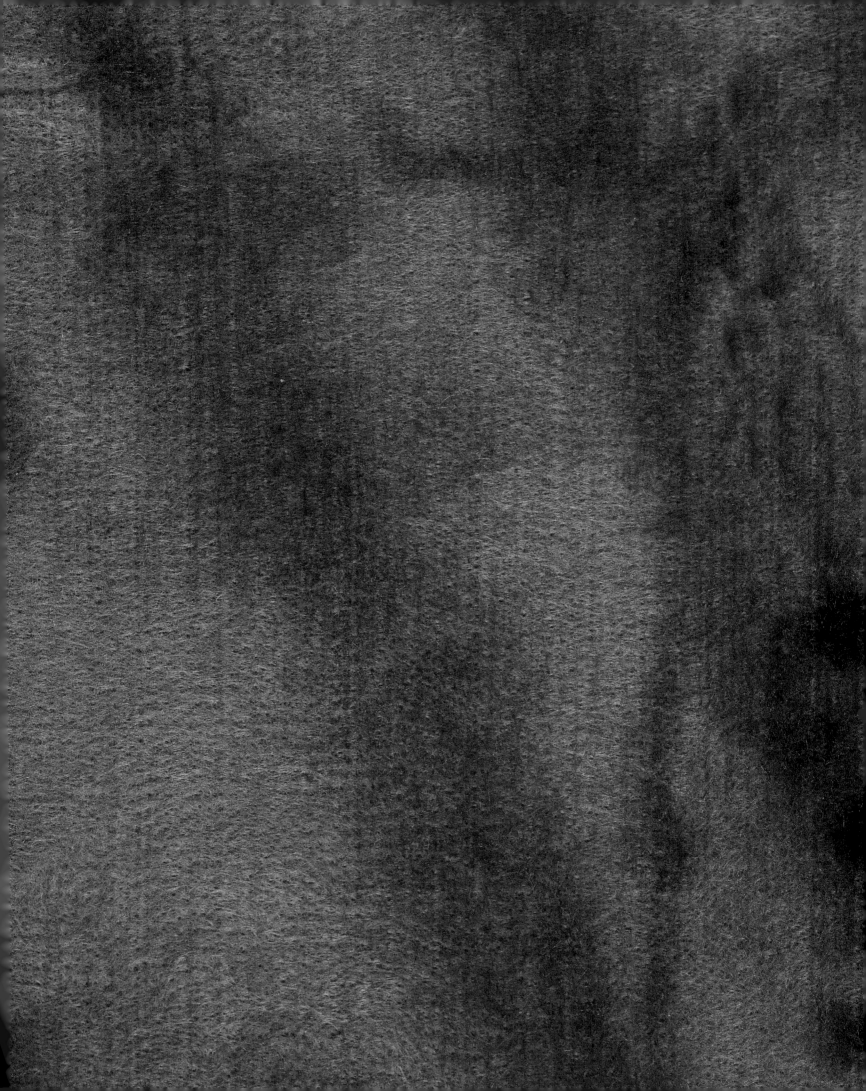

## Yoshiki Hishinuma

Yoshiki Hishinuma regards himself first
and foremost as a fashion designer.
He graduated from fashion design
school in Tokyo and says he only
started designing textiles because
"I was looking for the right material for
my creations but I could find nothing
to satisfy me." Since 1992 he has
produced two new Paris collections
a year and is regarded as a rising star
among young Japanese fashion
designers. But unlike the established
fashion design names such as Issey
Miyake and Yoji Yamamoto, who never
design their own textiles but work
closely with their favourite designers,
Hishinuma successfully controls the
whole design process and is a strong
and adventurous presence on the
contemporary scene.

Even as a textile designer, his work
is changing character. When he first
appeared in *The International Design
Yearbook*, Hishinuma's work surprised
with its graphic colour combinations in
"pop" patterns, reminiscent of Keith
Herring's illustrations and hand-drawn
prints. Since then his colours have
gradually become more subtle and his
patterns more complicated. This year
colour and drawn pattern have
disappeared from almost all of his
work. *Street Material*, for example,
qualifies as a print, but it is printed
from fallen leaves to emphasize the
texture of the real object. Hishinuma's
transfer from illusion of texture to real
texture is at its most adventurous in
*Tape Knit,* which comprises aluminium-
coated polyester cut into tape-like
strips and hand-knitted for use in a
simply cut evening dress. *Tape Knit* is
a development of an earlier Hishinuma
fashion statement: dresses made out
of cassette tape.

Yoshiki Hishinuma attributes his
change of direction to the fact that he
is getting older, even though he is only
in his thirties: "I have lost interest in
working on the surface. Human wrinkles
are texture, are they not? They show
maturity and spirit. I want to create
deeper spiritual work through texture."

15

16

17

18

**19**

**20**

**21**

**22**

**Yoshiki Hishinuma**

page 154 **13.** *Tape Knit*
Aluminium-coated polyester. Handmade one-off

page 155 **14.** *Fire print*
Novoloid (fireproof material developed by NASA in 1968
for spacemen and fire-fighters)
Handmade one-off

**15.** *Tape Knit*
Aluminium-coated polyester. Handmade one-off

**16, 18, 20.** *Wrinkle print*
Polyester. Handmade one-off
W: Approximate width of printing machine is 100cm (39½ in)

**17, 19.** *Street Material*
Polyester. Handmade one-off

**21.** *Destroyed synthetic material*
Polypropylene. Handmade one-off

**22.** *Metallic Dream*
100% cotton. Handmade one-off

**23.** *Marble*
Marble-dyed polyester with polyurethane coating. Handmade one-off

**24.** *Hand cut*
Polyester. Handmade one-off
100% polyester disposable material is torn at random

**23**

**24**

25

### Reiko Sudo

Unlike Hishinuma or Hamai, Reiko Sudo studied hand weaving at college. This background has not only enabled her to make her own samples, it has allowed her to work for the leading Japanese textile designer Junichi Arai, whose brilliant Jacquards stemming from a traditional weaving background have dominated previous editions of the *Yearbook*. Sudo is now working as the principal designer for Arai's Nuno Corporation, sharing a similar taste and attitude towards combining Japanese tradition with modern design and new technology.

Sudo's latest work shows this very clearly. Her *Cracked Cloth* series (in Japanese it is called *Voro Voro* series, meaning literally "ragged") grew from an interest in traditional kimonos and old mattress covers that have been patched and repaired over time so that even the patches are worn and the result is a collage of different materials of different ages. "It tells us the history of a person's life and the colours of the periods they lived through. That is beautiful – real Japanese culture," explains Sudo, whose interest in ragged materials was reflected in the prevalence of a ragged look at the 1993 Paris fashion shows.

She achieves her effect on *Cracked Quilt* by using a material made of quilting wool and rayon together and printing with a substance that burns out the rayon fibre. To create *Cracked Cloth Newspaper*, a newsprint variant on the ragged theme, Sudo bonded the newspaper to the polyester cloth with vinyl chloride and subjected it to heat. As the negative parts of the design dissolve in the melting-off process, so the newspaper motif is incorporated into the textile. The sheer invention and beauty of Reiko Sudo's work demonstrates why Japanese textile design is currently far ahead of US and European practice.

Reiko Sudo

**25.** *Cracked Quilt*
Wool, rayon. W 108cm (42½ in)  Repeat 45cm (17¾ in)
Manufacturer: Nuno Corporation, Japan

**26.** *Cracked Cloth Newspaper*
Polyester, newspaper print, vinyl chloride
W 105cm (41⅜ in)
Manufacturer: Nuno Corporation, Japan

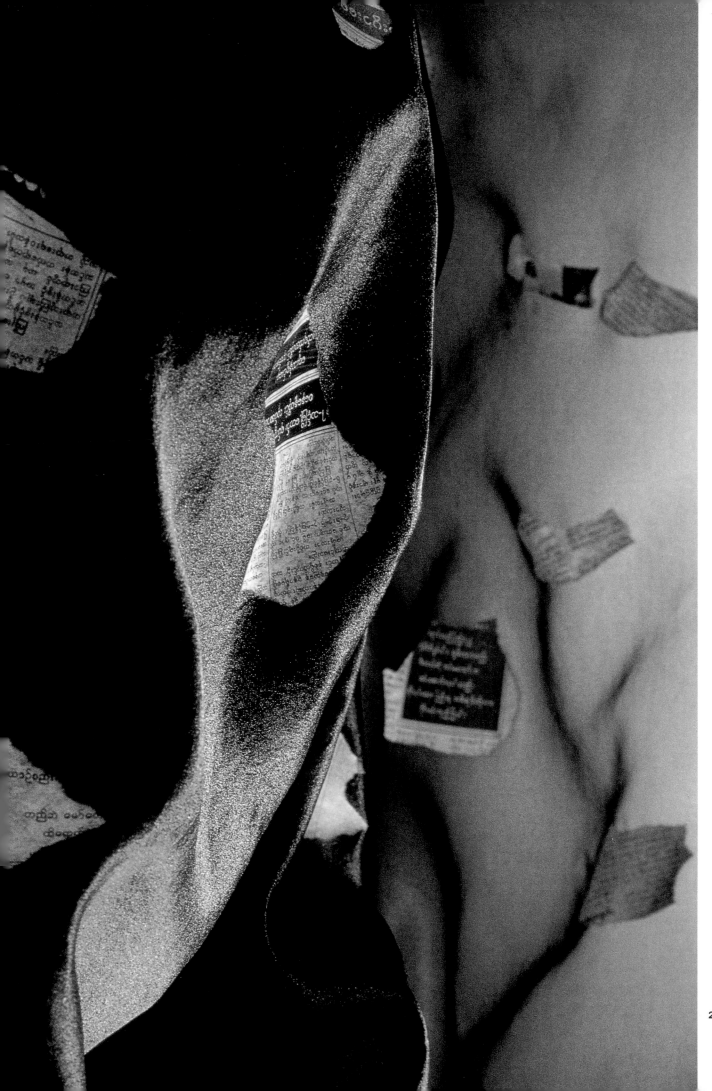

29

30

31

32

33

34

## Helle Abild

Helle Abild is the only non-Japanese textile designer in Ron Arad's selection. Based in New York since autumn 1992, she is a Danish designer who works in the Off The Wall design studio for a wide range of clients – from Dansk to Walt Disney. As a designer of garments herself, Abild makes little distinction between fabric and fashion in her designs. What inspires her is the opportunity to try out new techniques and ideas which will find practical use in the long term.

Abild trained in the textile department of the Danmarks Designskole and in the product and furniture department at the Royal Academy of Fine Arts in Copenhagen. As a designer in Denmark, she worked on many diverse projects: fashion shows; textile design for SAS (Scandinavian Airline Systems); furniture design in the lobby of the Royal Danish Theatre; and jewellery, prints and fabrics for a children's television production. Her penchant for creating fabrics based on off-beat ideas is best expressed in *Art Farming*, a series that grew out of the idea of a field ploughed by a computer-controlled, driverless tractor. Abild studied aerial shots of Danish farmland, noting how the land has different layers according to the composition of turf, flowers and crops. By using such materials as flat PVC with rubber on top, and pigment on hand-dyed velvet, she created a similar three-dimensional effect. *Art Farming* was created as a one-off installation and then printed. Abild envisages application on curtains and bedspreads.

Another collection, *Components for Radio,* develops the theme of weird and wonderful computer-driven decoration. Abild went to her local computer store and bought a mixed bag of components solely for their shapes and colours. She scanned the components directly into the computer, placing the bits on a flat-bed scanner without even photographing them. The images were then repeated, coloured and masked to achieve certain effects. Abild's sophistication and boldness in using repeat industrial imagery conjures up the spirit of the pioneer Soviet Constructivist textile designers. She wants to continue to design textiles on computer but is wary of its pervasive influence. "Different things take different tools," she says. "A lot of people become overpowered by the technology and they just end up printing out ugly images."

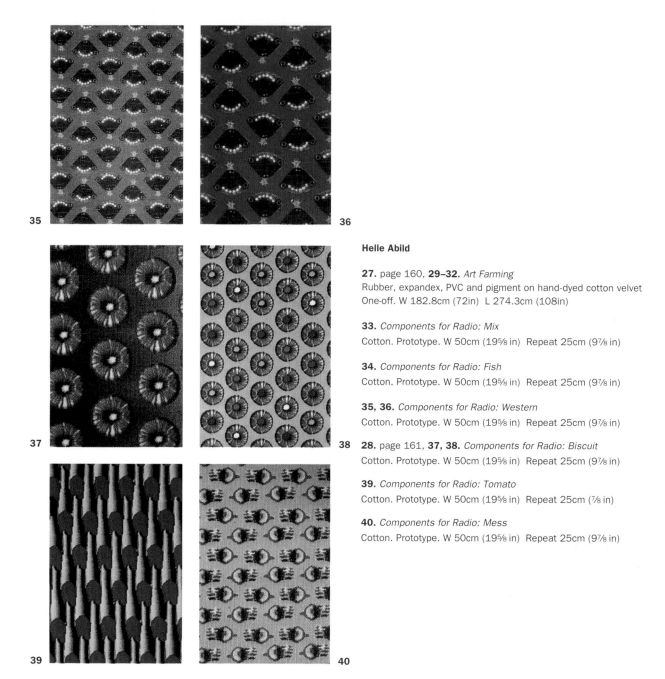

**35**

**36**

**37**

**38**

**39**

**40**

**Helle Abild**

**27.** page 160, **29–32.** *Art Farming*
Rubber, expandex, PVC and pigment on hand-dyed cotton velvet
One-off. W 182.8cm (72in)  L 274.3cm (108in)

**33.** *Components for Radio: Mix*
Cotton. Prototype. W 50cm (19⅝ in)  Repeat 25cm (9⅞ in)

**34.** *Components for Radio: Fish*
Cotton. Prototype. W 50cm (19⅝ in)  Repeat 25cm (9⅞ in)

**35, 36.** *Components for Radio: Western*
Cotton. Prototype. W 50cm (19⅝ in)  Repeat 25cm (9⅞ in)

**28.** page 161, **37, 38.** *Components for Radio: Biscuit*
Cotton. Prototype. W 50cm (19⅝ in)  Repeat 25cm (9⅞ in)

**39.** *Components for Radio: Tomato*
Cotton. Prototype. W 50cm (19⅝ in)  Repeat 25cm (⅞ in)

**40.** *Components for Radio: Mess*
Cotton. Prototype. W 50cm (19⅝ in)  Repeat 25cm (9⅞ in)

**Kaori and Chiaki Maki**

Both the Maki sisters, Kaori and Chiaki, trained in textile design at Rhode Island School of Design in the USA. Chiaki, the elder of the two, set up the Maki Textile Studio after studying in Japan with Junichi Arai, travelling to Mexico, Guatemala and El Salvador to explore the history and folklore of natural dyed weaving, and then opening a workshop in New Delhi. In 1990 she was joined in the company by her younger sister Kaori, who had worked in America for interior textile designer Jack Lenor Larsen and in Japan for one of the largest textile producers. Now they work closely together as a team: Kaori Maki does most of the designing, while Chiaki is responsible for some design and for all production and direction.

The Maki sisters are interested above all in texture. The pattern of the Jacquard, for example, comes from the weaving and is not printed. But why have the workshop in India? Chiaki Maki explains: "Nowadays in Japan there is no longer a craft-weaving industry as few kimonos are made. If we want to use a traditional Japanese technique to create texture, it is too expensive for us. But in India, as in Thailand and Indonesia, craft weaving is still an industry. Their technique to make saris, for example, is of good quality."

While most saris today are made of cheap materials, the Maki sisters favour using a wild pure silk – Tasser silk – which is hand-spun and has "great texture". Produced only in India, it is a natural golden brown colour. It is usually bleached before dyeing, but the Maki sisters use it in its natural colour for the warp of their fabrics in combination with cotton, wool or linen.

42

43

44

45

46

47

48

49

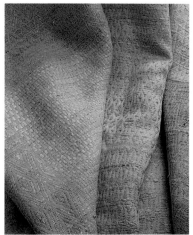

**Kaori Maki**

page 164 **41.** Jacquard *Cords A*
Wool, hand-spun wild silk. Limited batch production
W 50cm (19⅝ in)
Width repeat 5.6cm (2⅛ in)  Length repeat 34cm (13⅜ in)
Manufacturer: Maki Textile Studio, Japan

**42.** *Jacquard*
Silk, synthetic rubber yarn, cotton, rayon. One-off
W 45cm (17¾ in)  Width repeat 45cm (17¾ in)
Manufacturer: Maki Textile Studio, Japan

**43, 45, 47.** Jacquard *Triangle*
Linen, Hand-spun wild silk. Limited batch production
W 60cm (23½ in)
Width repeat 4cm (1½ in)  Length repeat 7cm (2¾ in)
Manufacturer: Maki Textile Studio, Japan

**44.** Jacquard *Little Diamond*
Linen, hand-spun wild silk. Limited batch production
W 60cm (23½ in)
Width repeat 4cm (1½ in)  Length repeat 4cm (1½ in)
Manufacturer: Maki Textile Studio, Japan

**46, 49.** *Jacquard*
Wool, hand-spun wild silk. Limited batch production
W 150cm (59in)  L 240cm (94½ in)
Width repeat 144cm (56¾ in)  Length repeat 220cm (85⅞ in)
Manufacturer: Maki Textile Studio, Japan

**48.** Jacquard *Movement*
Linen, hand-spun wild silk. Limited batch production
W 60cm (23½ in)
Manufacturer: Maki Textile Studio, Japan

50
51

52
53

**50, 53. Chiaki Maki** Jacquard *Sandy*
Wool, hand-spun wild silk. Limited batch production
W 146cm (57½ in)  L 225cm (88⅝ in)
Width repeat 12cm (4¾ in)  Length repeat 43cm (16⅞ in)
Manufacturer: Maki Textile Studio, Japan

**51, 52, 54. Chiaki Maki** Jacquard *Une*
Linen, hand-spun wild silk. Limited batch production
W 60cm (23½ in)
Width repeat 4cm (1½ in)  Length repeat 12cm (4¾ in)
Manufacturer: Maki Textile Studio, Japan

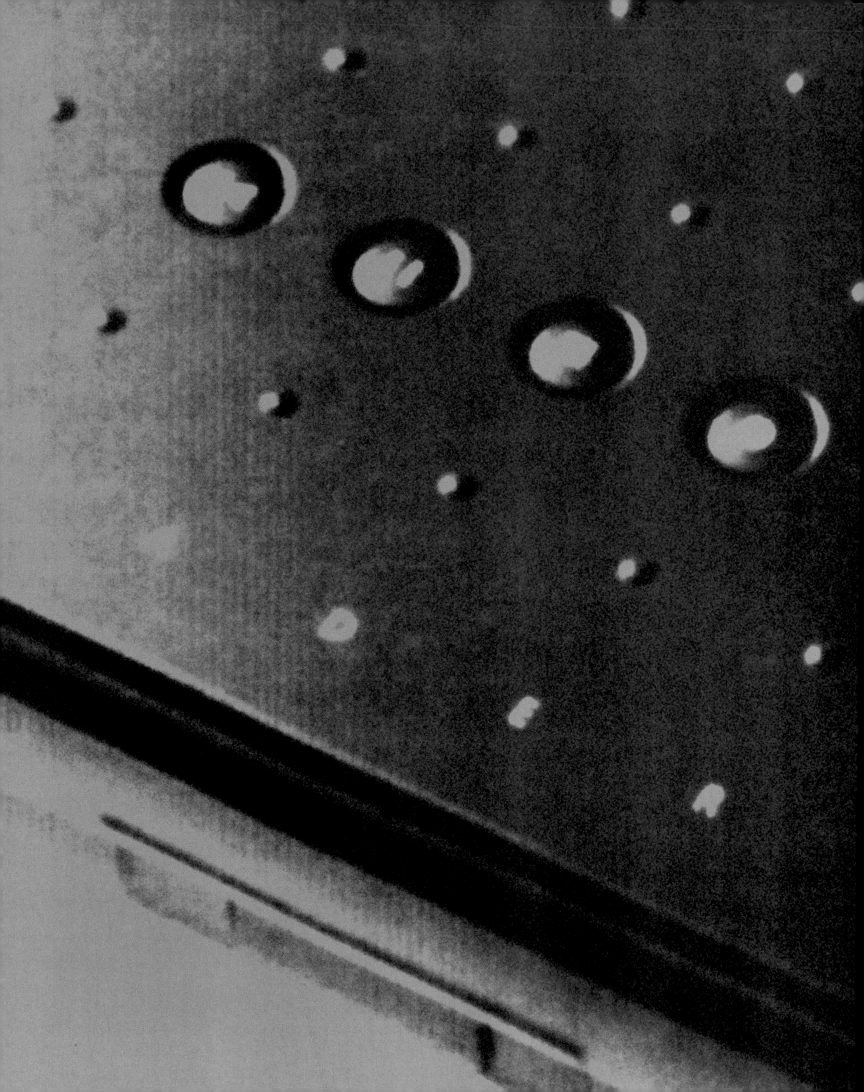

Detail: **Mario Bellini** Portable computer *Quaderno*

Despite all the debates and polemics about post-Modernism, deconstruction and product semantics which have swept through international product design in recent years, it is surprising to see how manufacturers remain resistant to change. Shaken by recession, consumer electronics design in particular still adheres to the old functionalist principles of technical Modernism – with nondescript "black box" design softened at the edges but not entirely eradicated by new product forms. Ron Arad's selection, therefore, can be viewed in the context of what he refers to as "my search for a new language of objects which is not in the conventional idiom of industrial design".

Arad believes that the industrial design profession is remarkably conservative considering its vanguard role in product development. He ruled out many competent products during the selection on the grounds that "they look too much like industrial design to me". Repetitive design clichés and superfluous features were severely judged. On the other hand, the useless decorative object also found no place in Arad's selection; "I am resistant to things without a function," he remarked.

# Products | 171

Encouragingly, his choice of products highlights the extent to which the major multinationals are now trying to develop a new design language. Philips has sponsored Ettore Sottsass to design a new range of mobile media furniture, and Susani and Trimarchi to create the kitchen appliances of the future. Siemens-Nixdorf has unveiled a series of six exercises in rethinking the mobile telephone, while Toshiba has launched new design concepts in audio-visual equipment which break down systems into more characterful component parts. Mitsubishi is among the companies backing the work of California consultant Doug Patton in developing jewel-like remote controls for home entertainment systems. All these products are committed to making electronic equipment more expressive on a human level, incorporating a sense of craft refinement in a world of baffling high technology. "They may not have all the answers but at least they are reaching out to explore new ideas," says Arad.

There is, of course, a long way to go. Video cameras and camcorders still largely promote the virtues of "professional" styling over product intelligibility and ease of use. Most of the new generation of notepad computers still cling to stereotypical techno-executive imagery rather than exploring the tactile world of books and paper on which the new technology is now based. But elsewhere, usually outside the realms of multinational mass production, functional innovation and visual flair combine to produce work of the highest calibre in Ron Arad's selection. Nowhere is this better expressed than in James Dyson's *Dual Cyclone* vacuum cleaner, Kazuo Kawasaki's titanium wheelchair or Andreas Dober's endless-chain clock.

1

## Clocks

The concept of time passing makes clock design one of the most beguiling of industrial design exercises, encompassing as it does both a physical and metaphysical dimension. Designers have played with clock faces in all kinds of different and decorative ways but few have really challenged conventional methods of recording time.

Ron Arad's selection of clocks, however, reflects the concern to suggest new conceptual ways to express the passage of time: **Jochen Henkels'** *Configuration Clock*

"describes kinetic design instead of precise time" using three de-centralized balsa and foam hands; the *Abaxial* clock by **Karim Rashid** has hands which move beyond the clock face and penetrate the space in which time is passing; but the most compelling image chosen by Arad is the *Catena* clock by Stuttgart-based designer **Andreas Dober**. Made of copper, brass and stainless steel, this uses the idea of the endless chain to express the passing of time in a totally new way.

**1. M & Co. (Tibor Kalman and Scott Stowell)** *Global Alphabet Blocks*
Solid Pennsylvania poplar. Printed with five writing systems: Arabic, Cyrillic, Hebrew, Latin and Japanese.
H 5cm (2in)  W 5cm (2in)  D 5cm (2in)
Manufacturer:  M & Co. Labs, USA

**2. Andreas Dober** Clock *Catena*
Stainless steel, brass, copper. Prototype
H 50cm (9⅝ in)  W 7cm (2¾ in)  D 7cm (2¾ in)

**4**

**3**

**5**

**3. Kazuo Kawasaki** Clock
*Mikros Hola*
ABS
H 10.1cm (4in)  W 10.2cm
(4⅛ in)  D 4.1cm (1½ in)
Manufacturer: Takata
Lemnos, Japan

**4. Karim Rashid** Clock *Abaxial*
Cast and spun aluminium, steel,
gold plate, silver plate or honed
aluminium
Limited batch production
H 22.5cm (9in) when hands
are pointing down and
30cm (12in) when hands
are in 12.00 position.
W 11cm (4⅜ in)  D 8.8cm (3½ in)
Manufacturer: Gallery 91, USA

**5.** (and opposite) **Jochen Henkels**
*Configuration Clock*
Wood, balsa-wood, foam
Prototype
H 45cm (17¾ in)
W 30cm (11⅞ in)  D 8cm (3⅛ in)

## Portable computers

When the businessman sitting next to you on the train opens his briefcase, the chances are he will not be pulling out a newspaper or a sandwich. The personal portable computer has become the essential accessory to executive travel. US-based Grid Systems knows this well and has become a leader in the field, working with design consultants IDEO to develop an entire new generation of products. The *Grid Convertible*, designed by IDEO's Mark Biasotti, marks a further step ahead. An ingenious mechanical design enables this keyboard-based laptop to be transformed into a pen-based notebook-style computer.

Grid's latest work logically builds on past developments, but what are we to make of Olivetti's dramatic entry into the field? Olivetti has raised the stakes considerably by launching the **Mario Bellini**-styled *Quaderno*. This device is just the size of an A5 notepad and much is made of the fact that it is a lot smaller than rival models. Olivetti that whereas other machines take up the entire briefcase, forcing the executive to carry two bags, the *Quaderno* is genuinely portable. The miniscule size of the keyboard has been criticized as making typing harder, however. There are also technical features such as a voice-processing facility which critics argue make the machine too complicated. Nobody doubts the sureness of Bellini's design touch, but one suspects that in trying to occupy a middle ground between electronic organizer and a fully fledged notebook computer, this product is in danger of becoming neither.

6

7

8

**6. Mario Bellini** Portable computer *Quaderno*
ABS
H 3cm (1⅛ in) W 14.8cm (5¾ in) D 10.5cm (4⅛ in)
Manufacturer: Olivetti, Italy

**7. Mark Biasotti** Pen/laptop notebook computer *Grid Convertible*
Die-cast magnesium, plastic mouldings
H 3.5cm (1¼ in) W 30.5cm (12in) D 26.7cm (10½ in)
Manufacturer: Grid Systems, USA

**8. Toshiba Corporation Design Centre** Pen computer *Dynapad T100X*
Plastics
H 4cm (1½ in) W 27cm (10⅝ in) D 21.4cm (8⅜ in)
Manufacturer: Toshiba Corporation, Japan

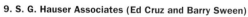

9

**9. S. G. Hauser Associates (Ed Cruz and Barry Sween)**
Computer peripherals *BlackCurrant Product Line*
Injection-moulded ABS, stamped metal
Consists of a power back-up, a simultaneous memory back-up,
a mini server and a personal memo printer. Stacked system:
H 15cm (6in)  W 18.5cm (7¼ in)  D 24.7cm (9¾ in)
Manufacturer: PK Electronics, USA

**11**

**10**

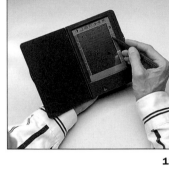

**12**

**10. S. G. Hauser Associates**
**(Ed Cruz, Barry Sween, Leonard Porche and Erich Kruse)**
Notebook computer *Getgo*
ABS, elastomeric keyboard. Prototype
H 3.4cm (1¼ in)  W 30.5 cm (12in)  D 20.3cm (8in)

**11. Siemens Nixdorf (Axel Loritz)** *Notepad computer*
Plastics, glass
Open: 2 x A4 size  closed: A4 size
Manufacturer: Siemens Nixdorf Information Systems, German

**12. Kenneth Grange** Electronic organizer *Pen Pad PDA 600*
Polycarbonate, ABS, polyester, glass laminate
H 2.7cm (1⅛ in)  W 11.5cm (4½ in)  L 16cm (6½ in)
Manufacturer: Amstrad, UK

**13. Sharp Corporation** Electronic Organizer *IQ-9000*
Plastic
H 2.5cm (1in)  W 18cm (7⅛ in)  L 10.2cm (4⅛ in)
Manufacturer: Sharp Corporation, Japan

**13**

## Notepad computers

Despite the revolution in information technology over the past decade, some executives have resisted the idea of typing in commands. As a result, the light pen-activated computer which replaces a keyboard with the electronic equivalent of a pencil and jotter has become the Holy Grail in business communications. The selection here represents the state of the art in terms of sophistication of software, functions and styling.

It is interesting to observe the extent to which designers have felt able to depart from the established techno-imagery of existing portable electronic products to develop a more humanistic style based on associations with books, pens and paper. Not very far, to judge by recent products. The technically-innovative *Dynapad* pen computer produced by the **Toshiba Corporation Design Centre** is faithful to the visual conventions (see page 176). However, Amstrad's pocket-sized *Pen Pad PDA 600*, designed by British consultant Kenneth Grange of Pentagram, does explore a new direction. Meanwhile, a concept study by **S.G. Hauser Associates**, the *Getgo*, shows how the notebook computer could work in the educational market, incorporating  multimedia capability. Just as existing notebook computers are carried home by executives, so the *Getgo* goes home from school with the student, with homework assignment programmed in.

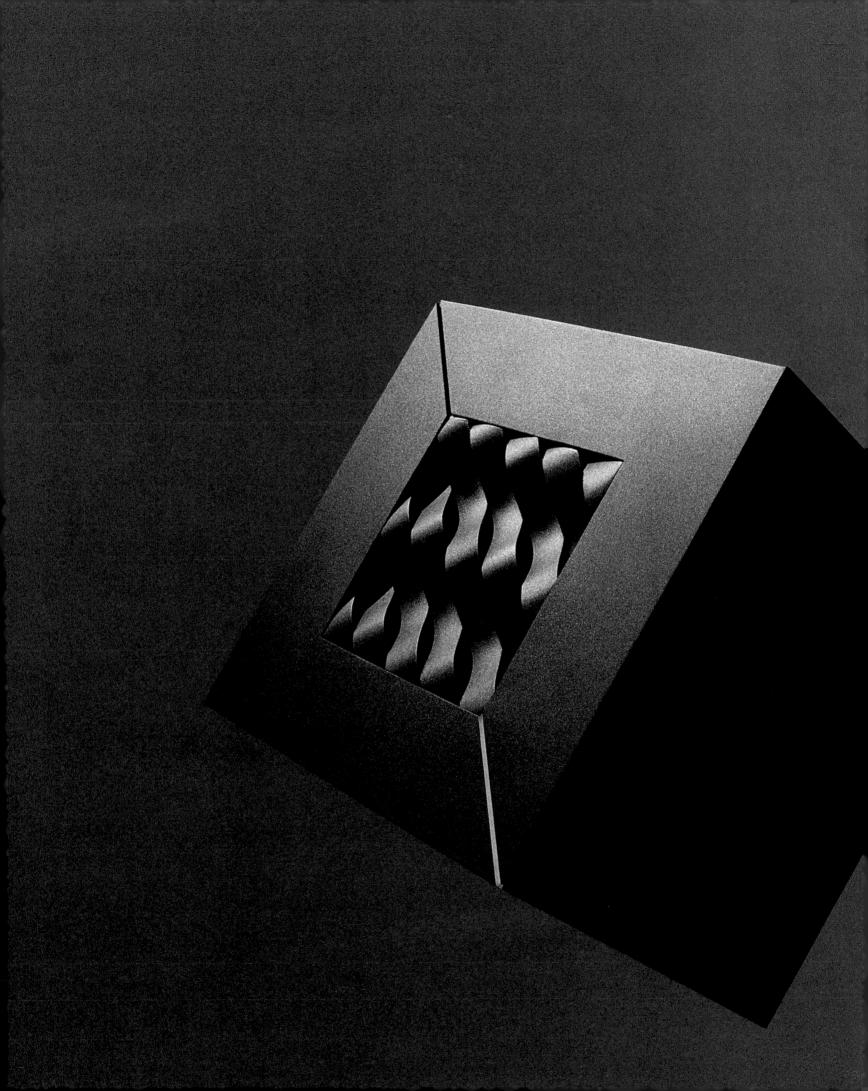

(page 179) **14. Doug Patton** CPU computer *Wave I*
ABS, cold-formed steel. Prototype
H 35.5cm (14in)  W 35.5cm (14in)  L 35.5cm (14in)
D 35.5cm (14in)
Manufacturer: Fountainhead Computers, USA

**15. Doug Patton** *IR blaster and control box*
ABS,  acrylic
Fills a room with infra-red for VCR, TV and cable
communication.
H 5cm (2in)  W 20.3cm (8in)
L 20.3cm (8in)  D 15cm (6in)
Manufacturer: Insight Telecast, USA

**16. Doug Patton** Remote control *Opuc*
ABS, acrylic. Prototype
The control does not have to be pointed at the set.
H 3.5cm (1¼ in)  Di 7.5cm (3in)
Manufacturer: Mitsubishi, USA

**17. Doug Patton and Ken Mori** *Personal Action Device*
ABS, acrylic. Prototype
Can be used to operate a telephone,
TV, computer, home security system or VCR.
H 10cm (4in)  W 12.5cm (5in)  D 1.7cm (¾ in)
Manufacturer: Patton Design, USA

**18. Doug Patton, Ken Mori and Steve Ewing**
*Insight Remote*
ABS, acrylic
H 23cm (9in)  W 6.3cm (2½ in)  D 1.3cm (½ in)
Manufacturer: Insight Telecast, USA

**19. Doug Patton** Remote control *Palmate*
ABS, acrylic
H 2.6cm (1⅛ in)  W 5.4cm (2⅛ in)  L 8.9cm (3½ in)
Manufacturer: Go Video, USA

**15**

**16**

**17**

**18**

**19**

**20. Doug Patton** Remote control *Quiver III*
ABS, acrylic. Prototype
H 7.5cm (3in)  W 10cm (4in)  D 0.4cm (⅛in)
Manufacturer: Patton Design, USA

20

## Doug Patton

Californian design consultant Doug Patton of Patton Design believes that, despite their technological wizardry in new product development, the large electronics manufacturers are currently missing a trick when it comes to remote controls. Although, as the main interface device with the user, these units to control home entertainment systems should have the highest standards of design, they are usually treated as an afterthought and given little real consideration.

As a result, Patton says, there is an abundance of "rectilinear matt-black techno-bricks and few genuinely new concepts in user tools". He wants to redress the balance and has produced a series of conceptual exercises which demonstrate how the universal remote control of the future, for everything from videos to audio and lighting systems, might look and work. Some concepts are voice-activated, others work on the principle of a worrystone or magic wand. All are much more sensuous than existing controls and linked to human emotions. "It is all about creating a remote control that is personal to whoever owns it," says Patton, "like a special pen or watch or piece of jewellery. How do you create someone's favourite object? It is all about getting back to a craft approach in technological products."

Mitsubishi and Insight Telecast have already commissioned new user tools from Patton, who also acts as consultant to Hewlett Packard and is well known as the designer of the conceptual Apple 2000 workstation which linked advanced Apple Macintosh technology to furniture design.

21

22

**21. Sony Corporation** *Discman 92A-054*
H 2.8cm (1⅛ in)  W 12.7cm (5in)  D 14.5cm (5¾ in)
Manufacturer: Sony Corporation, Japan

**22. Sony Corporation** Clock radio *92A-080*
H 12.4cm (4⅞ in)  W 34.3cm (13½ in)  D 18.4cm (7¼ in)
Manufacturer: Sony Corporation, Japan

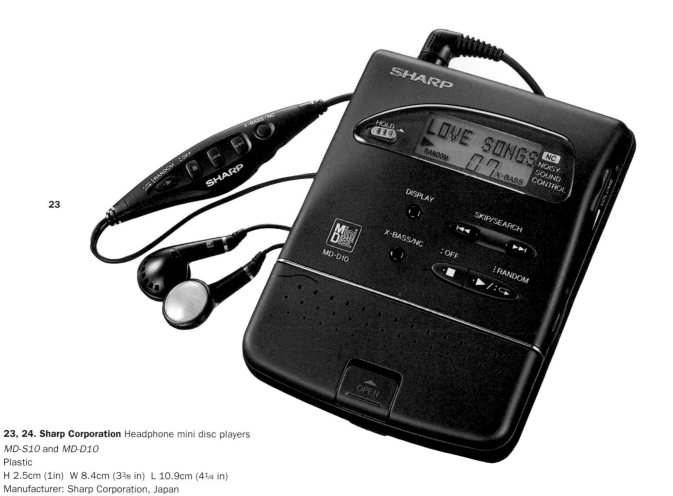

**23, 24. Sharp Corporation** Headphone mini disc players
*MD-S10* and *MD-D10*
Plastic
H 2.5cm (1in)  W 8.4cm (3⅜ in)  L 10.9cm (4¼ in)
Manufacturer: Sharp Corporation, Japan

**25**

**28**

**27**

**26**

**25. Siemens Design (Dov Rattan)** Mobile telephone *Handheld D-Net*
Aluminium
H 2.5cm (1in)  W 5.5cm (2⅛ in)  L 18.2cm (7⅛ in)
(closed) H 2.5cm (1in)  W 5.5cm (2⅛ in)  L 14.8cm (5⅞ in)
Manufacturer: Siemens, Germany

**26. Siemens Design (Hatto Grosse)** Mobile telephone *Handheld D-Net*
PU foam
H 3cm (1⅛ in)  W 5.8cm (2⅜ in)  L 20.7cm (8⅛ in)
(closed) H 3.6cm (1⅜ in)  W 5.8cm (2⅜ in)  L 14.9cm (6in)
Manufacturer: Siemens, Germany

**27. Siemens Design (Wolfgang Münscher)** Mobile telephone *Handheld D-Net*
Die-cast aluminium, ABS plastics
H 2.5cm/1.6cm (1in/⅝ in)  W 5.8cm (2⅜ in)  L 18.2cm (7⅛ in)
(closed)  H 2.5cm /1.6cm (1in/⅝ in)  W 5.8cm (2⅜ in)
L 14.8cm (5⅞ in)
Manufacturer: Siemens, Germany

**28. Siemens Design (Stephan Apetauer)** Mobile telephone *Handheld D-Net*
Die-cast aluminium, plastics
H 3cm (1⅛ in)  W 5.8cm (2⅜ in)  L 17.5cm (6⅞ in)
(closed) H 2.4cm (1in)  W 5.8cm (2⅜ in)  L 13.5cm (5⅜ in)
Manufacturer: Siemens, Germany

**29. Siemens Design (Hatto Grosse)** Mobile telephone *Handheld D-Net*
Plastics
H 2.7cm (1⅛ in)  W 5.7cm (2¼ in)  L 21cm (8¼ in)
(closed) H 3cm (1⅛ in)  W 5.7cm (2¼ in)  L 14.4cm (5⅝ in)
Manufacturer: Siemens, Germany

**30. Siemens Design (Axel Loritz and Jens Pattberg)** Mobile telephone
*Handheld D-Net*
Glass, aluminium
H 2.3cm (⅞in)  W 5.2cm (2in)  L 15cm (6in)
Manufacturer: Siemens, Germany

**31. Jürgen Schmid** Mobile telephone *Handy*
ABS. Prototype
H 3cm (1½ in)  L 17cm (6⅝ in)  D 8cm (3⅛ in)
Manufacturer: Teko, Germany

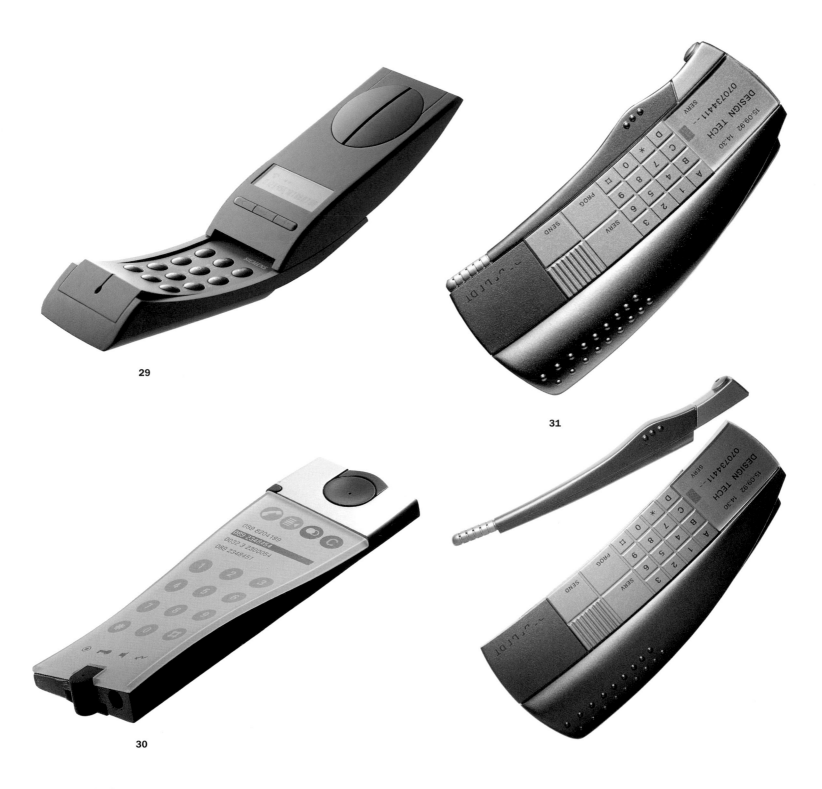

29

31

30

## Telephones

As telecommunications markets around the world have been de-regulated, so the telephone has become a symbolic design object in recent years, reflecting new styles and advances in design thinking. This was not always the case, however. For 50 years, two designs dominated: in Europe, the *DB 1001* phone designed in 1931 by the Norwegian artist Jean Heiberg for Ericsson with a sculpted Bakelite body; in America, the similarly shaped Bell telephone designed in 1937 by Henry Dreyfuss.

The telephone has been a utilitarian piece of equipment for half of this century, but today, in an era of liberalized markets and cordless technology, it is expressive of the fashion accessory. It is hardly surprising that, in trying to soften the mobile telephone's militaristic image, Swatch has crossed over into the cellular phone market with a sleek new model designed in Milan by **Enrico Quell** and **Fabrizio Galli**; or that **Siemens Design** has shown a series of six styling exercises which explore more engaging new forms.

32

33

34

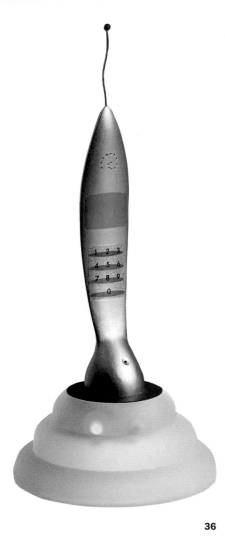

36

### 32. Plan Creatif/Crabtree Hall Telephone *Amarys*
ABS
H 6.5cm (2½ in)  W 16.5cm (6½ in)
D 21.5cm (8½ in)
Manufacturer: France Telecom, France

### 33. Jürgen Schmid *Mobile telephone*
ABS. Prototype
H 7cm (2¾ in)  L 25cm (9⅞ in)  D 13cm (5⅛ in)

### 34. Siggi Fischer *Telephone*
Plastic
H 9cm (3½ in)  W 23cm (9in)  D 23cm (9in)
Manufacturer: Vericom, Germany

### 35. Fabrizio Galli and Enrico Quell *Cellular Swatch*
ABS
H 17cm (6⅝ in)  W 6.3cm (2½ in)  D 3.1cm (1⅛ in)
Manufacturer: Swatch Telecom, Switzerland

### 36. Tadao Amano Telephone *Prossimo*
ABS, glass. Prototype
H 29cm (11⅜ in)

### 37. Marianne Stokholm and Gad Zorea Wall telephone
*Kirk Lotus*
ABS
H 22cm (8⅝ in)  W 15cm (6in)  D 7.5cm (3in)
Manufacturer: Kirk Telecom, Denmark

### 38. Marianne Stokholm and Gad Zorea Table telephone
*Kirk Lotus*
ABS
H 9.5cm (3¾ in)  L 25cm (9⅞ in)
D 13cm (5⅛ in)
Manufacturer: Kirk Telecom, Denmark

## Tadao Amano/Marianne Stokholm and Gad Zorea

Tadao Amano – one of nine Milan-based Japanese designers who exhibited new designs at a city-centre exhibition during the 1993 Milan Furniture Fair – takes the cordless telephone to a Starck-inspired sculptural limit. But perhaps a more unusual design in Ron Arad's selection is the *Kirk Lotus* telephone designed for Kirk Telecom in Denmark by Marianne Stokholm and Gad Zorea. This has a strongly graphic personality in the composition of differently-shaped elements connected by the black lines of telephone cords; there are table and wall-mounted versions.

35

38

37

39

**39. Izuru Tanaka and Osamu Yonekawa**
VHS video camera *NV-S78*
*ABS*
H 11.5cm (4½ in)  W 7.2cm (2⅞ in)
L 24.2cm (9⅜ in)
Manufacturer: Matsushita Electronic
Industrial Co., Japan

**40. Seiichi Watanabe and Mitsuo Takanaga**
Video camera *NV-CS1*
ABS moulding, plastic
H 11.4cm (4⅛ in)  W 7.1cm (2¾ in)
L 17.8cm (7in)
Manufacturer: Matsushita Electronic
Industrial Co., Japan

40

41

**41. Sharp Corporation** Video camera *Viewcam VL-HL100U*
ABS, metal
H 14.8cm (5⅞ in)  W 19.9cm (7⅞ in)  D 7.8cm (3⅛ in)
Manufacturer: Sharp Corporation, Japan

**42. Philips Corporate Design** HDTV professional camera *LDK 9000*
Magnesium
Camera head:
H 21.8cm (8½ in)  W 14.3cm (5⅝ in)  D 35.9cm (14⅛ in)
Manufacturer: Broadcasting Television Systems, Germany

**43. Sharp Corporation** LCD colour TV *4E-L1*
Plastic, low-reflection TFT LCD panel
H 2.9cm (1⅛ in)  W 12.5cm (5in)
L 12.4cm (4⅞ in)
Manufacturer: Sharp Corporation, Japan

**44. Yamaha Design Laboratory** Digital
percussion *DD-3*
Polystyrene, ethylenepropylene
H 8.5cm (3⅜ in)  W 26.5cm (10⅜ in)
D 21.9cm (8½ in)
Manufacturer: Yamaha Design Laboratory,
Japan

**45. Yamaha Design Laboratory** Music
accompaniment player *QR10*
PS, silicon rubber
H 4.6cm (1⅞ in)  W 24.3cm (9½ in)
D 24.5cm (9⅝ in)
Manufacturer: Yamaha Design Laboratory,
Japan

**46. Toshiba Corporation Design Centre**
New concepts in audio-visual
equipment design
ABS, acrylic, rubber
H 9.5cm (3¾ in)  W 14.5cm (5¾ in)
D 3cm (1⅛ in)
Manufacturer: Toshiba Corporation,
Japan

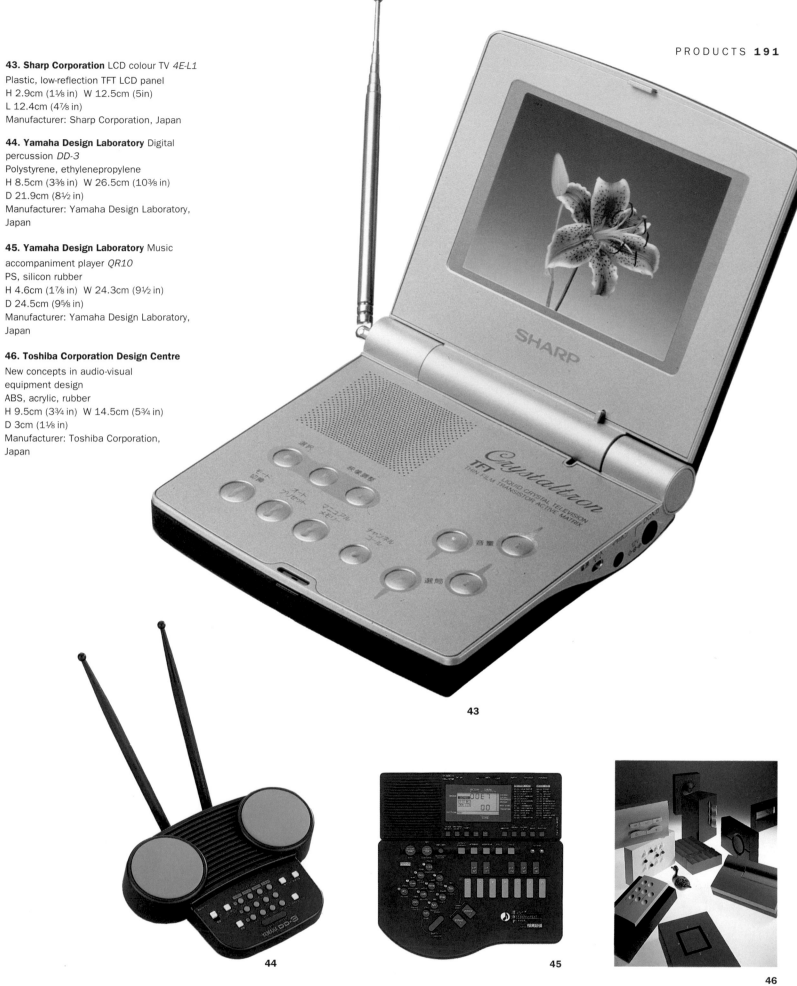

43

44

45

46

**47**

**47. Dov Rattan** *Personal fax machine*
Plastics
H 1cm (3⁄8 in)  W 25cm (97⁄8 in)  L 34cm (133⁄8 in)
Manufacturer: Siemens, Germany

**48. S. G. Hauser Associates (John von Buelow)** *Smart Label Printer Pro*
ABS injection-moulded plastic
H 15cm (6in)  W 10.4cm (41⁄8 in)  L 18.5cm (71⁄4 in)
Manufacturer: Seiko Instruments USA, USA

**49. Doug Patton** Stapler *Apexon*
Formed metal, ABS
H 6.3cm (21⁄2 in)  W 3.4cm (11⁄4 in)  L 12.7cm (5in)
Manufacturer: Apex Manufacturing, Japan

**50. David Farrage** *Pen*
Stainless steel. Prototype
Manufacturer: Royal College of Art, UK

**51. Enzo Mari** Multi-use box *Flores*
Technopolymer resin
H 6cm (23⁄8 in)  W 31cm (121⁄4 in)  D 15cm (6in)
Manufacturer: Bruno Danese, Italy

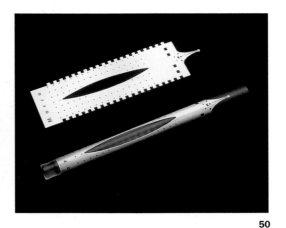

**48**                    **49**                    **50**                    **51**

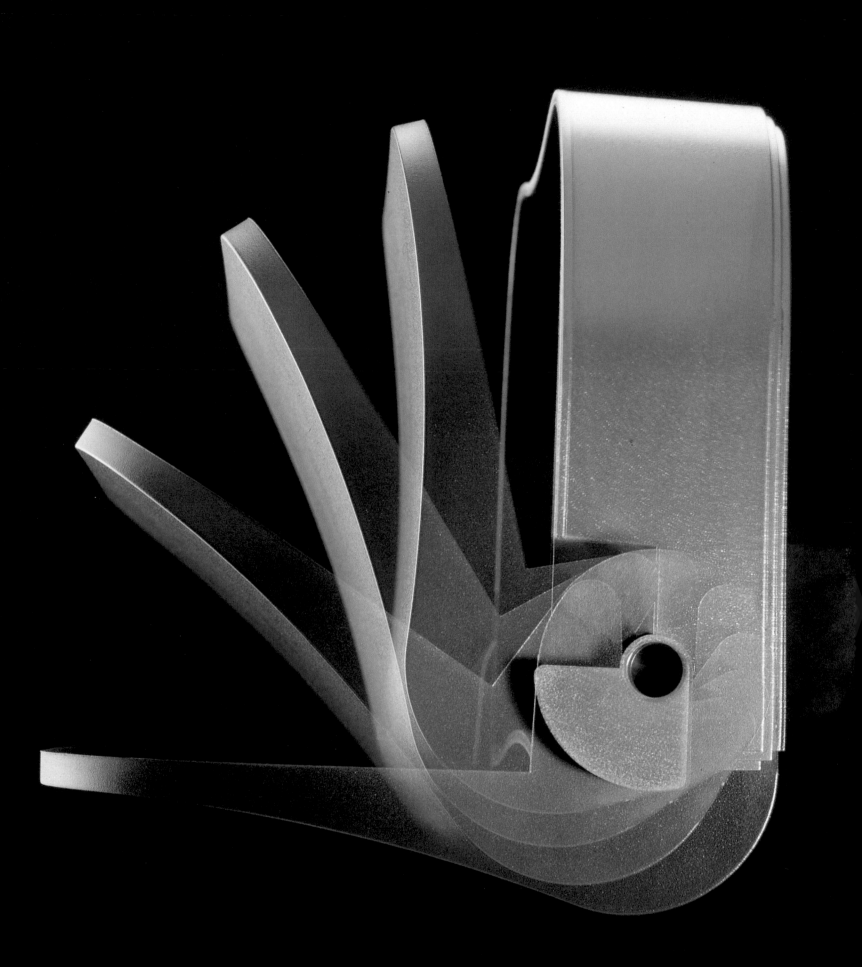

52

## Ettore Sottsass

The major multinationals are responding in different ways to the growing charge that consumer electronics design is all about characterless "boxes" of technology and does not reflect contemporary culture. Philips in Germany, for example, has launched the Philips Design Edition to involve leading designers and architects such as Massimo Iosa Ghini, Andrée Putman and Ettore Sottsass in projects of a more unusual, aesthetic and visionary nature. The latest Philips product to emerge from this initiative is the *Magic Media Container* by Sottsass. This is a system of mobile, modular media furniture which can be used in a variety of different combinations: there are roller-tables for the sets and pull-out filing units for accessories and software.

According to Sottsass, the rationale for the design is based on the paradox between the media, which is always on the air with new information and always changing, and our tendency to place our television and video sets firmly in one isolated place and never move them. "This is ridiculous," says Sottsass. "We need to use them for forming and shaping the space available to us, easily and freely." The system enables users to place the different units in individual combinations as a "multi-media collage". The project marks the first time that Sottsass – a long-time consultant to Olivetti – has worked for Philips Consumer Electronics.

**52. Ettore Sottsass** *Magic Media Container*
Chrome metal, lacquered wood, radica. Limited batch production
Audio console with large filing area:
H 170cm (66⅞ in)  W 90cm (35½ in)  D 55cm (21¾ in)
TV console:
H 65cm (25⅝ in)  W 90cm (35½ in)  D 55cm (21¾ in)
Large filing unit:
H 200cm (78¾ in)  W 40cm (15¾ in)  D 55cm (21¾ in)
Manufacturer:  Philips Design Edition, Germany

**53. Denis Santachiara** TV and VCR stand *Girino*
H 52cm (20½ in)  W 78cm (30¾ in)
Manufacturer:  Domodinamica, Italy

53

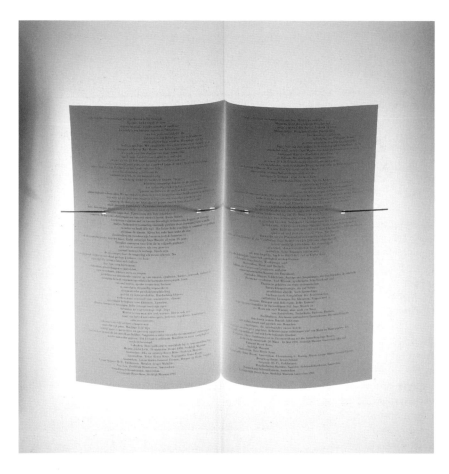

54

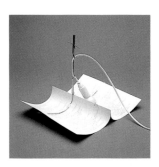

**54. Reyer Kras** Catalogue light *Licht Licht*
Stainless steel, spring wire, lexan sheets
Limited batch production
H 28cm (11in)  W 34cm (13⅜ in)  D 29cm (11⅜ in)

**55. Dissing and Weitling Arkitektfirma** *Air Titanium glasses*
Titanium wire, silicone rubber
H 4cm (1½ in)  W 12.5cm (5in)  D 14cm (5½ in)
Manufacturer: Lindberg Optic Design, Denmark

**56. GK Sekkei Incorporated** Pager *Pocket Bell*
Polycarbonate
H 5.5cm (2⅛ in)  W 3.4cm (1⅜ in)  D 1.3cm (½ in)
Manufacturer: NTT Mobile Communications Network, Japan

### Dissing and Weitling

A decade ago, if you wore spectacles you flaunted your style – bright primary colours, bold moon-like shapes. Today the trend is towards the reverse – spectacle frames so subtle and invisible that people barely notice they are on your nose. Gerhard Fuchs's *Minimal Art* glasses for Silhouette, featured in last year's *International Design Yearbook*, signalled the strong move towards minimalism in eyewear. This year the *Air Titanium glasses* by Danish architecture and industrial design firm Dissing and Weitling confirm the trend. The frames are made of titanium wire – chosen because of strength and lightness – and require no soldering joints, screws or rivets. Despite its invisibility, the design has made a major impact: Japan's Ministry of Trade and Industry awarded the product its prestigious Good Design Grand Prize of 1992.

55

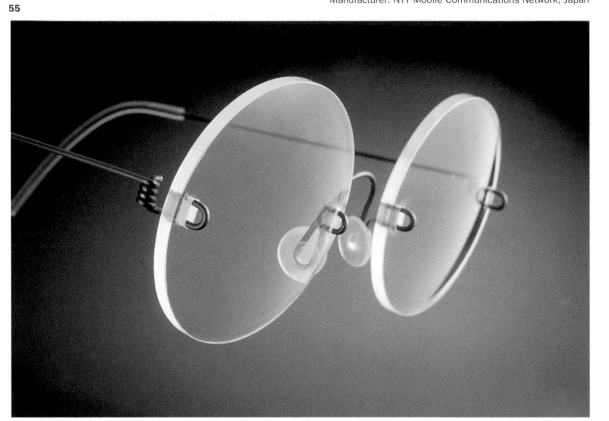

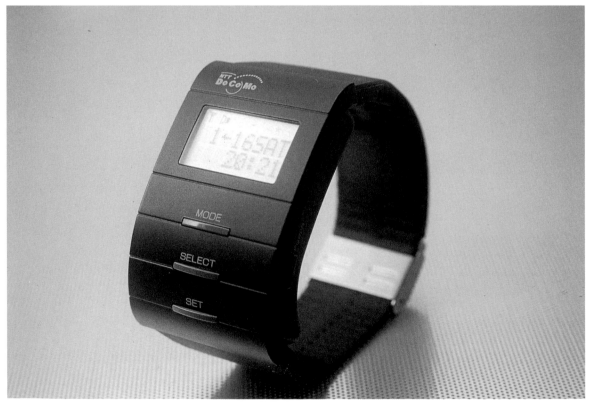

56

## Razors

British traditions in the technology of wet-shaving date back to Victorian times. Now they have found a contemporary outlet in the work of British designers in Europe and the Far East. The accent is on combining technical innovation with visual flair to give the shaver a better all-round product. The *Protector* razor for Wilkinson Sword in Germany, designed by **Kenneth Grange** of Pentagram, features a special swivel twin blade with safety protector wires to avoid accidental cuts. **FM Design's** travel razor for Taiwanese manufacturer Hoyo Inc. is made from extruded aluminium with two moulded rubber finger grips which also serve to retain it in a compact one-piece case.

57

58

60

**57. Kenneth Grange** Razor *Protector*
Chrome-plated die-cast metal, plastics
W 4cm (1½ in)  L 12cm (4¾ in)  D 4.3cm (1⅝ in)
Manufacturer: Wilkinson Sword, Germany

**58. Emanuela Frattini** Umbrella *Dome*
Wood, metal, aluminium, Velcro, nylon. Standard size
Manufacturer: EFM, USA and Italy

**Carla Weisberg** Umbrella *Swirl*
Wood, metal, aluminium, Velcro, nylon
Standard size
Manufacturer: EFM, USA and Italy

**M & Co. (Tibor Kalman)** Umbrella *Sky*
Wood, metal, aluminium, Velcro, nylon. Standard size
Manufacturer: EFM, USA and Italy

**59. FM Design** *Razor*
Extruded aluminium, thermoplastic rubber
W 3cm (1½ in)  L 13cm (5⅛ in)
Manufacturer: Hoyo, Taiwan

**60. Emilio Ambasz** Range of bags and suitcases *X-pand bags*
Steel, aluminium, die-cut plastic, leather, elastic
The bags come in a range of sizes.
Attaché case:
H 33cm (13in)  L 45cm (17¾ in)  D 7cm (2¾ in)
Manufacturer: Ajioka, Japan

59

**61. S. G. Hauser Associates (Larry Tang)** *Pro-Formance Putters*
Stainless steel
H 3.8cm (1⅝ in)  W 11.4cm (4½ in)  L 89cm (35in)
Manufacturer: Taylor Made Golf Co., USA

**62. Doug Patton, Erik Jung, Dennis Grudt and Steve Ewing**
Luggage, *Andiamo* and *Valeroso*
ABS, polyethylene
Each range has suitcases in 7 sizes.
Manufacturer: Andiamo, USA

61

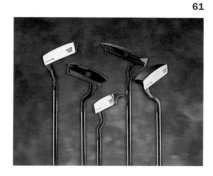

62

**Masatoshi Sakaegi**

Since leaving art school, Japanese ceramics designer Masatoshi Sakaegi has worked in the Aichi Prefecture, which accounts for 65 per cent of Japanese ceramics production. He concentrated initially on tableware but has recently become more interested in wall tiles, with the aim of using ceramics to create a fabric-like texture. Sakaegi's latest work was inspired by a trip to Finland which revealed to him how much post-war Japanese ceramics and glass have been influenced by Finnish design. "It is so simple and yet so sophisticated," he explains. That is the effect achieved in the *Waving Motion* and *Tension* relief wall tiles. They allow users the freedom to design their own walls by manipulating and combining asymmetrical patterns.

Sakaegi works by laying extruded ceramic strands or "noodles" on to a rippling base before firing them together. He says working in ceramics provides a lot of creative freedom: "The moulds are cheaper so you do not need a big factory or expensive tooling, and you do not have to have long runs."

**64**

**63. Masatoshi Sakaegi** Unit tile *Waving Motion*
Ceramic
H 18cm (7⅛ in) W 9cm (3½ in) D 7.5cm (3in)
Manufacturer: Sakaegi Design Studio, Japan

**64. Masatoshi Sakaegi** Relief wall tile *Tension*
Ceramic
H 18.6cm (7⅜ in) W 9.3cm (3⅝ in) D 2.4cm (1in)
Manufacturer: Nihon Touheki, Japan

65

66

**65. Massimo Iosa Ghini** Door handle and coat hook *Delphina*
Brass
Door handle:
H 6.3cm (2½ in)  L 14.5cm (5¾ in)  D 6.3cm (2½ in)
Coat hook:
H 6.5cm (2⅝ in)  L 18.2cm (7⅛ in)  D 6.3cm (2½ in)
Manufacturer: Olivari, Italy

**66. Davide Mercatali** Taps *Girotondo*
Mixer:
H 17cm (6⅝ in)  W 11.8cm (4½ in)  D 6cm (2⅜ in)
Tap:
H 7.5cm (3in)  W 7.2cm (2⅞ in)  D 7.2cm (2⅞ in)
Manufacturer: Fratelli Fantini, Italy

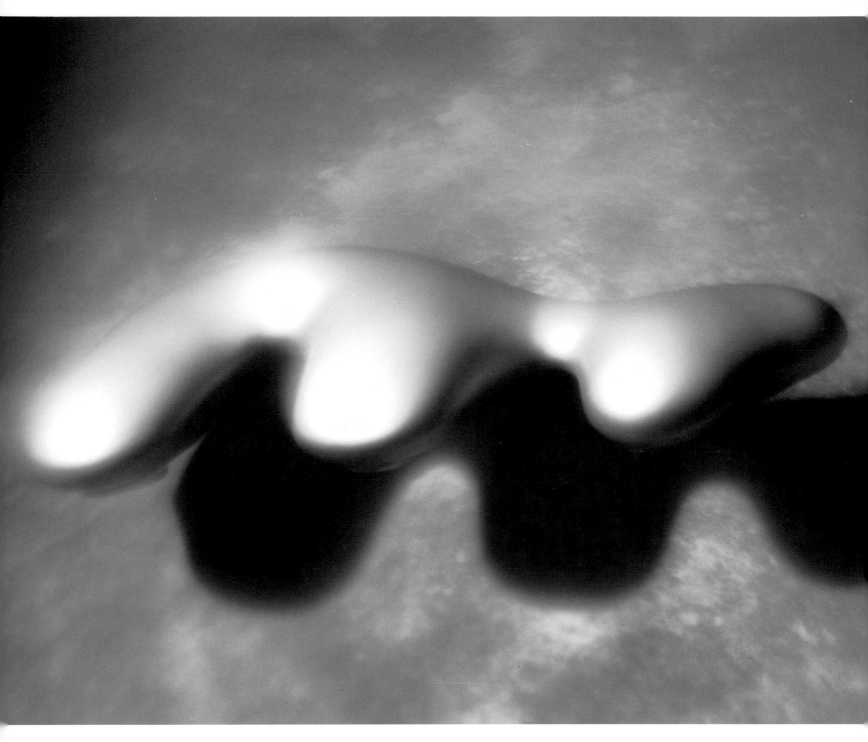

**67. Toshiyuki Kita** *Automatic tap*
Brass
Discharges soap, water and hot air when the sensor is activated.
H 7.4cm (3in)  W 42cm (16½ in)  D 17.4cm (6⅞ in)
Manufacturer: Toto, Japan

**68**

**69**

**70**

**71**

**72**

**73**

**74**

**75**

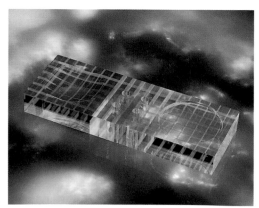

**76**

**77**

**68. Denis Santachiara** Humidifier *Ciminiera*
Contains a 25w clear bulb.
H 180cm (70⅝ in)  W 40cm (15¾ in)
D 40cm (15¾ in)
Manufacturer: Domodinamica, Italy

**69. Hannu Kähönen** Floor brush and dustpan
*Kurki*
Steel, plastic, wood, natural bristle
Prototype
H 95cm (37½ in)  W 17.2cm (6¾ in)
D 22.1cm (8¾ in)

**70. Winfried Scheuer** Wastepaper bin
*Aero Flatpack*
Laser-cut aero ply. Prototype
H 35cm (13¾ in)  W 25cm (9⅞ in)
L 32cm (12½ in)

**71. Friedrich Sulzer** Waste bags *Tribelle*
Polyoxymethylene, polypropylene,
polyethylene. Prototype
W 43cm (16⅞ in)  D 6cm (2⅜ in)

**72. Jasper Morrison** Mirror *Progetto 9310*
Glass
H 80cm (31½ in)  W 60cm (23½ in)
D 15cm (6in)
Manufacturer: Cappellini, Italy

**73. Konstantin Grcic** Coat hanger with brush
*Progetto 9215*
Beechwood
H 12cm (4¾ in)  W 42cm (16½ in)
Manufacturer: Cappellini, Italy

**74. Casimir Reynders** CD rack *Gill*
Maple or cherrywood
Limited batch production
H 80cm (31½ in)  W 19cm (7½ in)
D 19cm (7½ in)
Manufacturer: Casimir Reynders, Belgium

**75. Emanuela Frattini** Picture frame *Quarters*
American cherrywood, maplewood, glass,
US quarters, stainless steel
H 25.5cm (10in)  W 20.3cm (8in)
H 17.8cm (7in)  W 12.7cm (5in)
H 15cm (6in)  W 10cm (4in)
H 12.7cm (5in)  W 8.9cm (3½ in)
Manufacturer: EFM, USA and Italy

**76. Setsuo Kitaoka** *Tooth brush stand
and soap tray*
Acrylic. Prototype
H 12cm (4¾ in)  W 11cm (4⅜ in)
D 11cm (4⅜ in)
Manufacturer: The Body & Bath Shop, Japan

**77. Andreas Mikkelsen** *Book end for CDs/cassettes*
Pewter, stainless steel
H 14cm (5½ in)  W variable
D 14cm (5½ in)
Manufacturer: Royal Copenhagen, Denmark

78

**78. Johanna Grawunder** Jewellery boxes *Trucks*
Wood, chromed metal, plastic car reflectors,
Perspex
Limited batch of 50
Manufacturer: Argentaurum, Belgium

**Boxes**

Boxes provided an unusual sub-theme at the 1993 Milan Furniture Fair. Much of the interest centred on two very different types of boxes produced by representatives of two generations of designers in the city. In one corner: the veteran Italian designer **Enzo Mari**, whose *Flores* container for Danese was exhibited in the stylish showroom of sister company Cassina (see pages 192–3). In the other corner (literally on a street corner): **Johanna Grawunder**, the young American architect and partner in Sottsass Associati, who mounted an exhibition of 14 jewellery boxes in the back of a truck.

The *Flores* storage container, made entirely of technopolymer resin, is based on a supreme piece of technical invention by Mari: this desktop object avoids the need for separate screws, hinges and other components due to the way the lid is joined to the base of the box. The sculptural form is a pleasing counterpoint to the nondescript styling that afflicts so much office machinery. Grawunder, meanwhile, has incorporated found objects such as car reflectors in her bold and imaginative *Trucks* series of jewellery boxes. Both projects adopt different strategies but share a similar spirit of adventure to create designs of refinement and intelligence.

**79. Kenneth Grange** Jug kettles *JK300* and *JK100*
Moulded polypropylene
H 23cm (9in)  W 21.5cm (8½ in)  Di 13.2cm (5⅛ in)
Manufacturer: Kenwood, UK

**80. Metamoderne** *Toaster*
Metal, rubber. Prototype
H 22cm (8⅝ in)  W 33cm (13in)  D 13cm (5⅛ in)

**Marco Susani and Mario Trimarchi** Kitchenware *New Tools*
Prototype
**81**. *Microwave oven:*
Polished stainless steel, plastic material, ceramic
H 30cm (11⅞ in)  Di 40cm (15¾ in)
**82**. *Electric steamer:*
Plastic material
H 30cm (11⅞ in)  L 45cm (17¾ in)  D 20cm (7⅞ in)
**83**. *Microclimatic bowls:*
Plastic material, aluminium
H 40cm (15¾ in)  L 40cm (15¾ in)  D 40cm (15¾ in)
**84**. *Recharging tray:*
A plate to recharge the batteries of the cordless tools
**85**. *Juice squeezer/pitcher:*
Plastic, rubber, glass
H 45cm (17¾ in)  Di 15cm (6in)
Manufacturer: Philips Corporate Industrial Design,
The Netherlands

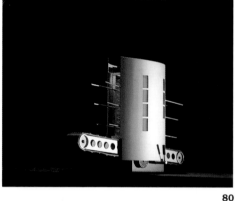

79                    80

81          82          83          84          85

**Marco Susani and Mario Trimarchi**

Marco Susani and Mario Trimarchi are industrial designers and
teachers at the Domus Academy in Milan. Their *New Tools* for the
kitchen result from design research into small domestic appliances of
the future, supported by Stefano Marzano, director of Philips Corporate
Industrial Design in Eindhoven. The designers set out to create kitchen
machines more closely related to the culture and ritual of food
preparation and eating. "There is no reference to a white plastic look",
say the designers. The aim was to make the *New Tools* comfortable,
natural and respectful of old cultural traditions in the kitchen.

An electric steamer, for example, updates the traditional system of
wooden baskets, while a rollable bread warmer features a soft mat
with a heating element to keep bread at the right temperature and
softness at the table.

All the tools were designed to be unobtrusive, to "disappear" on the
table when not in use. All utilize existing technologies, although the
designers admit that in some cases they require further development
to be industrially feasible.

86

**86. Slany Design Team** Cookware *Silit 2000*
Silargan (a metal-containing ceramic surface covering
a solid core of ferromagnetic silit steel)
The exterior of the pot remains cold.
Low cookpot with sliding lid:
H 7.5cm/8.5cm/10.5cm (3in/3⅜/4⅛ in)
Di 16cm/20cm/24cm (6½ in/7⅞ in/9⅜ in)
Tall cookpot with sliding lid:
H 10.5cm/13cm/15cm (4⅛ in/5⅛ in/6in)
Di 16cm/20cm/24cm (6½ in /7⅞ in/9⅜ in)
Saucepan without lid:
H 7.5cm (3in)  Di 16cm (6½ in)
Saucepan with lid:
H 8.5cm (3⅜ in)  Di 20cm (7⅞ in)
Manufacturer: Silit Werke, Germany

**87. Guy Dyas** Vacuum cleaner *Vacman*
Cast aluminium, ABS, rubber. Prototype
H 123cm (48⅜ in)  W 68cm (26¾ in)  D 31cm (12¼ in)

**88. Guy Dyas** *Microwave oven*
ABS, ceramic, polycarbonate. Prototype
H 26cm (10¼ in)  Di 32cm (12½ in)
Manufacturer: National Panasonic, Japan

**89. James Dyson** Vacuum cleaner *Dyson Dual Cyclone*
Metallic flake, ABS, polycarbonate
H 112cm (44in)  W 35.5cm (14in)  D 30.5cm (12in)
Manufacturer: Dyson Appliances, UK

### James Dyson

Conventional vacuum cleaners swiftly clog up with dirt and have a cumbersome paper or cloth bag which needs emptying, says British designer-inventor James Dyson. He claims that traditional machines lose 70 per cent of their power after vacuuming just 500 grams of dust – barely a cupful. Dyson's *Dual Cyclone* vacuum cleaner does away with the need for bags and provides greatly improved performance by harnessing the power of two cyclones to clean via an 800mph cyclonic action. Dirt is sucked up and spun through a see-through bin in a five-stage filtration process. The bin is easy to unclip and empty. The cleaner feels lightweight due to the clever use of product geometry: the centre of gravity is in the motor by the wheels. Other design features include a handle which unclips to become a telescopic hose with a four-metre reach.

James Dyson has already enjoyed design success with the cylone vacuuming principle, working with Silver Reed and Johnson Wax. Now his Bath-based company has branched out from design and research into manufacturing this domestic model. Previous Dyson market inventions have included the *Ballbarrow*, a wheelbarrow with a pneumatic ball-wheel.

88

### Guy Dyas

Guy Dyas is a British industrial design graduate of the Royal College of Art who is currently working in Tokyo as a product designer for Sony. Unusually for a staff designer, he has made quite an impact in Japan due to his one-man show in the Loft Gallery at Seibu, the major Tokyo department store. Dyas exhibited a range of prototypes which reflect his concern to incorporate fantasy, spirit and playfulness into electrical and electronic products which usually lack such qualities.

Dyas finds the current language of industrial design sterile in its continuing adherence to technical Modernism. His prototype microwave oven fundamentally reassesses a product type which convention dictates should look like a television. Sponsored by National Panasonic, his design reconfigures the product beneath a glass dome to provide a better view of the food cooking and to make the oven easier to use. A transparent ceramic perforated door seal is scarcely visible under the dome.

The *Vacman* vacuum cleaner, meanwhile, adopts conventional technology but takes a more extreme sculptural approach: the motor is housed in a cast aluminium head with eyes acting as headlights. "I set myself the challenge of imagining what would happen if the vacuum cleaning concept had been introduced to one of the great inventors or artists of long ago," explains Dyas. "For example, how would Leonardo da Vinci have viewed the technology – with wonder or fear?"

89

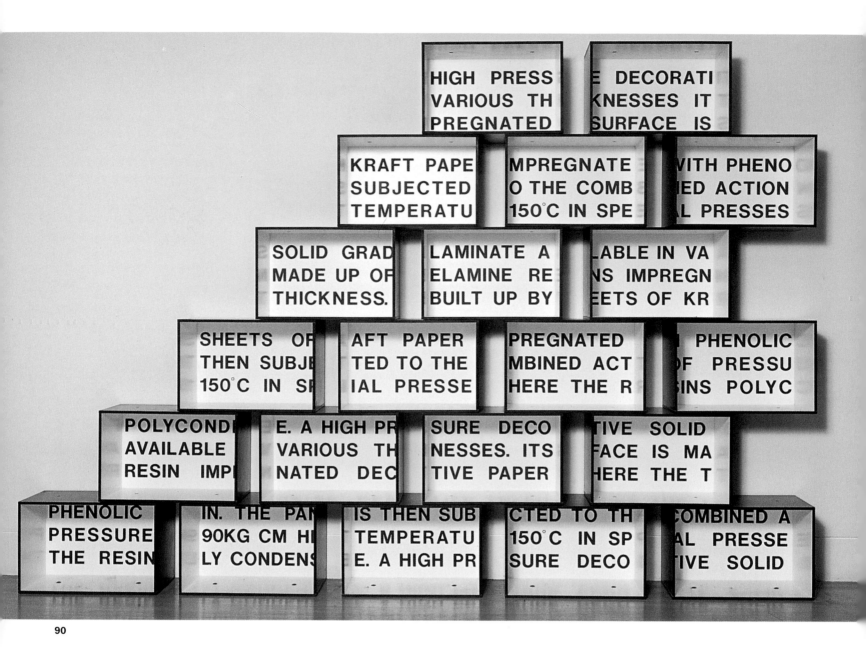

**90. Jane Atfield** *Storage boxes*
Solid core laminate. Prototype
Words are engraved on the rear of the boxes using
a shop sign machine.
H 34cm (13⅜ in)  W 52cm (20½ in)  D 34cm (13⅜ in)
Manufacturer: Royal College of Art, UK

91

92

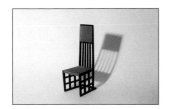

93

94

95

96

97

98

## Miniatures

If you can collect classic cars, doll's houses and famous
football trophies in miniature, then why not classic furniture?
That at least appears to be the reasoning behind new
collections of furniture miniatures from the **Vitra Design
Museum** and from Austrian lighting company **Woka**, which has
issued a series of Wiener Werkstätte pieces (Hoffmann, Moser,
Wagner *et al*) made by Galerie Ambiente using the same stain,
paint and lacquer finishes to the wood as the originals. There
is a consolation in the smaller scale of the miniatures for those
of us who would like to own the originals: they come with a
smaller price tag – although not all that small!

**Galerie Ambiente**

*Furniture miniatures*
Beechwood
The miniatures are constructed
on a scale of 1:6.

**91.** Josef Hoffmann
Table *Quadratl*
H 13cm (5⅛ in)
W 6cm (2⅜ in)
D 6cm (2⅜ in)

**92.** Otto Wagner *Desk*
H 17.5cm (6⅞ in)
W 17.5cm (6⅞ in)
D 11cm (4⅜ in)

**93.** Josef Hoffmann
Chair *Dr Salzer*
H 21.7cm (8½ in)
W 7.8cm (3⅛ in)
D 8.2cm (3¼ in)

**94.** Otto Wagner *Stool*
H 7.5cm (3in)
W 7.3cm (2⅞ in)
D 7.3cm (2⅞ in)

**95.** Josef Hoffmann
*Nest of tables*
H 12.5cm (5in)
W 9cm (3½ in)
D 7.5cm (3in)

**96.** Josef Hoffmann
*Purkersdorfer Armchair*
H 11cm (4⅜ in)
W 10.1cm (4in)
D 10.5cm (4⅛ in)

**97.** Josef Hoffmann
*Sitzmaschine*
H 18.5cm (7¼ in)
W 10.5cm (4⅛ in)
D 14cm (5½ in)

**98.** Josef Hoffmann
*Purkersdorfer Chair*
H 16.7cm (6½ in)
W 7.3cm (2⅞ in)
D 7.2cm (2¾in)

**99. Vitra Design Museum**

*Furniture miniatures*
Manufacturer: Vitra Design
Museum, Germany

99

**100**

## The NovoPen

The NovoPen is one of the most remarkable success stories in modern industrial design. It is a device which enables diabetes sufferers to inject themselves with insulin swiftly, accurately and conveniently – without the need to grapple with unwieldly and unsightly syringes, swabs and bottles.

When the lightweight "insulin pen" concept was first launched in the mid-1980s, turning a medical syringe into a device with the image of a discreet writing tool, it marked a revolution in the treatment of diabetes. Danish manufacturer Novo Nordisk won a number of international awards as a result. Ron Arad has selected the latest insulin pen products to emerge from Novo Nordisk's research and development department. Designed in plastic and stainless steel by **Steve McGugan**, the *NovoPen 3* and *NovoPen 1.5* use 3ml and 1.5ml insulin cartridges respectively.

**100. Novo Nordisk (Steve McGugan)**
Insulin administration devices
*NovoPen 3* and *NovoPen 1.5*
Plastic, stainless steel
*NovoPen 3*:
L 16.4cm (6⅜ in)
Di 1.6cm (¾ in)
*NovoPen 1.5*:
L 15.3cm (6in)  Di 1.5cm (⅝ in)
Manufacturer: Novo Nordisk,
Denmark

**101. Kazuo Kawasaki**
Folding wheelchair *Carna*
Titanium
H 84cm (33in)  W 56cm (22in)
D 89.6cm (35¼ in)
Manufacturer: SIG Workshop
Co., Japan

**101**

## Kazuo Kawasaki

Japanese designer Kazuo Kawasaki has been in a wheelchair for the past 18 years, following a car accident at the age of 27 which left him paralysed from the waist down. The *Carna* wheelchair represents what has become for him the greatest design challenge of his life. After his accident, he needed to find the perfect wheelchair but discovered that there was little innovation in wheelchair design because a limited market meant that the costs were high. Most wheelchairs are normally made to individual specifications, but says Kawasaki, there is a big problem with that. "Accident victims have no previous experience of wheelchairs. It's not like a suit, is it? So it can't really be tailor-made. And if a tailor-made one doesn't fit, a mass-produced wheelchair like those provided at airports will be even more uncomfortable."

Kawasaki took a long time to develop a good working relationship with a manufacturer. Most, he says, were too keen to incorporate new ideas without fully testing or integrating them. The *Carna* was eventually developed with SIG Workshop Co., a small company which operates like a traditional craft workshop. It is made of titanium, an expensive, lightweight material, to meet Kawasaki's objective that the wheelchair should weigh no more than 6kg. "A wheelchair is not just a piece of medical equipment for me," says Kawasaki. "It is my legs and feet. So the most important thing is to keep the weight down. We're designing sneakers, not boots. Disabled people do not want to change shoes between indoors and outdoors, so the wheelchair has to be a car outdoors and a chair indoors – easily folded and carried by hand." Kawasaki is continuing to experiment with weight reductions and fashionable colours in developing his design.

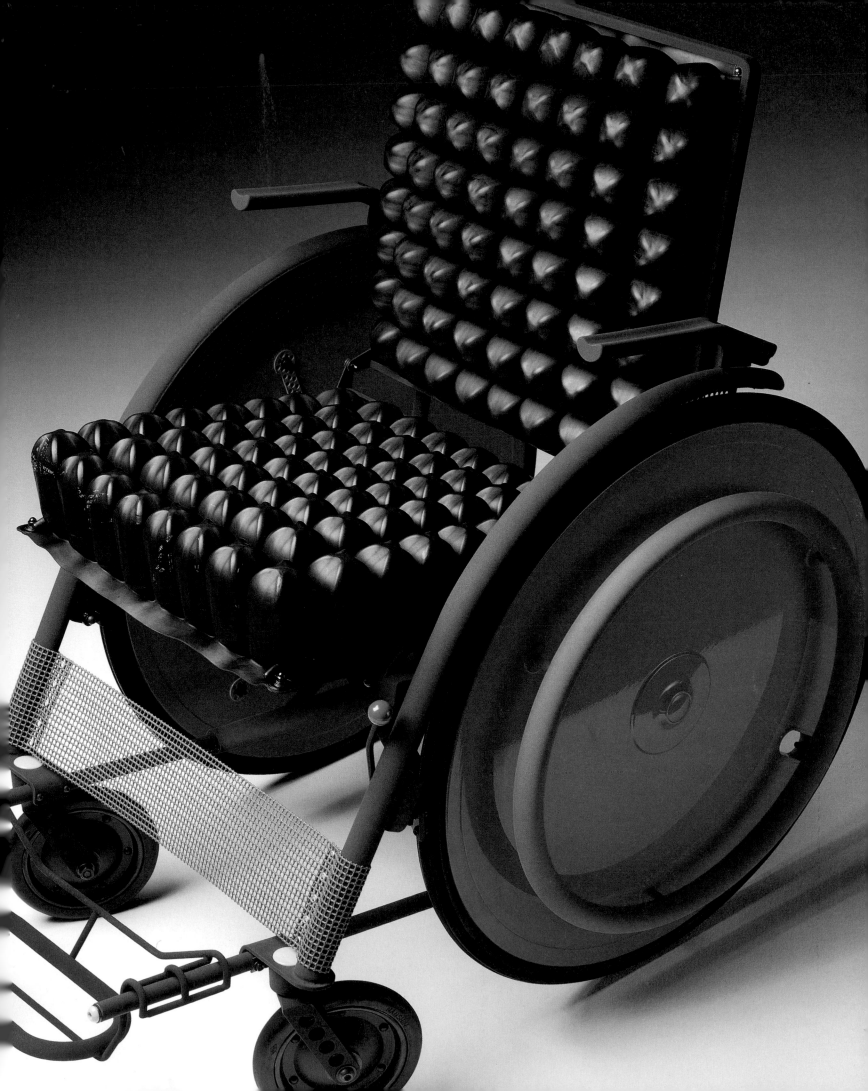

The publisher and editors would like to thank the designers and manufacturers who submitted work for inclusion in this book; Junko Popham for her help in collecting Japanese contributions, and the following photographers and copyright holders for the use of their material:

# Photographic Credits

**Arunas** 1.118 (page 78)

**Toshi Asakawa** 5.76

**Tod Babick** 5.4

**Maria Vittoria Corradi Backhaus** 1.123

**Aldo Ballo** 2.21, 3.4, 5, 25

**Florian Bilges** 1.110

© **Michael Bohme Photo Design** 2.37

**Santi Caleca** 3.27, 5.78, 5.81–85

**Alister Clarke** 1.121

**Maarten Corbijn** 1.117

**Caren Dissinger** 2.19, 20

**Guy Dyas** 5.87

**Mike Edwards** 3.6

**Siggi Fischer** 5.34

**Mitsumasa Fujitsuka** 1.126, 3.14, 5.101 (pages 210, 211)

**Nob Fukuda** 5.67

**David Granger** 1.65

© **Léon Gulikers** 3.9, 10, 11

**Doug Hall** 1.79, 2.12

**Scott Hawkins** 1.63, 66, 3.38

**Michael Hemsley** 1.115, 116

**Yuuki Higuchi** 4.41–54

**Cecile Hohenlohe** 2.40

**Image Studios** 1.88

**Craig Kershaw** 1.118

© **Ralph Klein** 1.119

**Ilmari Kostiainen** 5.69

**Dan Kramer** 3.23, 42

**Miyuki Kume** 1.58

**Mariette Landon** 1.80

**Till Leeser** 1.87

**R. Matsunaga** 5.60

**Sue McNab** 4.26

**Trevour Meiin** 1.124

**Masaru Mera** 3.12, 13, 28, 29, 30

**Gunmar Merrild** 5.37, 38

**METAmoderne** 5.80

**John Montana** 1.92

**Luciana Mulas** 3.31

**Mundus** 1.95

**Occhiomagico** 5.65

**Takayuki Ogawa** 1.113, 114

**Grethe Lund Overgaard** 1.41

**Josef Pausch** 2.1, 38

**T. Pellegrini** 5.35

**Andreas Pohlmann/Felix Wey** 2.62–65

**Mark Preston** 1.75

**Prospero Rasulo** 1.132

**R.C.R.** 1.86

**Amy Reichman** 1.34

**Alan Richardson** 5.1

**Benvenuto Saba** 5.51

**Jordi Sarra** 1.70

**Katsuji Sato** 4.1–12

**Winfried Scheuer** 5.70

© **Schnakenburg & Brahl** 1.83, 84

**Heini Schneebeli** 1.108

**H.Seehuber** 5.31, 33

**Masafumi Sekine** 3.15, 16

**Roberto Sellitto** 1.68, 2.3, 4, 22, 23

**Michael Sieber** 1.6, 7, 8, 9

**Akira Shimizu** 1.120, 2.2, 3.2

**Yoshio Shiratori** 1.97

**Skalski** 3.41

**Christian Steiner** 2.9

**Studio Diametro** 1.94

**Studio Hablützel** 1.104

**Studio Visus** 2.11

**Terry Sutherland** 5.9, 10, 48, 61

**Symmetrical** 3.37

**Michael Tagger** 2.52

**Vincent Thfoin** 3.26

**Justin Thomas** 3.17, 19

**Frank Thurston** 5.88

**Rauno Träskelin** 2.35

**Emilio Tremolada** 3.7, 8

**Nick Turner** 5.12, 57, 79

**Thomas Vack** 1.64, 127, 2.30

**Hans van der Mars** 1.1, 5, 18, 109, 2.16

**Deidi von Schaewen** 1.73

© **Vernon Warren** 1.69, 112

**Joshua White** 1.131

© **Courtesy of Worshipful Company of Goldsmiths** 3.18

**Gionata Xerra** 5.6

**Kouta Yoshimizu** 2.17, 18

**Andrea Zani** 2.28

The photographs of Ron Arad's work, featured on pages 8–17 were taken by Christoph Kicherer, Alison Brooks and Howard Kingsnorth.

# Biographies

Every effort has been made to obtain details about the designers whose work is featured in this book, but in some cases information was not available. The figures following each entry refer to the illustrations of that designer's work (the number before the full point indicates the chapter number).

**Helle Abild** was born in Copenhagen in 1964 and graduated in textile design in 1989. A freelance textile designer, she has also designed furniture, including a sales counter for the Royal Theatre in Copenhagen. She has worked in London and is currently working in New York. 4.27–40

**Laura Agnoletto** and **Marzio Rusconi Clerici** were born in 1963 and 1960 respectively, and formed their design partnership in 1985. They have lived and worked in Los Angeles and London, and have exhibited in international group and solo shows. They create their objects mostly from industrial salvage. 2.3, 4

**Tadao Amano** was born in Yamanashi, Japan, in 1956. He graduated from the Musashino University of Art, then in 1987 worked in Angelo Mangiarotti's studio. Since 1988 he has worked as an independent industrial designer and architect. He has won prizes for his designs in both Italy and Japan. 5.36

**Emilio Ambasz** was born in Argentina in 1943. He gained a Master's degree in architecture from Princeton University, and was subsequently made a professor there. While still in his twenties, he helped to found New York's Institute of Architecture and Urban Studies and served as Curator of Design at the Museum of Modern Art. Among his buildings, the Museum of American Folk Art and Houston Center Plaza are especially well known. He has received international recognition and has won several awards for his work as an architect and interior and industrial designer, most recently the 1990 Quaternario Award for high technological achievement. He has exhibited widely, including the 1989 travelling show "Emilio Ambasz: Architecture Exhibition: Industrial and Graphic Design" which appeared at many venues in the USA and Canada. 5.60

**Stephan Apetauer** was born in 1962 and studied industrial design and product design at the Technical Colleges in Munich and Schwäbisch-Gmünd. He worked as a freelance designer for Andreas Weber Architektur and Design, before becoming a product designer at Siemens Design, Munich in 1991. He has lectured in product design at the Technical College in Schwäbisch-Gmünd, and his work has received several awards from the Industrie Forum Design, Hanover. 5.28

**Ron Arad** was born in Tel Aviv in 1951 and studied at the Jerusalem Academy of Art, and the Architectural Association, London (from 1974 to 1979). In 1981 he founded One Off Ltd with Dennis Groves and Caroline Thorman and in 1983 designed One Off's first showroom in Neal Street, Covent Garden. He started to exhibit both nationally and internationally, as well as hosting shows for other designers, notably Danny Lane, Tom Dixon and Jon Mills in 1986. In 1988 he won the Tel Aviv Opera Foyer Interior Competition with C. Norton and S. McAdam, and the next year formed Ron Arad Associates in order to realize the project, moving his premises to Chalk Farm, London. As well as the design and construction of the new One Off Design Studio, furniture gallery and workshop in 1990, recent projects have included the Poltronova *Split* series of furniture; two Vitra Editions – the *Schizo Chair* and a design for an office chair, and the Moroso *Soft Volumes* and *Spring* collections; and the design of various interior installations and domestic architectural projects, such as a house in Schopfheim for a German publisher. Recent exhibitions include "Breeding in Captivity", a one-man show at the Edward Totah Gallery, London; joint shows with Ingo Maurer at the Galleria Internos and the Galleria Facsimile, Milan; and "Gaz Naturel, L'énergie créative" at the Grand Palais, Paris. Pages 8–17, 2.62

**Zeev Aram** graduated from the Central School of Design, London after completing a course in furniture and interior design. He established Aram Designs and Zeev Aram & Associates in 1964. He is active in promoting modern design and in 1973 was instrumental in introducing Eileen Gray designs to the world market. The annual Aram Designs Graduate Show, established in 1988, gives design students from colleges throughout the UK the chance to exhibit their work. Zeev Aram is a Fellow of the Chartered Society of Designers and the Royal Society of Arts, and an Honorary Fellow of the Royal College of Art. 1.108

**Josep Aregall** was born in Barcelona in 1957 and since 1979 has designed and built commercial spaces, houses and offices. He has also designed exhibitions and temporary constructions, and has been Professor of Window Dressing and Temporary Constructions at the EINA Design School since 1985. He collaborated in the Barcelona Cinema Festival in 1987, 1988 and 1990 and the EINA-20 Years Exhibition. He designed the travelling exhibition for the presentation of the 1992 Barcelona Paralympic Games. 2.44

**Jan Armgardt** was born in 1947. He trained initially as a cabinet-maker and later in interior design. After gaining practical experience in a firm involved in furniture design, he opened his own furniture studio in Bensheim, Germany, in 1974. He collaborates with companies such as de Padova, de Sede, Knoll and Wittman, and besides furniture also designs kitchen and table accessories, office equipment and lamps. He has been the recipient of numerous awards and prizes. 1.20, 21, 23–25

**Pietro Arosio** was born in Lissone, Italy in 1946. After graduating from the Monza Art Institute in 1965 he worked as a designer for a firm specializing in institutional furniture. In 1972 he established his own industrial design practice. He received the Casaviva d'Oro first prize for his kitchen designs in 1983. His work has been exhibited at the Victoria and Albert Museum, London and the modern art museum, Die Neue Sammlung, Munich. 1.67

**Shigeaki Asahara** was born in Tokyo in 1948 and studied in Torino, Italy. Since 1973 he has worked as a freelance industrial designer in Tokyo. He exhibits internationally, and one of his projects is on permanent show at the Brooklyn Museum of New York. 2.49, 50, 51

**Jane Atfield** studied furniture design at the Royal College of Art, London from 1990 to 1992. 1.14, 15, 5.90

**Hiroshi Awatsuji** was born in Kyoto, Japan in 1929 and graduated from the Kyoto City University of Art. In 1964 he began his collaboration with the Fujie Textile Co. Ltd. In 1988 he became a professor at the Tama University of Arts. He has participated in exhibitions world-wide and is internationally recognized for his work. He received an Outstanding Award at the 3rd International Textile Competition in Kyoto in 1992, and later that year a Gold Award at the 38th ID Annual Design Review in the USA. 1.126

**Gijs Bakker** was born in Amersfoot, Holland in 1942. He studied at the College of Arts and Crafts (now the Rietveld Akademie), Amsterdam in the Department of Jewellery Design, and later at the Konstfackskolan, Department of Industrial Design in Stockholm. From 1962 to 1963 he worked as a designer at Van Kempen & Begeer in Zeist, then founded a studio with his wife in Utrecht. Until 1986 Bakker was a freelance designer for companies such as Bussum and Artifort Maastricht, as well as teaching (from 1971 to 1978) at the Academie van Beeldende Kunsten at Arnhem in the Department of Metal and Plastic Design. From 1987 to 1989 he was a partner in the design studio BRS Premsela Vonk in Amsterdam. Today he is Head of the "Man and Living" Department of the Academy of Industrial Design at Eindhoven, and design adviser for the Keramische Industrie Cor Unum, 's Hertogenbosch. In 1993 Bakker established Keizersgracht 518 in Amsterdam. His work can be seen in major design collections, including the Stedelijk Museum, Amsterdam; the Power House Museum, Sydney; the Denver Museum of Art; the Cooper-Hewitt Museum, New York; and the Victoria and Albert Museum, London.

**Bang Design** was founded in Sydney in 1989 by Bryan Marshall and David Granger. Both are graduates of industrial design, with degrees in environmental design from the School of Environmental Design at the University of Canberra. Before forming their own company, they spent six years working for manufacturers and design consultants. Bang Design's work has been exhibited and published widely in Australia. 1.63, 65, 66, 118, 3.38

**Mario Barbaglia** and **Marco Colombo** have worked in interior design since 1975. They became involved in industrial design in 1984 when they started a collaboration with PAF, creating the PAF Studio collection. Their designs have received awards internationally. 2.21

**Luigi Baroli** was born in the Milan province of Corbetta in 1951. Sincer taking a degree in architecture at the Milan Polytechnic, he has worked for the most part in interior design. He has created a co-ordinated image for a chain of clothing stores and is at present working on the design of a series of restaurants. He also designs jewellery. Since 1990 he has been in charge of the art direction of Baleri Italia's Milan showroom and the installations for the Baleri collection at events in Italy and abroad. 1.94

**François Bauchet** was born in 1948 and today practises interior and furniture design in Saint-Étienne, France. Interior design projects include the reception areas of the Musée d'Art et d'Industrie, Saint-Étienne and the Centre d'Art de Vassivière in Limousin. He has exhibited his work in Europe and Japan and has had several one-man shows at Galerie Néotù, Paris. His work can be seen in the permanent collection of the Musée des Arts Décoratifs in Paris. 1.3

**Mario Bellini** graduated in architecture in 1959 from Milan Polytechnic and now lives and works in Milan. He has designed for numerous Italian and foreign companies, including Olivetti, Cassina, Vitra, Erco, Rosenthal and Yamaha. As a member of the 17th Milan Triennale Executive Committee, he designed and curated the exhibition "Il Progetto Domestico" in 1986, and in 1988 co-directed the exhibition "La città del Mondo e il futuro delle Metropoli". He designed the series of exhibitions on "The Treasure of S. Marco in Venice" for some of the world's major museums, and designed "Italian Art in the 20th Century" in 1989 at the Royal Academy of Art, London. Recent architectural projects include an office and industrial complex in Milan; the exhibition and convention centre in the Villa Erba park, Lake Como; three residential buildings in the centre of Milan, now under construction; and an elementary school at Giussano, Milan, also under construction. From 1986 to 1991 he was editor of *Domus*, the monthly magazine of architecture, design and art. In April 1992 the Tokyo Design Centre opened a large exhibition dedicated to his activities in design and architecture. He has taught and given lectures and seminars at numerous international universities and cultural centres, and has won many awards for his work including the Compasso d'Oro (seven times). Twenty-five of his works are in the permanent design collection of the Museum of Modern Art in New York which in June 1987 dedicated a monographic exhibition to him. 3.4, 5, 5.6

**Jurgen Bey** was born in 1965 and graduated in 1990 from the Academy of Industrial Design in Eindhoven. He has a design studio with Jan Konings and has won several design competitions in Holland. 1.98

**Mark Biasotti** is a senior industrial designer with IDEO in Palo Alto, California. He received a BSID from San Jose State University, then worked for Hewlett Packard until joining IDEO. He has collaborated with companies such as Apple Computer and Tandeau. 5.7

**Thomas Bley** was born in Düren, Germany, in 1954 and studied graphic and industrial design in Aachen, Hamburg and New York. After a collaboration with Memphis Milan, he co-founded Zebra Design in New York in 1986. From 1988 to 1990 he was Professor of Industrial Design at Arizona State University and he is currently Professor for Design and Concept at Cologne College. 1.69

**Constantin Boym** was born in Moscow in 1955. He graduated from Moscow Architectural Institute in 1978 and from 1984 to 1985 studied for a Master's degree in design at the Domus Academy in Milan. He became a registered architect in the USA in 1988 and today has his own design consultancy in New York. He has designed award-winning products for many international companies including Morphos, Néotù and the Formica Corporation, and since 1986 has taught at the Parsons School of Design, New York. Recent awards include the ID Annual Design Award in 1988 and 1990. His work is included in the permanent collection of the Cooper-Hewitt Museum, New York. 1.40

**Andrea Branzi** was born in 1938 in Florence where he studied architecture. Together with Gilberto Corretti, Paolo Deganello and Massimo Morozzi, he founded the avant-garde group Archizoom Associates in 1966. From 1974 to 1976 he was involved with Global Tools, and in the late 1970s set up CDM, a Milan-based group of design consultants. He worked with Studio Alchimia and Memphis from the outset, designing furniture and objects and preparing shows and publications. He has contributed to leading architectural and design reviews, and his work has appeared in various leading design publications; two issues of *Space Design* and *Japan Interior Design* were devoted entirely to his work. He also teaches, holding conferences at universities in Italy and abroad. He founded the Domus Academy in 1983 and has been its cultural director and vice-president. He has had many one-man shows at the Milan Triennale and at galleries and museums around the world. All his projects were acquired in 1982 by the Communications Study Center and Archives at the University of Parma. In 1987 he won the Compasso d'Oro/ADI prize for his entire career. 1.26, 27, 32, 102, 2.63

**Juli Capella** and **Quim Larrea** were born in Barcelona in 1960 and in Córdoba in 1957, respectively. Capella studied industrial design and Larrea architecture. They have been partners since 1982. They were members of the editorial board of *El Croquis* magazine from 1983 to 1987 and were the founders of the Spanish design magazine *De Diseño*. At present they are editors of the architecture and design magazine *ARDI*. They have been consultants on the Sevilla '92 International Exhibition and the cultural Olympics of the Barcelona '92 Olympic Committee, and are also active in exhibition organization in Spain. They have received various awards and have taught at ELISAVA and EINA, as well as at the Universidad Internacional Menéndez Pelayo. 1.95

**Anna Castelli Ferrieri** studied at the University of Milan where she graduated in architecture. She taught industrial design at the Milan University School of Architecture from 1984 to 1986 and at the Domus Academy Postgraduate Design School from 1987. A co-founder of the Movement for Architectural Studies (MSA), she is a member of the National Institute for Town Planning (INU) and the Association for Industrial Design (ADI). Projects include the Kartell corporate buildings at Binasco, and the restoration and interior redesign of ancient buildings such as the Bramante cloister in Milan. From 1976 to 1987 she was Art Director for Kartell. Her industrial design projects have achieved international recognition through major design awards such as the Compasso d'Oro which she has received twice and the ID Annual Design Award, USA (1983). A number of her designs are included in the permanent collections of the New York Museum of Modern Art; the Design Museum, London; the Munich Stadtmuseum; the Jerusalem Museum of Israel; the Copenhagen Museum of Decorative Art; and the São Paulo Design Museum. 3.31

**Celina Clarke** and **Simon Christopher** founded ISM Objects in 1990 with the aim of creating modern products for inner-city living. Both partners hold degrees in industrial design from the Royal Melbourne Institute of Technology, and since graduating in 1988 have worked in the fields of furniture design, retail display design and packaging. 1.121

**Lluis Clotet** was born in Barcelona in 1941 and studied at the Escuela Tecnica de Arquitectura in Barcelona, graduating in 1965. In 1964 he founded Studio PER with the architects Pep Bonet, Cristian Cirici and Oscar Tusquets, and has collaborated in numerous projects with Tusquets. He is a founder member of Bd Ediciones de Diseño, for which he still designs furniture and objects. He received the FAD award for the best interior in Barcelona in 1965 and 1972, and for the best building in 1978 and 1979. He has also received the Delta de Oro on three occasions for his industrial design. He exhibits widely both nationally and internationally. 2.8

**Laslo Conek** was born in Srbobran, Yugoslavia in 1954 and graduated in industrial design in 1979. He moved to Italy in 1980 and today works for several companies as a consultant and designer. 1.22

**Christopher Connell** was born in Melbourne, Australia in 1955 and was educated in graphic design, applied art and interior design. He designed retail and commercial interiors before founding Modin Australia in 1990 and MAP (Merchants of Australian Products) in 1991, dealing with furniture and object design and design development. 1.24

**Gaetan Coolen** was born in Hasselt, Belgium, in 1960 and studied architecture. He has exhibited his work frequently in Belgium. 1.96

**Toni Cordero** was born in Lanzo Torinese, Turin in 1937. He studied architecture in Turin and in 1962 founded his own architectural practice. His most notable projects are the Alps Stadium and the Automobile Museum, both in Turin. In the field of product design his clients include Artemide, Driade and Morphos. In 1992 he designed a complete series of furniture and objects for Sawaya & Moroni and its new division Hop-Là. 1.35

**Pepe Cortes** was born in Barcelona in 1946. He trained at the ELISAVA school and later at EINA where he became a lecturer. In the early 1970s he co-founded the Grupo Abierto de Diseño, specializing in interior design. In the 1980s he collaborated with Oscar Tusquets, Eduard Samso and Alfredo Arribas. At this time he also started a collaboration with Javier Mariscal, creating furniture and lamps for industrial production. In 1983 Cortes received the FAD Award and in 1986 the Delta de Plata ADI-FAD. 1.52

**Edward Cruz** graduated from California State University at Long Beach and holds a Bachelor of Science degree in Industrial Design. He is currently a Project Manager at S. G. Hauser Associcates. 5.9, 10

**Simon de Boer** was born in The Netherlands in 1960 and was an *haute cuisine* cook when he started making furniture. He studied at the Rietveld Academy in Amsterdam and is at present a full-time designer of one-off and limited edition pieces. 1.117

**Michele de Lucchi** was born in Ferrara, Italy in 1951 and graduated from Florence University in 1975. During his student years he founded the "Gruppo Cavat", a group concerned with avant-garde and conceptual architecture. He worked and designed for Alchimia until the establishment of Memphis in 1981. Today he produces exclusive art-orientated handmade products, industrial consumer items and furniture in wood, metal, stone and other materials for companies serving specialized markets. His architectural activities range from shop design to large-scale office buildings and private apartment blocks. De Lucchi's work has received many awards and he has published and exhibited widely both nationally and internationally. 2.5, 6, 30, 3.36

**Piero de Martini** was born in Milan in 1939 and graduated in architecture in 1964. Since then he has worked freelance in the residential sector and on work and community environments, with special interest in restoration work and safeguarding the environment. He now devotes his time to research into housing-related problems and collaborates in the field of interior design with companies including Cassina, Monteni, Arteluce, Venini and Acerbis. In 1974 he won the third prize in the International Design Competition at Courtrai in Belgium. In 1986 he was invited by the Crafts Council of Victoria to give a number of lectures in Melbourne and Sydney. 1.133

**Bernhard Dessecker** was born in 1961 in Munich and studied interior architecture. From 1983 to 1984 he worked at Studio Morsa, New York and since 1984 has been a freelance designer, collaborating with the design team of Ingo Maurer. 2.43

**Matthias Dietz** was born in Frankfurt am Main in 1957, and from 1976 to 1980 studied ecology at the Free University and the Technical University, Berlin. In 1980 he studied industrial design at the Academy of Fine Arts, Berlin and the Academy of Visual Arts, Hamburg, and worked as a freelance designer. From 1985 to 1989 he was the Design Manager at Deutsche Leasing AG, Bad Homburg. During this time he worked with Bořek Šípek and David Palterer. Dietz Design Management GmbH was founded in 1989 offering a full range of design strategy, research, analysis and consultancy. Clients include Artemide, Belux, Silhouette International, the Vitra Museum, Moormann and Deutsche Lufthansa. Dietz has organized numerous design exhibitions and has published books on design. 2.53

**David D'Imperio** was born in Pennsylvania in 1960 and graduated from Kutztown University with a Bachelor of Fine Arts degree in graphic design in 1982. He currently lives and works in Miami. Since 1989 he has concentrated on furniture, lighting and exhibition design. Recent projects include a collection of display fixtures for Bergdorf Goodman, New York. His work has been shown annually at the International Contemporary Furniture Fair in New York, and in 1992 at the International Furniture Fair, Frankfurt, Germany. 2.19, 20

**Dissing and Weitling Arkitektfirma** was founded in 1971 by Hans Dissing and Otto Weitling as a continuation of the company originally established by Arne Jacobsen (1902–1971), one of the leading international architects and industrial designers of the Functionalist Movement in Denmark. Since 1971 Dissing and Weitling has continued to expand; today the firm comprises 11 partners, and approximately 70 professional architects and key designers. Their interests range from comprehensive consulting services, through industrial, architectural and urban design to large-scale civil engineering projects. Frequently invited to participate in domestic and international competitions, Dissing and Weitling has won several prestigious commissions, including the Town Hall in Mainz, the IBM Headquarters, Hamburg and the Nordrhein-Westfalen Art Museum in Düsseldorf. Clients include private individuals and companies, as well as local public authorities and national governments. Within the field of industrial design, the firm has been responsible for the design of furniture, medical diagnosis equipment, glasses, light fittings, heating and ventilation installations, telephone equipment, signage systems and graphic design. 5.55

**Nanna Ditzel** was born in 1923 in Copenhagen and graduated from the Industrial Arts and Crafts College in Copenhagen in 1946. Also in that year she established an industrial design studio in Copenhagen with Jørgen Ditzel, and since then has founded several practices in London and Copenhagen. She is active in the fields of furniture, textile, jewellery and tableware design and has belonged to numerous professional institutions, most recently being Chairman of the Danish State Arts Foundation's Committee for Industrial Arts and Design. She has received international acclaim for her work, winning the Gold Medal (with Jørgen Ditzel) at the Milan Triennale in 1960 and the Gold Medal at the International Furniture Design Competition, Asahikawa, Japan in 1990. In 1991 a film on the life and work of Nanna Ditzel was made by the Danish Ministry of Education. Examples of her work can be seen in the permanent collections of the Louisiana Museum of Modern Art, Humlebaek, Denmark; the Museum of Decorative Art, Copenhagen; the Nordenfjeldske Museum of Decorative Art, Trondheim, Norway; and Goldsmiths' Hall, London. 1.84, 85

**Tom Dixon** was born in Sfax, Tunisia in 1959 and moved to the UK when he was four. From 1981 to 1984 he was involved in nightclub promotion and event organization, forming Creative Salvage with Nick Jones and Mark Brazier-Jones in 1985. His studio, Space, is where his prototypes and commissioned works are made, including stage sets, furniture, sculpture, illuminated sculptures, architectural installations, chandeliers and numerous other objects. His clients include Cappellini, Comme des Garçons, Nigel Coates, Ralph Lauren, Vivienne Westwood and Terence Conran. Dixon is a visiting tutor at the Royal College of Art, the Architectural Association and Kingston Polytechnic. He has exhibited his work both individually and in group shows nationally and internationally. It can be found in the permanent collection of the Victoria and Albert Museum, London; the Musée des Arts Décoratifs, Paris; the Pompidou Centre, Paris; the Vitra Chair Museum, Basel; the Crafts Council and the Design Museum, London; and the Brooklyn Museum, New York. 2.40

**Andreas Dober** was born in Düsseldorf in 1960 and studied industrial design and product design at the Visual Arts Institute of Hamburg. Since 1989 he has worked as a product designer in Stuttgart. 5.2

**Stephan Doesinger** was born in 1968 in Salzburg, Austria. He studied industrial design in Linz from 1988. In 1992 he studied architecture at the University of East London under Pascal Schöning, and the same year founded his own studio for graphic and product design with Doris Kropfreiter in Linz. His designs have received much acclaim within Austria. 2.1, 38, 52

**Rodolfo Dordoni** was born in Milan in 1954 and graduated from the Polytechnic in 1979. After working in the offices of several architects in Milan he became interested in industrial design and at present works as consultant and designer to companies such as Artemide, Arteluce, Cappellini, De Sede, Driade, FontanaArte, and Foscarini. Dordoni is also involved in pavilion, shop and stand design, and architecture. 2.41

**Marie-Christine Dorner** was born in Strasbourg in 1960. She graduated from the École Camondo in 1984 and after working for several months in Paris travelled around the world before settling for a year in Tokyo. On returning to France in 1987 she founded her own design studio, specializing in furniture, interior and product design as well as architecture. In 1988 she created the funrniture for La Villa hotel, Paris, and in 1991 was a competition prizewinner for the conception of a new reception area and library at the Musée des Arts et Traditions Populaires in Paris. She has collaborated with companies such as Idée, Cassina, Scarabat, Artelano and Montis. Dorner teaches in Paris and at Quebec University in Montreal and is creating a new series of design courses with the Principal of the Fine Arts School in Reims. Besides one-woman exhibitions in galleries in Tokyo, Paris, New York, Geneva and Los Angeles, Dorner has also taken part in a number of shows including "Design Français 1960–1990" at the Pompidou Centre, "Avant-Première" at the Victoria and Albert Museum, London, and "Women in Design" at the Design Centre in Stuttgart. 1.81

**Donato d'Urbino** and **Paolo Lomazzi** were born in Milan in 1935 and 1936 respectively. In 1966 they started working with Jonathan de Pas in the fields of architecture, design, interior design and urban planning. (The three worked together until de Pas' death in 1991.) In the 1960s they created a series of inflatable designs which were shown at the World Exposition in Osaka and at the 14th Milan Triennale. This culminated in the creation of their inflatable chair, *Blow*, in 1967. They continued with similar designs, working for Acerbis, Artemide, Driade, Disform and others. They have exhibited their work widely and have shown at all the Compasso d'Oro exhibitions since 1979. They recently extended their work to include architecture, product and lighting design, and their output is documented in historical literature on Italian design, as well as in major international publications on industrial architecture and design. Examples of their work can be found in the permanent collections of the Museum of Modern Art, New York; the Victoria and Albert Museum and the Design Museum, London; the Pompidou Centre, Paris; the Kunstgewerbe Museum, Zurich; the Staatliches Museum für Angewandte Kunst, Munich; and the Jerusalem Museum, Israel. 1.123, 125

**Guy Dyas** was born in 1968 and trained at the Chelsea School of Art and the Royal College of Art, London. He has worked as a product and industrial designer for several companies, notably Sony Corporation in Tokyo. Since 1992 he has combined his work for Sony with freelance consultancy. He has exhibited his work in Japan. 5.87, 88

**James Dyson** was born in Norfolk, England in 1947 and studied furniture and interior design at the Royal College of Art, London. He has worked in interior, engineering and product design, and today heads Dyson Research, a team of young product design and mechanical engineering graduates. He has many clients in Japan, the USA and Europe, and is the holder of nearly a hundred registered patents. From 1988 to 1990 Dyson was the chairman of the new Board of Governors of Bath College of Higher Education, and from 1991 has been the external examiner on the industrial design engineering master's course at the Royal College of Art. 5.89

**Joachim Eckhardt** was born in 1960 in Cologne. He practised as a cabinet-maker from 1977 to 1980, then worked with Tobias Winter in Neesbach and with Willy Praml on theatrical design projects. In 1986 he founded the design group X99. He has exhibited his work in Germany and Italy. In 1993 he conceived and organized the art and culture festival "Stadt Land Fluss" in Limburg an der Lahn with Tobias Winter. 1.119

**Thomas Eisl** was born in the Tirol in 1947 and has lived and worked in England since 1969. 2.36, 37

**Steven Ewing** graduated from California State University, Long Beach in 1990 with a Bachelor of Science degree in Industrial Design. He is currently the Senior Industrial Designer at Patton Design in Irvine, California. He holds awards and patents and has been published for his work in design. 5.18, 62

**David Farrage** was born in England in 1969 and studied at Ravensbourne College of Design, Kent and, on an exchange programme, at the Academy of Industrial Design in Eindhoven. He graduated from the Royal College of Art, London in 1993 and has been working for Ross Lovegrove, studio X, London and the architectural and urban products company Sekisui Jushi in Osaka, Japan. 5.50

**Marco Ferreri** was born in Impéria, Italy in 1958 and in 1981 received a degree in architecture from Milan Polytechnic. At present he is collaborating with Angelo Mangiarotti and Bruno Munari. His clients include Luxo, FontanaArte, Danese, Nemo and Interflex. 1.68

**Siggi Fischer** was born in Cologne in 1954 and studied industrial design in Wuppertal. Since 1990 he has worked independently and has a list of clients which includes Thomas Schulte Designmanufaktur, Vericom GmbH and Best Friends Collection. He has exhibited his work in Germany, Italy and Japan. 5.34

**FM Design** is one of the four design-based companies that make up the Fether Miles Group. Based in London, FM Design develops products for European and world markets in the fields of furniture, retail, consumer products and transportation. Recent designs include luggage for Samsonite and several new ranges of Tupperware. 5.59

**Joseph Forakis** was born in 1962 in New York and graduated from the Rhode Island School of Design in 1985. He then worked as an industrial designer in the high technology and consumer product sectors and was Senior Project Manager for new product development at BioMedic Data Systems in New Jersey. He has also been involved in theatre set and exhibition design. In 1992 he received a scholarship to attend the Domus Academy in Milan. Also in that year he was awarded the Philips Award (second prize) in Italy for his work on the future of communication technology. 2.42

**Formfürsorge** is a design group founded by six industrial designers in Hanover in 1988. The group's work has been exhibited nationally and internationally and has won many prizes and awards. 1.110

**Susan Frank** and **David Frisch** were both born in Tucson, Arizona in 1965. They met at the University of Arizona and, after graduating with Bachelor's degrees in architecture, moved to Venice, California in 1989. They later studied at the Southern California Institute of Architects under Peter Shire, whose classes have a strong emphasis on furniture design, and in 1992 became his teaching assistants. They recently collaborated with their former teacher to produce two dining tables for a benefit auction for the Music Center in Los Angeles, and at present are working together on a number of private commissions for furniture and interior design projects. Their work has been published in leading design magazines. 1.131

**Emanuela Frattini** was born in Milan. She studied at the Polytechnic, receiving a doctorate in architecture in 1983. After working in Milan and London, she set up her own practice in New York in 1989 and created EFM Design in 1991. She has had her work published in numerous national and international design magazines and is a correspondent for *Domus*, *Art and Design*, *Architecture and Design* and *Interior Design*. She has exhibited widely, including the Knoll International exhibition at the Triennale in Milan, and in 1993 was given the Roscoe Award for a side chair. 5.58, 75

**Olivier Gagnere** was born in 1952 in Paris. From 1980 to 1981 he collaborated with Memphis and since then has worked for VIA, Néotù and Ecart. His furniture designs and his work in glass and terracotta have been widely exhibited internationally and he has received several awards. His work can be seen in the permanent collections of the Musée des Arts Décoratifs in Paris and Bordeaux and the Museum of Modern Art in San Francisco. 1.60

**Tzachi Gal** was born in Tel Aviv in 1952 and graduated in 1982 from the Bezalel Academy of Art and Design, Jerusalem with a major in industrial design. From this time until 1991 he ran an independent studio in Tel Aviv. He has since become chief designer for Neto Furniture Design Ltd. 1.90

**Fabrizio Galli** gained an architectural degree in Florence in 1983 and since 1981 has been involved in many aspects of design and architecture. In 1989 he began to work as an industrial design consultant for Mario Bellini's studio in Milan. He founded his own industrial design studio with Enrico Quell in 1990. He has participated in various exhibitions, and his work has been published both in Italy and abroad. 5.35

**Kristian Gavoille** was born in 1956 in Brazzaville, Africa and studied architecture in Toulouse. He has lived and worked in Paris since 1984. He collaborated with several architectural offices in Paris and Toulouse from 1984 to 1986. He then worked with Philippe Starck on a number of projects including the Royalton Hotel, New York and the Teatriz Restaurant in Madrid. In 1987 he received a grant from VIA which allowed him to produce a range of prototypes. He then began a collaboration with Disform and Néotù, and a range of his products was presented by these companies at the Milan Fair in 1988. He has worked on stage, exhibition and television set design, and since 1990 has become increasingly involved in interior design projects. Gavoille has exhibited his work widely within Europe. 1.106, 3.3

**Ilaria Gibertini** was born in 1970 in Parma, Italy, where she now lives and works. She received a degree from the Instituto d'Arte in Parma and continued her studies at the Università del Progetto in Reggio Emilia. She has collaborated with NEMO since 1992. 2.22

**Andrew Gillmore** is a furniture design student at the Royal College of Art, London. 1.48

**Lyn Godley** was born in 1956 in Oberlin, Ohio and received a Bachelor of Fine Arts degree from Ohio State University in 1978. She received a Master of Fine Arts degree from the University of Wisconsin at Madison in 1980, and has been a partner in Godley-Schwan since 1985. 2.7

**Glendon Good** was born in 1962 in Santa Monica, California and is a self-taught designer, engineer and artist. His work is becoming well known in the USA and was selected by Bergdorf Goodman for a special exhibition. He owns a gallery in SoHo called Modern Stone Age. 1.93

**Kenneth Grange** was educated at the Willesden School of Art, London and served in the Royal Engineers as a technical illustrator. He then worked for eight years in various architectural and design offices before establishing his own industrial design practice in 1959. A founder-partner of Pentagram in 1972, his work includes mass production items ranging from small appliances to the InterCity 125 train. In 1969 he was appointed Royal Designer for Industry and in 1984 was awarded the CBE. He holds Honorary Doctorates from the Royal College of Art, London (1985) and Heriot Watt University, Edinburgh (1986) and has served as Master of the Faculty of Royal Designers for Industry (1985-7), as well as being the President of the Chartered Society of Designers (1987). He has been the recipient of major design prizes including 10 annual Design Council Awards. 5.12, 57, 79

**Johanna Grawunder** was born in 1961 in San Diego and graduated in architecture from California Polytechnic State University in 1984, studying in Florence from 1983 to 1984. She has been a guest lecturer at California State University and in Florence, and was guest professor at the Hochschule der Künste, Berlin in 1991. At present she is a project architect with Sottsass Associati and has been a partner since 1989. Her work has been shown in several exhibitions, and in 1993 she presented a personal show called "Trucks" for Argentaurum Gallery, Antwerp and Knokke-Le-Zoute and Galleria Jannone, Milan. 5.78

**Konstantin Grcic** is a German furniture designer who is at present working freelance in London and Munich. He was born in 1965 and trained as a cabinet-maker, continuing his education at the John Makepeace School for Craftsmen and the Royal College of Art, London. 1.99, 5.73

**Hatto Grosse** was born in 1956. He trained as an industrial designer and toolmaker, and has been an industrial designer with Siemens Design since 1985. He received the Peter Stuyvesant Award in 1991 and awards from the Industrie Forum Design Hanover in 1991, 1992 and 1993. 5.26, 29

**Dennis Grudt** is an American designer who was born in 1950. He received a Bachelor of Science degree in Industrial Design from California State University, Long Beach in 1974. He worked for Design West, specializing in design engineering, and since joining Patton Design in 1989 has worked on computer, medical and consumer products. 5.62

**Monica Guggisberg** and **Philip Baldwin** established their glass and design studio near Lausanne, Switzerland in 1982. Their work focuses on one-offs and limited production items. Since 1985 they have collaborated with Rosenthal in Germany, and since 1989 with Steuben in the USA. Their work has been exhibited regularly in Japan, Europe and the USA, and they have received numerous awards in the USA, Germany, France and Switzerland. 3.23, 42

**Koji Hamai** was born in Japan in 1964 and graduated from the Bunka Fashion College. He believes strongly in the importance of the textile in fashion design and is well known for producing highly fashionable fabrics. He initially joined Miyashin Corporation in Hachioji where he acquired his knowledge of textile production. In 1986 he moved to the Issey Miyake Design Studio where he stayed until 1991, leaving to work as a freelance fashion designer. He has received many awards within Japan. 4.1–12

**S. G. Hauser Associates** was established in 1966 and today is a leading industrial design firm employing 25 industrial designers, engineers and graphic designers. Their client list includes many of America's leading corporations in healthcare, office equipment and consumer products, such as Apple Computer, NCR, Samsonite, Baxter Healthcare Corporation and Seiko Instruments. 5.9, 10, 48, 61

**Jochen Henkels** was born in 1956 in Solingen, Germany. He studied at the Solingen Workshop for Wood and Metal, then studied industrial design at Wuppertal University. From 1986 to 1989 he studied under Dieter Rams at the Hochschule für Bildende Künste in Hamburg. He has worked as a freelance designer since 1989. 5.5

**Robert Heritage** was born in Birmingham, England in 1927 and studied furniture design at the Royal College of Art, London, receiving his Master's degree in 1951. He started his private practice as a design consultant in 1953, specializing in furniture and product design. He has received 13 design awards from the Council of Industrial Design since 1958, and in 1966 was given the British Aluminium Design Award. From 1974 to 1985 he was Professor of Furniture Design at the Royal College of Art. He was appointed a Royal Designer for Industry in 1963 and was awarded the C.B.E. in 1980. 2.48

**Matthew Hilton** was born in 1957. He studied furniture design at Kingston Polytechnic, London until 1979, then, after working for several years as an industrial designer in London, he started his own design work in 1984. At present he is designing for SCP, Disform, XO, Idée and Alterego. He regularly exhibits his work at the Milan and Cologne Furniture Fairs. 1.58

**Yasuyuki Hirai** is a furniture design student at the Royal College of Art, London. 1.77

**Yoshiki Hishinuma** is a fashion and textile designer who was born in Sendai, Japan in 1958. He has presented collections since 1984, showing both in Japan and Europe. He designs theatrical costumes and in 1990 created the uniform and monument for the Friendship Pavilion in the International Green and Greenery Exhibition in Osaka. 4.13–24

**Mathias Hoffmann** was born in 1954 in Ulm, Germany. After leaving school he went to Munich where he worked as a freelance artist before beginning an apprenticeship in Rolf Benz's design studio in 1971. In 1980 he became an independent designer and today employs seven permanent collaborators, specializing in shop design and the planning of trade fair stands for various clients. He has been a recipient of awards in Germany and from the Design Council in New York. 1.56

**Knud Holscher** was born in 1930 and studied at the School of Architecture, Royal Academy of Fine Arts, Copenhagen. He has been responsible for numerous large-scale award-winning public works in Norway, as well as smaller projects in France, Germany, Switzerland, Austria, Bahrain and the UK. Today he is a partner of Krohn and Hartvig Rasmussen Architects and Planners, with whom he has worked since 1968. From 1968 to 1988 he was professor at the School of Architecture, Royal Academy of Fine Arts, and in 1979 was made a Member of the Danish Design Council. In 1990 he became design consultant for ERCO Leuchten, Germany and was awarded a prize from the Industrie Forum Design, Hanover for a range of lamps designed for that company in 1993. He is a member of the Federation of Danish Architects, the Association of Academic Architects, the Council of Practising Architects and Industrial Designers Denmark. 2.47

**Richard Hutten** was born in 1967 and graduated in 1991 from the Academy of Industrial Design in Eindhoven. 1.5

**Takenobu Igarashi** is internationally known as a designer and sculptor specializing in graphic and product design. His work includes calendars designed for the Museum of Modern Art, New York and sculptures for the Nissan "Infiniti" showrooms in the USA. His work can be found in the permanent collections of various museums around the world, and he has design offices in Los Angeles and Tokyo. 3.12, 13, 28–30

**Massimo Iosa Ghini** was born in Borgo Tossignano, Italy in 1959 and graduated in architecture from Milan Polytechnic. Before working with Ettore Sottsass and Memphis in 1986, he was involved in drawing cartoons for international magazines. In 1987 he launched his first collection, *Dinamic*, for Moroso which received awards worldwide. Since then he has been a leading figure in the design world, holding one-man shows internationally and judging design awards. In 1991 he presented a collection of furniture which continued research he had been doing on the moulding of wood. Important interior design projects include the planning of the fashion store chain Fiorucci and the planning and design of the Renault Italy showrooms. Since 1992 he has held two major retrospectives, one at the Steininger Gallery, Munich and the second at the Inspiration Gallery, in the Axis Building, Tokyo. 1.64, 5.65

**James Irvine** was born in London in 1958 and graduated from the Royal College of Art in 1984. He then moved to Italy, working as a consultant designer for Olivetti with Ettore Sottsass and Michele de Lucchi. He participated in "12 New Memphis 86" and became a member of the group Solid. In 1987 Olivetti arranged a cultural exchange for him with Toshiba in Tokyo where he carried out research in industrial design. On his return to Milan he designed industrial products for Olivetti with Michele de Lucchi, eventually becoming responsible for a new range of mini computers and work stations. In 1988 he opened his own studio in Milan designing interiors, furniture and industrial products, and collaborating with various companies including Alessi, Cappellini and Fantini. In 1990 Irvine taught as a visiting lecturer at the Domus Academy, Milan. 1.59, 82

**Hans Jakobsen** trained as a carpenter until 1986, then studied design for four years in Denmark. His aim is to combine simplicity, function and beauty in his designs, a concept reinforced during his stay with a Shaker community in 1988, as well as in the three months he spent working in a Japanese design office in 1990. 1.42

**Richard Jung** is an American designer, born in 1960. He graduated in 1984 in industrial design from California State University, Long Beach. He is currently vice-president of Patton Design. He has contributed to many national and international award-winning projects in the areas of computers, consumer electronics, medical equipment and furniture. 5.62

**Hannu Kähönen** was born in 1948 and graduated in graphic and industrial design from the University of Helsinki in 1975. He has achieved considerable fame within Finland, and gives cultural, educational and commercial seminars at home and abroad. In 1981 he founded Creadesign Studio and in 1985 Moform Co. He has produced over 50 product, exhibition and corporate image designs, including the colour, interior design and image of the local train service of the Finnish State Railways. His work can be seen in the permanent collections of the Museum of Applied Arts, Helsinki; the Staatliches Museum für Angewandte Kunst, Munich; the Design Centre, Stuttgart; and the Jerusalem Museum, Israel. 2.35, 5.69

**Tibor Kalman** was born in Budapest in 1949 and studied journalism at New York University. In the early 1970s he worked for Barnes & Noble Bookstores, eventually becoming their design director. In 1979 he founded the multi-disciplinary design firm M & Co. His watch collection is on permanent display in the Museum of Modern Art, New York. 5.1, 58

**Wolfgang Karolinsky** studied musical composition at Vienna University. He opened an antique lighting shop in 1977. Today, his company, Woka Lamps, has built up an international reputation for its faithful reproduction of classic designs by Hoffmann, Loos and the Wiener Werkstätte. He employs over 20 people producing highly crafted handmade pieces. In 1986 he organized a competition at the Academy of Applied Arts in Vienna, inviting students to produce lighting designs. The three winning designs were then put into production by Woka Lamps. At present Karolinsky is supervising a growing collection of contemporary lamps, each month selecting a new design to produce. His work is exhibited internationally. 2.39

**Yaacov Kaufman** lives in Tel Aviv and works in Jerusalem, Tel Aviv and Milan. He is involved mainly in furniture and lighting design, collaborating with Italian-based manufacturers such as Arflex, Lumina, Seccose and Tecno. He has exhibited his work in Israel, and lectures at the Bezalel Academy of Art and Design in Jerusalem. 1.28–31, 44

**Kazuo Kawasaki** was born in Fukui City, Japan in 1949 and graduated from Kanazawa University. Before founding his own company, Ex-Design Inc., in 1980, he worked for Toshiba developing and designing hi-fi audio products. Today he is involved in design theory and practice, business strategies, community revitalization, traditional crafts, interior design and computers. His work is represented in the permanent collection of the Cooper-Hewitt Museum, New York, and he has been the recipient of numerous prizes, including the 1992 ICSID Excellence Award. 3.39, 5.3, 101

**David Kawecki** was born in 1949 and today lives and works in San Francisco. He became a designer following an eclectic range of studies, and his varied career has included employment in music, carpentry, construction work, software development, fine art restoration and industrial automation. He has been active in furniture, graphic and industrial design. 1.37

**Perry A. King** and **Santiago Miranda** were born and educated in Britain and Seville, respectively. In 1976 they founded King Miranda Associati in Milan and today are active in interior, graphic and product design. Their award-winning work in furniture and lighting, as well as their work in the design of computer equipment interface, has received much attention in recent years. In 1989 they were awarded the Spanish National Design Award. 1.34, 2.28

**Toshiyuki Kita** was born in Osaka, Japan in 1942. He has been working in the field of environmental product design since 1969 in Milan and Japan, and is also involved in traditional Japanese craft design. In 1987 he took part in the celebration of the Pompidou Centre's 10th anniversary, and in 1990 was awarded the Delta de Oro in Spain. His work forms part of the permanent collections of the Museum of Modern Art, New York and the Design Museum, London. 5.67

**Setsuo Kitaoka** was born in 1946 in Kochi Prefecture and graduated from the Kuwasawa Design School in Tokyo in 1974. Kitaoka Design Office was founded in 1977. 5.76

**Makoto Komatsu** was born in 1943 in Tokyo and from 1970 to 1973 was Assistant to Professor Stig Lindberg at Gustavsberg Porcelain in Sweden. He has achieved national acclaim through various design awards, and his work can be seen in the permanent collections of the Museum of Modern Art, New York and the Victoria and Albert Museum, London. 3.14

**Komplot Design** was founded in 1987 by Poul Christiansen and Boris Berlin. Boris Berlin was born in Leningrad in 1953 and graduated from the Institute of Applied Arts and Design there in 1975. He worked for VNIITE in Leningrad and was a freelance designer of industrial products and graphics, moving to Denmark in 1985. Poul Christiansen was born in 1947 and graduated in architecture from the Royal Academy of Fine Arts, Copenhagen in 1973. He worked for IB and Jørgen Rasmussen and designed furniture for Søro Stolefabrik, DK, Lübke and Brunner. Komplot Design is involved in the fields of industrial, furniture and graphic design for Thonet, Klaessons AB and Copenhagen Airports. It has received awards in Denmark and Japan and in 1992 took part in the 18th Milan Triennale. 1.72

**König & König** was founded in 1993 by brothers Matthias and Thomas König whose earlier enterprise, MTM Studios, had been in existence since 1990. Matthias was born in 1961. He studied architecture in Mainz and worked as an independent furniture designer. Thomas, who was born in 1958, received a design diploma from Darmstadt University in 1988, and before joining his brother worked as a freelance desiger for D-Tec in collaboration with Markus Börgens. 1.91

**Jan Konings** was born in 1966 and graduated in 1991 from the Academy of Industrial Design in Eindhoven. He has a design studio with Jurgen Bey (Konings and Bey) and has won several design competitions in Holland. 1.98, 109

**Harri Korhonen** was born in 1946. He has received prizes for exhibition design and design management, and his work has been published in leading design magazines. 1.62

**Reyer Kras** was born in 1940. He started his career as a freelance designer and later became a lecturer in industrial design at the University of Delft and in design history at the University of Leiden. He is currently chief curator of applied art and design at the Stedelijk Museum in Amsterdam. 5.54

**Erik Krogh** was born in 1942 and educated as a cabinet-maker and furniture designer at the Danish School of Art and Design and the Royal Danish Academy. He has owned his own design studio since 1979. He has lectured at the Royal Danish Academy and the Interior Design School, and today is head of the Institute of Industrial Design at the Danish Design School, and the Chairman of the Danish State Workshop for Arts and Design. He frequently exhibits his work within Denmark and has received national recognition. 1.41, 50

**Erich Kruse** is a graduate of the Hochschule für Bildende Künste in Brauchschweig, Germany and holds a Bachelor of Arts degree in Industrial Design. He worked in graphic design and corporate identity for Einsatz Art in Hamburg and in 1981 founded his own industrial and corporate design consultancy Hesse and Kruse, Designer (later, Design: Kruse). He joined S. G. Hauser Associates in 1992 after moving to the USA. He has been awarded the Good Industrial Design award seven times and in 1983 won the Braun Prize. His work has been published in various design magazines. 5.10

**Axel Kufus** was born in Essen in 1958. He served a carpentry and joinery apprenticeship, then worked in wood and bronze workshops in Bischofsheim from 1979 to 1982. In 1985 he studied industrial design at the Hochschule der Künste, Berlin, and since 1986 has been a partner in the Crelle Workshop. He has worked with Jasper Morrison and Andreas Brandolini for Utilism International, and since 1989 has collaborated with Jonas Milder in New York. 1.71

**Shiro Kuramata** (1934–1991) was born in Tokyo and trained at the Tokyo Technical High School of Art and the Kuwasawa Institute of Design. In 1965 he created his own design office. As well as his celebrated glass armchair of 1976, and a number of other equally elegant but innovative pieces of furniture, Kuramata has designed interiors, notably for Issey Miyake and Esprit. He participated in the first three Memphis shows, and also had various private exhibitions in Japan and London. In 1981 he received the Japan Cultural Design Prize. 1.101

**Masayuki Kurokawa** was born in Nagoya, Japan in 1937 and graduated in architecture from Nagoya Institute of Technology in 1961. In 1967 he completed a Doctorate at the Graduate School of Architecture, Waseda University, Tokyo, and founded Masayuki Kurokawa Architect and Associates. 1.120, 2.2, 3.2

**Stanislaus Kutac,** an interior designer, was born in 1960 and trained in Germany and at the Domus Academy, Milan. 1.9

**Louis A. Lara** was born in New York in 1964 and studied industrial design at the Pratt Institute. Since 1986 he has designed a wide range of products including lighting and furniture for both private clients and manufacturers. In 1989 he founded Lara Designs Inc. His furniture designs have sold throughout the United States and abroad and have been included in gallery exhibitions across the country. 3.37

**Stuart Lee** was born in North Yorkshire, England in 1965 and trained as a mechanical engineer at the Imperial College of Science and Technology in London. After a period working independently he took a Master's degree at the Royal College of Art. He has worked in Europe, Japan and the United States and is currently with Smart Design in New York. His work has been published internationally and exhibited in the Aram Design Gallery and the Design Museum in London, and Gallery 91 in New York. 3.41

**Lievore y Asociados** was created in 1977 by Alberto Lievore (born in Buenos Aires in 1948) who is now a partner with Jeanette Altherr and Manel Molina. The company is active in all areas of design, but best known for its furniture for which it has won several national and international prizes and awards. Clients include Perobell, Kron, Simeyco, Andreu and Divano. The company is increasingly recognized for its interior design projects, including exhibition design and corporate image schemes. 1.70, 100

**Axel Lorltz** was born in 1959 and studied industrial design at the Technical College of Darmstadt. Before joining Siemens Design he worked for Studio Bonetto in Milan and Triumph Adler Design Study in Nuremberg. He received Industrie Forum awards in 1990 and 1991. 5.11, 30

**Vico Magistretti** was born in Milan in 1920 and graduated in architecture in 1945. Since 1967 he has been a member of the Academy of San Luca in Rome. As well as teaching at the Domus Academy in Milan, he is an honorary member of the Royal College of Art in London where he is a visiting professor. He has been the recipient of numerous major awards including the Gold Medal at the 9th Milan Triennale in 1951, the Compasso d'Oro in 1967 and 1979 and the Gold Medal of the Society of International Artists and Designers in 1986. He has exhibited widely in Europe, the USA and Japan, and his work can be seen in the most important design collections world-wide. 1.76, 2.13

**Chiaki Maki** was educated at the Rhode Island School of Design and received a Bachelor of Fine Arts in Textile Design in 1985. Before creating Maki Textile Studio in 1989, she worked for various clothing companies in New York and Tokyo. She was a finalist in the International Textile Contest sponsored by the Japanese Fashion Foundation in 1986, 1987 and 1990, and has exhibited her work widely in Japan. 4.50–54

**Kaori Maki** was educated at the Rhode Island School of Design and received a Bachelor of Fine Arts in Textile Design in 1988. She then began a professional internship with Jack Lenor Larsen in New York. Before joining her sister Chiaki Maki in the Maki Textile Studio in 1992, she worked as a freelance textile designer in New York, Thailand and Japan. In 1987 she was nominated for the Grand Prix in the American Section of the International Textile Design Contest and was again a finalist in that section in 1988. 4.41–49

**Enzo Mari** was born in Novara in 1932 and studied at the Academy of Fine Art in Milan. In 1963 he co-ordinated the Italian group Nuove Tendenze and in 1965 was responsible for the exhibition of optical, kinetic and programmed art at the Biennale in Zagreb. He has also taken part in several Biennales in Venice and in the Triennale, Milan. In 1972 he participated in "Italy: The New Domestic Landscape" at the Museum of Modern Art, New York. Mari is involved in graphic and industrial design, publishing and the preparation of exhibitions. He has recently been occupied with town planning and teaching and has organized courses for the History of Arts faculty at the University of Parma and the Architecture faculty at Milan Polytechnic. He has been awarded the Compasso d'Oro on three occasions and was President of the Association for Industrial Design from 1976 to 1979. His work can be found in the collections of various contemporary art museums including the Stedelijk Museum, Amsterdam; the Musée des Arts Décoratifs, Paris; and the Kunstmuseum, Düsseldorf. 5.51

**Ingo Maurer** was born in 1932 on the Island of Reichenau, Lake Constance, Germany and trained in typography and graphic design. In 1960 he emigrated to the United States, working as a freelance designer in New York and San Francisco before returning to Europe in 1963. He founded Design M in Munich in 1966, and since then his lighting designs have achieved world recognition. He has exhibited widely, most recently "Ingo Maurer: Making Light" at the Museum Villa Stuck, Munich and "Licht Licht" at the Stedelijk Museum in Amsterdam, and his work forms part of the permanent collections of many museums, including the Museum of Modern Art, New York. 2.25, 26, 27

**Steve McGugan** was born in Vancouver in 1960 and studied product design at the Art Center College of Design from 1979 to 1981. He has worked as an in-house designer for Bang and Olufsen and David Lewis Industrial Design. In 1988 he formed his own design consultancy in Copenhagen, working in all areas of product design. He has received the Danish Design Council's ID prize twice and recently won first prize in the Forma Finlandia Design Competition for the best plastic product in production. His work is displayed in the permanent collection of the Museum of Modern Art, New York. 5.100

**Philip McNally** graduated from the Furniture Design Department of the Royal College of Art, London in 1992. 1.47

**Alberto Meda** was born in Como, Italy in 1945 and graduated in mechanical engineering from Milan Polytechnic in 1969. He worked at Magneti Marelli as assistant to the production manager, and at Kartell as executive producer before starting a freelance practice collaborating with a number of clients including Gaggia, Kartell, Centrokappa, Lucifero, Cinelli, FontanaArte, Luceplan, Ansaldo, Montedison, Mandarina Duck and Carlo Erba. He has been awarded numerous international prizes including the Compasso d'Oro in 1989 for his *Lola* lamp and Design Plus in 1992 for his *Titania* lamp. 3.40

**Luca Meda** was born in Chiávari, Italy and attended the Hochschule für Gestaltung in Ulm, Germany. In 1961 he started a professional relationship with Aldo Rossi, working on a number of architectural projects in Italy, as well as corporate image design, exhibitions and interior design. 1.103

**Alessandro Mendini** is the publisher of the design magazines *Casabella, Modo* and *Domus*. For several years he has been the theorist of avant-garde design, co-founding the Global Tools Group in 1973 as a counter-movement to established Italian design. In 1978 he started his collaboration with Studio Alchimia in Milan and developed the so-called "banal design" which sought to change items in daily use into new and ironical objects. In 1983 he became Professor of Design at the University of Applied Art in Vienna, and from 1983 to 1988 collaborated with designers such as Achille Castiglioni, Riccardo Dalisi and Aldo Rossi in Casa della Felicità for Alessi. Interior design projects include the Groningen Museum in Holland and – with Yumiko Kobayashi – the Paradise Tower, Hiroshima. 2.15

**Davide Mercatali** was born in Milan in 1948. He worked for agencies, publishing companies and private clients in the fields of visual and product design before gaining a university dregree in architecture in 1973. From 1974 to 1977 he collaborated with Maurizion Dallasta on industrial and promotional designs. He then established a partnership with Paolo Pedrizzetti with whom he eventually opened a design studio. From 1982 to 1987 their client list included Fantini, Domus, Olivari and others. Their series of taps and bath accessories, *I Balocchi*, produced by Fantini, was chosen for the Compasso d'Oro in 1979. In 1988 Mercatali founded the International Design Association and organized INGENUO, a collection of innovative projects designed for Japanese industry by young European designers. In 1989 he helped to create MAS, a society concerned with the development of design in Spain. Since 1991 he has been working independently, collaborating with companies which specialize in plumbing fixtures, door handles, accessories, utensils and small household appliances, such as Zeus/Noto, Bernini/Progetti, Indy, Dolomite and Fantini. In 1993 he became Art Director of Metals. 5.66

**METAmoderne** was created in 1988 by Volker Dowidat, Christoph Ermisch, Wolfgang Hein, Armin Knoll, Bernard Neelen and Torsten Wittenberg. The company, which creates products and furniture, has participated in international design competitions and has exhibited in Germany and the Netherlands. 5.80

**Andreas Mikkelsen** was born in 1928. From 1952 to 1955 he trained at the Copenhagen School of Economics and Business Administration, after which he joined the management of Georg Jensen Silversmiths in Copenhagen. He was managing director from 1983 to 1985 and then Artistic Director and Head of Product Development of the Royal Copenhagen Group. Since 1989 he has been a designer for Georg Jensen. 5.77

**Josep Mora** was born in Barcelona in 1953. He is a lecturer in Aerodynamics at the Engineering School of Barcelona and the Escola Elisava and is a specialized designer in his own right of light vehicles and complex mechanical objects. He has also collaborated with leading project manufacturers, namely Polinax, Stua, Mobles 114 and Andreu Nort, and has received national recognition for his work. 1.89

**Hikaru Mori** was born in Sapporo, Japan in 1964 and graduated in Design from Tokyo University of Fine Art in 1987. In 1988 he was awarded the Rotary Foundation Scholarship and continued his studies in Milan. Whilst in Milan, where he now lives and works as a freelance designer, he was awarded a Diploma in interior design from the Institute of Design and also collaborated with the furniture company Sawaya & Moroni for two years. He was awarded a Master's degree from the Tokyo University of Fine Art in 1991. 2.23

**Kenneth Mori** was born in 1965 in Los Angeles and educated at the California State University, Long Beach where he received a Bachelor of Science degree in Industrial Design. He has collaborated with Xerox Corporation Industrial Design/Human Interface Group, Patton Design and Ashcraft Design. 5.17, 18

**Jasper Morrison** was born in London in 1959 and studied at the Kingston School of Art and the Royal College of Art, winning a Berlin scholarship in 1984. In 1986 he established his own design office in London. He designs for Sheridan Coakley (SCP), Cappellini and Vitra, and lectures at the Hochschule der Künste, Berlin and Saarbrücken, the European Institute of Design, Milan and the Royal College of Art, London. He has exhibited widely in Europe and the UK, most notably for Vitra in Milan, at the Kunstmuseum in Düsseldorf and at Galerie Néotù, France. 1.57, 61, 108, 5.72

**Pascal Mourgue** was born in 1943 in Neuilly-sur-Seine, Paris and is a graduate of the École Nationale Supérieure des Arts Décoratifs. Since 1969 he has been designing furniture, carpets, tableware and even trimarans. He has exhibited his work widely within Europe, and in 1984 was elected "Designer of the Year" by the Salon du Meuble de Paris, an honour which was also to be bestowed by the Grand Prix de la Création de la Ville de Paris in 1992. His work can be seen in the permanent collection of the Musée des Arts Décoratifs in Paris. 1.80

**Ursula Munch-Petersen** was born in 1937 in Denmark and was educated at the School of Arts and Crafts, Copenhagen. Later studies included a brief period at the Escuela de Diseño y Artesanias in Mexico in 1968 and at the Academy of Fine Arts, Department of Room and Mural Arts, Copenhagen. Since 1973 she has taught at the School of Applied Arts, Copenhagen. She has had her own workshop since 1978, and began her collaboration with Royal Copenhagen in 1987. She has received various awards for her work, both within Denmark and in Germany. 3.24

**Wolfgang Münscher** was born in 1944. He studied architecture at the Hochschule der Künste, Berlin, and architecture and communication design at the Technical College of Mainz before joining Siemens Design in 1972. For the last six years he has been working mainly in the area of telecommunications design. He has received awards from the Nordrhein-Westfalen Design Centre and several Industrie Forum awards, most recently in 1993. 5.27

**Kish Munshi** was born in 1947 in Srinagar, Jammu and Kashmir State, India. He received a degree in mechanical engineering and post-graduate qualifications in product design from the Indian Institute of Technology, Bombay and the Royal College of Art, London. He gained experience at the Technical University of Hanover, and the Université de Technologie de Compiègne, France and with Sottsass Associati in Italy. Today he is a full professor and co-ordinator on the Product Design Programme at the Industrial Design Centre, IIT Bombay and is management adviser to more than thirty industrial organizations. He has published articles in professional publications internationally and has presented papers at conferences in Switzerland, France, Hungary, Japan and Hong Kong. 2.14, 3.22

**Hauke Murken** was born in 1963 in Wilhelmshaven, Germany. He spent several years in furniture restoration before studying industrial design at the Hochschule der Künste, Berlin. Since 1990 he has participated in national exhibitions and in 1993 won first prize in the competition Design Plus '93 at the International Furniture Fair, Frankfurt for his folding table *Last Minute*. 1.127

**Lorenzo Negrello** and **Paolo Scagnellato** were born in 1953 and 1952 respectively, and both graduated in architecture in Venice. They have been working together professionally since 1981. Their studio deals with design and technical assistance, mainly in the areas of furniture and seating for offices. Since 1986 they have also been designing small electrical appliances for the home and motor-cycle accessories. In 1991 two of their products were selected for the Golden Compass award. 1.86

**Marc Newson** was born in Sydney in 1962 and graduated from the Sydney College of Art in 1984. In 1985 the Powerhouse Museum acquired some of his designs for their permanent collection, at the same time offering him a Craft Council Grant to devise new work. Since 1987 he has worked periodically in Japan for Idée, creating, amongst other designs, the *Insect* chair. 1.2, 128, 3.20

**Paolo Pallucco** is an Italian furniture designer, architect and manufacturer born in Rome in 1950. He established Pallucco Italia in 1980, producing new designs and re-editions of modern classics and putting his own creations into production. In 1984 he started Pallucco Design to work on projects independently of his other company. He works in conjunction with Mireille Rivier. 2.64

**David Palterer** was born in Haifa, Israel in 1949 and completed his architectural studies at the University of Florence in 1979. From then until 1989 he combined teaching at the Faculty of Architecture in Florence with guest lecturing and his own design work. He has collaborated with manufacturers such as Alterego, Driade, Artelano, Artemide, Acerbis International, Swid Powell and Zanotta, and has achieved international acclaim for his product design as well as his architectural and interior design schemes. Recent projects include the restoration and enlargement of San Casciano Theatre (with Professor Luigi Zangheri); the Florence Air Terminal; and an Italian restaurant in Arata Isozaki's cultural centre in Mito, Japan. His designs can be seen in the permanent collections of the Kunstgewerbe Museum, Vienna; the Uméleckoprumyslové Museum, Prague; the Israel Museum, Jerusalem; and the Musée des Arts Décoratifs in Montreal. 1.33, 3.7–11

**Roberto Pamio** has worked near Venice since graduating in architecture in 1968. His projects include both domestic and industrial design for clients such as Cadel, Matteo Grassi and Leucos. He has worked in the USA, Australia, Mexico and Japan, as well as in Italy. 2.11

**Doug Patton** graduated from California State University, Long Beach with a Bachelor of Science in Industrial Design. Today he is principal of Patton Design which specializes in human interface design, mechanical engineering and industrial design. His clients include Apple Computer, Hewlett Packard, Hitachi, Mitsubishi, Philips and 20th Century Fox. He has received over 70 design awards and engineering patents, and his work can be seen in the permanent collection of the Smithsonian Institute, New York. 5.14–20, 49, 62

**Jorge Pensi** is a Spanish architect and industrial designer, born in 1946 in Buenos Aires. He has worked in Barcelona since 1977, specializing in the design of furniture, lighting, fittings and product image. He has been associated with Perobell, the SIDI group, Amat, Herriola-B.Lux and the magazine *On Diseño*. He has achieved wide acclaim for his designs, most notably the *Toledo* chair for which he was given the first Award Selection SIDI-1988, two silver Deltas and an Award Design-Auswahl 90 from the Stuttgart Design Centre. He has lectured in Spain, England and the USA. 3.33

**Maurizio Peregalli** was born in Varese, Italy in 1951. He was responsible for the interior design and planning of Giorgio Armani boutiques in Milan, London and New York and also the shop's Emporio Armani. He is the co-founder and art director of Zeus, and in 1984 designed a chair and table collection for the company. He is also a partner in Noto which produces the Zeus collections. 1.38, 39, 49, 129

**Charles Perry** lives in the USA where he has received considerable recognition for his commissioned work for public places. He received the Prix de Rome in 1964 and the National Academy of Design Award (Best of Show, Sculpture) in 1987. Design projects include jewellery and puzzle collections, trophies for the Top 30 Architects Award and the Frank J. Scallon Surgical Award, as well as chair designs for Krueger International. He has lectured widely within the USA and has been professor in residence of both Dartmouth College in Rome. He has participated in many group shows in museums and galleries internationally. His work can be seen in the permanent collections of the Museum of Modern Art, New York, the Art Institute of Chicago and elsewhere. 1.88

**Gaetano Pesce** was born in 1939 in La Spezia, Italy and studied architecture at the University of Venice, graduating in 1965. He lives and works in New York although he also has a studio in Paris. He is currently a professor at the Institute d'Architecture et d'Études Urbaines in Strasbourg, and for a number of years taught at the Cooper Union in New York. In addition, he has been a visiting professor at architecture and design schools in Europe, the USA and the Far East. Pesce's expertise ranges from architecture through to industrial design, sculpture, music and urban planning, and he has worked with many manufacturers such as Cassina, B & B Italia, Knoll International and Vitra International. Projects undertaken within the last year include a series of chairs and stools for Bernini SpA; the *Vesuvio* coffee pot and its packaging produced by Zani and Zani; and the presentation of the *Seaweed Chairs* at an exhibition held at the Gallery Mourmans in Knokke-Le-Zoute, Belgium. In 1993 he exhibited his experimental range of glassware, C.I.R.V.A., twice: at the Peter Joseph Gallery in New York and at the Fundazione Danese, Milan. His work can be seen in most of the major design museums, including the Museum of Modern Art and the Metropolitan Museum in New York, and the Pompidou Centre and the Musée des Arts Décoratifs in Paris. 1.11, 12, 3.1, 43–46

**David Peschel** studied ceramics at Wayne State University, Detroit and Rhode Island School of Design, receiving a Bachelor of Industry degree in 1989. At present he works for Smart Design. His work can be seen in the permanent collections of the Cooper-Hewitt Museum, New York and the Montreal Museum of Decorative Arts. 3.41

**William Petrie** is a furniture design student at the Royal College of Art, London. 1.74

**Paolo Piva** was born in Ádria, Italy in 1950. He studied at the University Institute of Architecture and the International University of Art in Venice, specializing in industrial design and the visual arts. His design work has been mainly in the architectural field. In 1980 he was invited by the Kuwaiti government to design the Kuwait Embassy in Qatar. He was awarded the Compasso d'Oro in 1987 and in 1990 won first prize for his design of a public area in the centre of Vienna. Piva is a Professor of Design at the Hochschule für Angewandte Kunst in Vienna. 1.54

**Plan Créatif/Crabtree Hall** is a joint venture company formed in 1990 by the French design group Plan Créatif and the English interior design group Crabtree Hall. It is active in the fields of graphic, interior and exhibition design and has received national recognition for its designs. In 1993 the *Amarys* range of telephones was awarded the Janus de l'Industrie. 5.32

**Pol International Design** is the design company of Pol Quadens who received European acclaim for his collection of CD racks in 1988. The desk lamp *Ned-Land* was created in January 1993 and made its first appearance at the 1993 Milan Furniture Fair. 1.130, 2.24

**Leonard Porche** graduated from California State University. He worked for S. G. Hauser Associates and Walt Disney Imagineering, before founding Design Backup Services in California. 5.10

**Andrée Putman**, the Parisian interior designer, initially studied music at the Paris Conservatoire with François Pulenc. After several years as a stylist and journalist, she founded the design company Créateurs et Industriels, working with fashion designers such as Issey Miyake and Jean Charles de Castelbajac. Today, her own enterprise, Ecart International, focuses on the production and revival of classic furniture design and modernist accessories. She has worked with deSede, Charles Jourdan, Sasaki and Toulemonde Bochart among other companies, and her interior design projects have brought her world fame. These include the Morgans Hotel, New York; the Wasserturm Hotel, Cologne; Le Lac, Japan; villas and shops for the clock and watch company Ebel; offices for the French Minister of Culture; an art museum in Rouen; and the Museum of Modern Art in Bordeaux. 1.73

**Enrico Quell** has a degree in industrial design and since 1981 has worked in professional studios gaining experience in both industrial design and graphics. In 1984 he began to work as an industrial design consultant for Olivetti in Milan. Then in 1990 he founded his own industrial design studio with Fabrizio Galli. He has participated in various exhibitions, and his work has been published both in Italy and abroad. 5.35

**Karim Rashid** received a Bachelor of Industrial Design degree in 1982 from Carleton University in Ottawa, Canada. He did his graduate studies in Italy under Ettore Sottsass and Gaetano Pesce, then moved to Milan for a one-year scholarship at the studio of Rodolfo Bonetto. On his return to Canada he worked for seven years with KAN Industrial Designers in Toronto as head designer on projects ranging from hi-tech products to furniture. He also co-founded and designed the Babel Collection (a clothing range for men and women) before setting up North Studio, a conceptual-based studio producing objects for exhibitions and galleries world-wide. Rashid has been a faculty member at the Ontario College of Art and a full-time assistant professor at the Rhode Island School of Design. His work has received international recognition. 1.78, 79, 2.12, 3.35, 5.4

**Prospero Rasulo** was born in 1953 in Stigliano, Matera, Italy and graduated from the Milan Academy of Fine Arts. In 1980 he opened a studio dedicated to printing, sculpture and stage decoration and worked in stage, video and exhibition design. He collaborated with Alchimia and Alessandro Mendini, and during the same period worked with the Occhiomagico studio, designing scenery for videos, photographs and exhibitions. In 1987 he founded the design, art and architecture gallery Oxido with Gianni Veneziano. Oxido subsequently became the trademark for a collection of furniture and art objects called Oxido Zoo. Since then Rasulo has begun to create mass-produced lines, working with companies such as Foscarini, Poltronova, Metals and BRF. 1.132

**Dov Rattan** was born in Israel in 1954. He studied at the Bezalel Academy of Art and Design in Jerusalem and in 1985 won a scholarship for industrial design in Germany. He has been working as an industrial designer at Siemens Design since 1986. In 1987 to 1988 he was a guest lecturer at the Art Academy of Jerusalem, Israel. He has won several awards from the Industrie Forum, Hanover and the Nordrhein-Westfalen Design Centre. 5.25, 47

**Tejo Remy** was born in 1960 and graduated in 1991 from the Art Academy of Utrecht. In 1992 he was awarded the Talentenbörsepreise at the Handwerkmesse in Munich. His work can be seen in the permanent collections of the Stedelijk Museum, Amsterdam and the Museum Boymans-van Beuningen, Rotterdam. 1.1, 10, 2.45

**André Ricard** was born in Barcelona in 1929. He trained as an industrial designer and is well known for his packaging designs. He sits on many committees and was president of the MID'90 Design Fair in Barcelona. He is currently vice-president of the Barcelona Design Centre. He has written books about design, and his work has received international acclaim. 3.34

**Robert le Héros** is a home furnishings company founded in 1987 by four art school graduates, Blandine Lelong, Isabelle Rodier, Corinne Hellein and Christelle le Dean. They have clients in both the private and public sectors, and are at present diversifying from largely textile production to tableware and accessories. 3.32

**Cheryl Stuart-Ruine** and **Paul Ruine** were born in New York in 1951 and 1947 respectively. Cheryl received a Master's degree in Art, with a speciality in sculpture and photography, from the Pratt Institute in New York. Paul studied jewellery design in the 1960s before opening an antique shop in New York specializing in twentieth-century design. Ruine Design Associates, founded in 1987, produces furniture, lighting, accessories, fabric and jewellery, often signed and in limited editions. 1.92

**Toby Russell** was born in London in 1963 and trained at the Camberwell School of Art and Design. He works mainly in pewter and silver, creating vessels, boxes, bowls, dishes and trophies. He has taken part in many exhibitions in London, and his work has been published widely in major national magazines and newspapers. 3.17–19

**Masatoshi Sakaegi** was born in 1944 in Chiba-ken, Japan. In 1983 he founded the Masatoshi Sakaegi Design Studio which specializes in ceramic and melamine tableware. He has won many awards for his work. In 1991 he became an assistant professor at the Art University of the Province of Aichi. 3.21, 5.63, 64

**Bryce Sanders** was born in Chicago and received his initial architectural and design training at Washington University, St Louis. After graduating he moved to New York and studied at Columbia University's graduate school of architecture and planning, receiving his Master of Architecture in 1985. He has worked in a number of major architectural offices, including Gwathmey Siegel & Associates and Bausman Gill Associates. Bryce Sanders Design was launched in 1992. 1.122

**Denis Santachiara** was born in Reggio-Emilia, Italy, and now lives and works in Milan. He collaborates with major European manufacturers such as Oceano Oltreluce, Artemide, Kartell, Vitra, Yamagiwa, Domodinamica and Zerodisegno. His work has been exhibited in private and public galleries, and he has taken part in the Venice Biennale and Documenta Kassel, as well as the Milan Triennale in 1982, 1984, 1986 and 1988. 1.43, 45, 2.31–34, 5.53, 68

**Winfried Scheuer** was born in Calw, Germany in 1952. He worked as a trainee in the styling department of Mercedes-Benz in Sindelfingen, before studying at the Royal College of Art, London from 1979 to 1981. He has worked in London as a self-employed industrial designer since 1986 and has exhibited his work at Documenta Kassel and the Luci Exhibition, Memphis, Milan. He is a visiting lecturer at the Royal College of Art, London and the Hochschule der Künste, Berlin. 5.70

**Jürgen R. Schmid** was born in 1956 and studied at the Fachhochschule für Gestaltung in Schwäbisch-Gmünd, Germany. In 1983 he founded his design studio Design Tech in Ammerbuch near Tübingen. Its client list of 50 includes Bosch, Mercedes-Benz and Dunlop. Schmid has received numerous design awards in Germany and has been represented in the Design Selection, Stuttgart. 5.31, 33

**Wulf Schneider** was born in 1943 and studied interior design and industrial design at the Staatliche Akademie der Bildenden Künste, Stuttgart. Before founding the Büro für Gestaltungskonzeptionen in 1975, he worked for various architectural firms. Wulf Schneider and Partner are involved in architecture, and interior, industrial and graphic design and have been commissioned by Bosch, Daimler-Benz, IBM Germany, Thonet and Thyssen, as well as various government departments. They have received several national awards. Wulf Schneider is currently Professor of Industrial Design at the Fachhochschule, Munich. 1.87

**Masafumi Sekine** was born in Saitama Prefecture, Japan in 1949. He studied crafts at the Tokyo National University of Fine Arts and Music, graduating in 1971, then undertook postgraduate study in metal carving. In 1982 he was awarded the Grand Prix at the Japan Crafts Design Association Exhibition. His work can be seen in the permanent collection of the National Museum of Modern Art, Tokyo. 3.15, 16

**Slany Design Team** was founded in 1956 in Esslingen, Germany by Hans-Erich Slany, Reinhard Renner and Klaus Schön. Today they employ 17 designers and have an international client list. 5.86

**Ettore Sottsass**, born in 1917 in Innsbruck, is one of the most important designers of this century. He completed his architectural studies in 1939 at the University of Turin and since 1947 has been working as a designer in Milan. In 1958 he became the chief consultant for design at Olivetti and was responsible for a number of innovative design concepts in information electronics. In 1980 he founded Sottsass Associati. During this period of consultancy Sottsass became involved in experimental projects, starting with the radical architecture of the sixties. This work was followed up with the Memphis Group, which initiated the New Design of the eighties. Sottsass's clients include major manufacturers such as Alessi, Cassina, Mitsubishi, Olivetti, Seiko, Zanotta, Esprit and Knoll. Among his recent architectural projects are interior furnishings for Esprit; the "Zibibbo" bar in the Il Palazzo hotel, Japan; the Daniel Wolf apartment block in Colorado; and a hotel and shopping mall in Kuala Lumpur. His work has been exhibited in numerous galleries and museums. 5.52

**Sottsass Associati**, established in 1980, has international clients in the fields of architecture, interior design, industrial design, graphics and corporate identity, including Apple Computer, Olivetti, Alessi, Coca Cola, Mitsubishi, Matsushita and Cassina. Sottsass Associati's partners are Ettore Sottsass, Marco Susani, Johanna Grawunder, Mike Ryan, James Irvine and Mario Milizia. 1.55

**Philippe Starck** was born in Paris in 1949. After a period of activity in New York, he returned to France where he has since built up an international reputation. He has been responsible for major interior design schemes, including François Mitterrand's apartment at the Elysée Palace; the Café Costes; and the Royalton and Paramount hotels in New York. He has also created domestic and public multi-purpose buildings such as the head-quarters of Asahi Beer in Tokyo. As a product designer he works for companies throughout the world, collaborating with Alessi, Baleri, Baum, Disform, Driade, Flos, Kartell, Rapsel, Up & Up, Vitra and Vuitton. His many awards include the Grand Prix National de la Création Industrielle. His work can be seen in the permanent collections of the major design museums. 1.107, 2.10, 3.25–27

**Christian Steiner** was born in 1961 and studied at the Hochschule für Angewandte Kunst in Vienna under Richard Sapper, Alessandro Mendini, Boris Podrecca and Paolo Piva. Since 1990 he has been a freelance designer based in Vienna. 2.9

**Marianne Stokholm** was born in 1946 in Copenhagen and graduated in architecture in 1974. Since 1983 she has been a partner in Stokholm/Zorea with Gad Zorea. 5.37, 38

**Davin Stowell** was born in 1953 in Corning, New York State and received a Bachelor of Industrial Design degree from Syracuse University in 1976. He founded the product design studio Davin Stowell Associates in 1978, and in 1985 created Smart Design with Tom Dair, Tamara Thomsen and Tucker Viemeister. His expertise lies in consumer product design, planning, marketing communications, graphic identity and international manufacturing liaison. He has managed design projects for a broad range of clients including Oxo, Copco, Corning Glass Works, International Playtex, Kepner-Tregoe and 3M. He also lectures for professional organizations and has served on juries for design competitions. Stowell has been the recipient of numerous IDEA awards and eight Annual ID Design Review selections. 3.41

**Scott Stowell** is one of the lead designers for the New York design practice M & Co. 5.1

**Reiko Sudo** was born in Ibaragi Prefecture, Japan and educated at the Musashino Art College. From 1975 to 1977 she assisted Professor Tanaka in the Textile Department. Before co-founding Nuno Corporation in 1984, she worked as a freelance textile designer and has since designed for the International Wool Secretariat, Paris and for the clothing company Threads, Tokyo. At present she is the Director of Nuno Corporation and K. K. Arai Creation System and a lecturer at the Musashino Art University. She has exhibited both nationally and internationally, and her work can be seen in the permanent collections of the Museum of Modern Art and the Cooper-Hewitt Museum, New York; the Museum of Art Rhode Island School of Design; the Philadelphia Museum of Art; the Museum of Applied Arts, Helsinki; and the Montreal Museum of Decorative Arts. 4.25, 26

**Friedrich Sulzer** was born in 1962. He trained in furniture-making and carpentry, receiving a National Diploma in 1988, then studied industrial design at the École Nationale Supérieure de Création Industrielle/Les Ateliers in Paris. In 1990 he created a range of urban furniture for the Parc Oceanique de Kerguelen which was the subject of an exhibition entitled "Entre Mer et Ville" at the Pompidou Centre in Paris in 1991. Since 1992 he has worked as a freelance designer in France and Germany, as well as carrying out research on the new technologies in furniture design at the Kunstakademie, Stuttgart. 5.71

**Marco Susani** works as an independent designer in Milan dealing mainly with electronic products. He also teaches and carries out research at the Domus Academy post-graduate school of design. In the past he has been a partner of Sottsass Associati and a consultant for Olivetti Design Studio. His work was shown at the Milan Triennale in 1985 and 1992 and at the Beaubourg Centre in Paris in 1986 and 1991. 5.81–85

**Barry Sween** received a Bachelor of Science degree in Industrial Design from California State University of Long Beach in 1991 and was also an exchange student at the University of Essen, Germany. He worked for ID Two in San Francisco and for California Medical Products, Long Beach, before joining S. G. Hauser Associates. 5.9, 10

**Martin Szekely** was born in 1956 in Paris where he now lives and works. He began to design furniture in 1979 and has won acclaim in Europe and Israel. Though still active in the fields of furniture and interior design, he has diversified since 1991 into object and industrial design, creating jewellery boxes for Schatzl, crystal desk accessories for Swarovski, luggage for Delvaux and clocks for Hour Lavigne. His most recent furniture collection was a series of wooden pieces for Zeus. He has exhibited his work both in France and abroad, and examples can be seen in the permanent collections of numerous museums including the Musée des Arts Décoratifs, Paris; the Cooper-Hewitt Museum, New York; the Israel Museum, Jerusalem; and the Kunstgewerbe Museums in Berlin and Cologne. 1.46

**Shin Takamatsu** was born in Shimane Prefecture, Japan in 1948 and studied at Kyoto University where he received a Bachelor of Architecture in 1971 and a Ph.D. in 1980. The same year he established Shin Takamatsu Architects and Associates in Kyoto, followed in 1992 by Takamatsu & Lahyani Architects Associates in Berlin. He has received national and international acclaim for his work, including an award from the Venice Biennale in 1985 and the Annual Prize from the Architectural Institute of Japan in 1989 for the Kirin Plaza project, Osaka. 1.13

**Mitsuo Takanaga** was born in Toyama, Japan in 1951 and trained at the Takaoka Industrial Arts High School. In 1970 he joined the television division of Matsushita Electric Co. and in 1978 the VTR division of Matsushita Electric Industrial. 5.40

**Izuru Tanaka** was born in Tokyo and studied at the Nihon University College of Art. In 1989 he joined the AV Design Centre at Matsushita Electric Industrial Co. 5.39

**Larry Tang** graduated in 1981 from the Arizona State University and attended the Art Center College of Design. He worked for Beckman Instruments before becoming a senior designer at S.G. Hauser Associates. He specializes in medical equipment, consumer products and sporting goods. 5.61

**Ali Tayar** is the designer for Parallel Design Partnership, New York. He trained as an architect at the University of Stuttgart and the Massachusetts Institute of Technology. His designs range from table and shelving systems to an architect's parallel ruler. He also works as a consultant on architectural and high-tech projects. 1.105

**Jan Tesar** was born in 1952 in Czechoslovakia, but today is a French citizen. He specialized in stone cutting at a professional school of sculpture, trained further at the École des Beaux Arts in Paris, then spent two years in Rome from 1981 to 1983. In 1991 he was invited to Kyoto by the Japan Foundation where he has had solo exhibitions. In 1992 he created a series of sculptural lights in collaboration with Idée. 2.17, 18

**Matteo Thun** was born in Bolzano, Italy, in 1952. He attended the Oscar Kokoschka Academy in Salzburg and graduated in architecture from the University of Florence. He was a partner of Sottsass Associati and a member of the Memphis Group from 1979 to 1984. At present he deals mainly with industrial design, architecture, furnishings and corporate culture for product design, graphics and packaging. He exhibits and lectures widely both nationally and internationally, and his products have won numerous awards. He is also a member of the jury for various design competitions. His works appear in the permanent collections of many leading art and design museums, including the Cooper-Hewitt Museum, New York and the Victoria and Albert Museum, London. 1.36

**Kurt Thut** is an architect and designer who was born in 1931. 1.104

**Mario Trimarchi** is Director of the industrial design programme at the Domus Academy and a consultant for the Olivetti Design Department in Milan. His design for the bank cash dispenser *CD 6300* for Olivetti was awarded the Premio SMAU in 1990. 5.81–85

**Shigeru Uchida** was born in Yokohama, Japan in 1943 and graduated from the Kuwasawa Design School in Tokyo in 1966. He established the Uchida Design Studio in 1970, followed in 1981 by Studio 80 with Toru Nishioka. He has lectured at universities and design schools in Japan, the USA and Italy and at IDEAS'93 in Melbourne. Uchida is best known for his interior design projects which include the Wave Building in Roppongi, Tokyo, the Il Palazzo hotel in Fukuoka and La Ranarita in Azumabashi, Tokyo. Product design clients include Alessi, Esprit and Chairs. He has exhibited internationally, and his work can be found in the permanent collections of the Metropolitan Museum of Art, New York; the Denver Art Museum; the San Francisco Museum of Modern Art; and the Montreal Museum of Decorative Arts. 1.113, 114

**Masanori Umeda** was born in Kanagawa, Japan in 1941 and graduated from Kuwasawa Design School in Tokyo in 1962. In 1967 he moved to Italy to work for the studio of Achille and Pier Giacomo Castiglioni in Milan, and for Ettore Sottsass, participating in the Memphis collection. In 1986 he established U-Meta Design Inc. in Tokyo. Major projects include the interior design for the restaurant and bar, Ginza MG Planet; the *Mutsugoro* cup and saucer; the *Xspace* office toilet system for INAX Corporation; the interior design for Tomato Bank in Okayama; and the *Getsuen* chair, *Ros* chair and *Antherium* table for Edra. He has exhibited widely and his designs can be seen in the permanent collections of the Museum of Modern Art, Kyoto; the Metropolitan Museum of Art, New York; the Montreal Museum of Decorative Arts; and the Denver Art Museum. 1.97

**Gerard van den Berg** trained in furniture design and began working as a freelance in 1972. He founded the Montis seating factory in 1974 with his brother. Clients include Wittmann, Perobell, Molteni and Artelano. He designs not only furniture but also exhibition stands, shop/office interiors and lamps. In 1990 he sold his shares in Montis to a second brother and founded the design consultancy Gerard van den Berg Design in Breda. He has received several prizes and awards, and his *Loge* design was recently purchased by the Design Museum in London. 1.85

**Tucker Viemeister** was born in Ohio and graduated from the Pratt Institute in 1974. In 1979 he began working with Davin Stowell and six years later founded Smart Design, of which he is now vice-president, with Tom Dair and Tamara Thomsen. Smart Design is an industrial design consultancy specializing in product design, packaging and graphics. Viemeister has lectured extensively, recently giving presentations at the Pompidou Centre in Paris and the Cooper-Hewitt Museum Millennium conference in New York. He has taught at the Pratt Institute and Parsons School of Design, New York, the California Institute of the Arts, Valencia, the University of Cincinnati and the École Nationale Supérieure de Création Industrielle, Paris. His work has been selected for the Presidential Design Achievement Award, the ID Annual Design Review (eleven times), IDEA Awards (six times) and Forma Finlandia. 3.41

**John von Buelow** was born in 1957 in Santa Monica, California and studied industrial design at San Jose State University. He has worked with S. G. Hauser Associates since 1982. His projects have won recognition in the Hanover competition, IDEA competitions and various design magazines. 5.48

**Uwe Wagner, Reinhard Müller** and **Meyer Voggenreiter** belong to the Pentagon Group which was formed by five designers from Cologne (Wolfgang Laubersheimer, Meyer Voggenreiter, Reinhard Müller, Ralph Sommer and Gerd Arens) in 1985. Since then the group has created furniture in steel, neon, wood and stone, and has achieved international fame with an artists' café for the Documenta 1987 in Kassel. It has held numerous national and international exhibitions. 1.112

**Rod** and **Alison Wales** were born in 1950 and 1952 respectively. Rod Wales studied at Rycotewood College, Buckinghamshire College of Higher Education and Parham College, England. Alison Wales received a BA Honours in Fine Art from Reading University. She also studied at Rycotewood College, and from 1979 to 1980 was a trainee at John Makepeace Furniture Ltd. In 1981 they set up the Longbarn Workshop, specializing in high-quality one-off furniture and limited batch production furniture and accessories. In 1986 they were selected for the Crafts Council Index. Wales & Wales have received numerous awards including the Guild Mark given by the Worshipful Company of Furniture Makers in 1988. Both Alison and Rod are visiting lecturers at a variety of colleges and have exhibited their designs in the UK and Germany. Their work can be seen in the Victoria and Albert Museum's 20th-century collection. 1.115, 116

**Marcel Wanders** was born in 1963 and graduated in 1988 from the Art Academy in Arnhem. He has won several design competitions in the Netherlands and is at present a partner in WAAC's design consultancy. 2.16

**Seiichi Watanabe** was born in Tokyo in 1969 and trained in industrial design at the Salesian Polytechnic. In 1990 he joined the AV Design Centre of Matsushita Electric Industrial Co. 5.40

**Hannes Wettstein** was born in Ascona, Switzerland in 1958 and, after working in furniture design, decided to specialize in interior design and architecture. He has worked with Baleri Italia since 1985. 2.65

**Robert Wettstein** was born in 1960. He is a self-taught designer and since 1985 has had his own office in Zurich, collaborating with companies such as Anthologie Quartett and Artipresent in Germany. 1.6, 7, 8, 9

**Stefan Wewerka** was born in 1928 in Magdeburg, Germany. He studied architecture with Max Taut before working with the architectural practice Taut, Luckhardts and Scharoun in Berlin. He is active in all fields of design as well as working as a sculptor and painter and in films and publishing. His clients include Tecta, Montana, Källemo and Vitra. He has taught at the Washington University in St Louis, USA, as well as at Cornell University and the Kungelige Danske Kunstakademi, Copenhagen. Today he is the director of the Alfred Veven DuMont Kunstakademie in Cologne. 1.4

**Christopher Williams** was born in Surrey, England in 1949 and studied at the Guildford School of Art. After working for Allard and Co. as an interior designer, he joined the Conran Design Group as an industrial designer of domestic products. He took a Master's degree in glassware design at the Royal College of Art in 1976 and since then has been director of the Glasshouse and a freelance industrial designer. He has lectured at High Wycombe College of Art and at the Royal College of Art. 3.6

**Jack Woolley** studied mechanical engineering at Edinburgh University and industrial design at the Royal College of Art, London, and is at present a director of the Industrial Design Consultancy ISIS (UK) Ltd. His furniture and lighting designs have been exhibited in Japan, Italy, Germany and Paris. Other projects include the development of artificial limbs and the design of water pumps. 1.75

**Manuel Ybargüengoitia** was born in Barcelona in 1954 and studied drawing and industrial design in Barcelona and Girona. He is a member of FAD INFAD and the Official College of Decorators of Catalunya. 2.29

**Osamu Yonekawa** was born in 1957 in Osaka, Japan and studied at the Tokyo-Zokei University. In 1980 he joined the AV Design Centre, Matsushita Electric Industrial Co. Ltd and in 1992 the Industrial Design Centre, Matsushita Housing Products Co. 5.39

**Gad Zorea** was born in Israel in 1953 and studied at the Tel Aviv Art Academy. In 1979 he moved to Denmark and worked in ceramic design before becoming a partner in Stokholm/Zorea in 1983 with Marianne Stokholm. 5.37, 38

# Suppliers

**Helle Abild.** Off The Wall Design, 4th floor, 55 Mercer Street, New York, NY 10012, USA.

**Acerbis International SpA.** Via Brusaporto 31, 24068 Seriate, Italy. *Outlets* Argentina: Interieur Forma SA, Paraguay 541/555, 1057 Buenos Aires. Belgium: Artiscope-Zaira Mis, 35 Bd St Michel, 1040 Brussels. Brazil: Forma SA, Rua Alfredo Wolf 150, 06750 Taboao da Serra. France: Francis Helven, 21 Côte des Chapeliers, 26000 Valence. Germany: Gert Kastein, Fichtenstrasse 12, 6950 Mosbach. Greece: J. Deloudis A.E., Kifisias 217, Parnassou 2, Amaroussion, Athens. Holland: Biermans Kees, Parkstraat 9, 4818 Breda. Hong Kong: William Artists Int. Ltd, Furniture Division, 3F Shing Dao Ind. Bldg, 232 A Main Road, Aberdeen. Scandinavia: Interstudio, Ludersvej 4,Frihavnen, 2100 Copenhagen, Denmark. Spain: Axa International SA, Carretera Granollers, Sabadel Km, 13,5, 08185 Lica de Vall. Switzerland: Wohn Design Ag-Kaufmann Peter, Rychenbergstrasse 123, 8400 Winterthur. UK: Environment, The Studio, Southway House, 954 North Circular Road, London NW2 7JR. USA: Atelier International Ltd, c/o Int. Design Center, 30–20 Thomson Avenue, Long Island City, NY 11101.

**Alessi SpA.** Via Privata Alessi 6, 28023 Crusinallo, Novara, Italy. *Outlets* Denmark: Gense AS, 17 Maglebjergvej, 2800 Lyngby. Finland: Casabella OY, 24 Yliopistonakatu, 20100 Turku. France: Société Métallurgique Lagostina, 62 rue Blaise Pascal, 93600 Aulnay-sous-Bois. Germany: Van Der Borg GmbH, Sandbahn 6, 4240 Emmerich. Japan: Italia Shoji Co. Ltd, 5-4 Kojimachi, 1-chome, Chiyoda-ku, Tokyo 102. The Netherlands: Interhal BV, 8 Zoutverkoperstraat, 3330 CA Zwijndrecht. Sweden: Espresso Import, 10E Furasen, 42177V Frolunda. Switzerland: Guido Mayer SA, 9 rue du Port Franc, 1003 Lausanne. UK: Penhallow Marketing Ltd, 3 Vicarage Road, Sheffield S9 3RH. USA: The Markuse Corporation, 10 Wheeling Avenue, Woburn, MA 01801.

**Ajioka Co. Ltd.** 1-18-12 Hamacho, Nihonbashi, Chuo-ku, Tokyo, Japan.

**Alias Srl.** Via Respighi 2, 20122 Milan, Italy. *Outlets* France: Roger Von Bary, 19 rue Lafitte, 75009 Paris. Germany: Peter Pfeifer, Focus, 87 Leopoldstrasse, 40 Munich 8. Japan: Casatec Ltd, 2-9-6 Higashi, Shibuya-ku, Tokyo 150. The Netherlands: Kreymborg, 63 Minervaalan, 1077 Amsterdam. Sweden:

Design Distribution, 38A Doebelnsgatan, 11352 Stockholm. Switzerland: Renato Stauffacher, 2 Capelli, 6900 Lugano. UK: Artemide GB Ltd, 17-19 Neal Street, London WC2H 9PU. USA: International Contract Furniture, 305 East 63rd Street, New York, NY 10021.

**Alterego.** 572 Egelantiersgracht, Amsterdam 1015 RR, The Netherlands. *Outlets* France: Néotù, 25 rue du Renard, 75004 Paris. Hong Kong: Le Cadre Gallery, 10th Floor, Bay Tower, 2–4 Sunning Road, Causeway Bay. Italy: Driade SpA, Via Padana Inferiore 12, 29012 Fossadello di Caorso, Piacenza. Japan: Chambres d'Amis, 3-18-20 Minami-Aoyama, Minato-ku, Tokyo 107. UK: The Ikon Corporation, B5L Metropolitan Wharf, Wapping Wall, London E1 9SS.

**Amstrad Plc.** The Eden Group Ltd, The Chapel, Rainow, Ches. SK10 5SF, UK.

**Andiamo.** 11520 Warner Avenue, Fountain Valley, California 92708, USA.

**Andreu World SA.** Cno de los Mojones, KM 2.5, 46970 Alaquas, Valencia, Spain. *Outlet* UK: Kesterport Ltd, Kestrel House, 111 Heath Road, Twickenham, Middx TW1 4AH.

**Anibou Pty Ltd.** 726 Bourke Street, Redfern 2106, NSW 2016, Australia.

**Apex Manufacturing.** 32 Luang-Cheng Road, Tailhsiang, Taichung Hsien, 41213 Taiwan ROC, Japan.

**Aram Designs Ltd.** 3 Kean Street, Covent Garden, London WC2B 4AT, UK.

**Area Group Inc.** Units 36–37, 55 West Beaver Creek Road, Richmond Hill, Ontario L4B 1KS, Canada.

**Argentaurum.** 826–1 Zeedijk, Knokke-Le-Zoute 8300, Belgium.

**Jan Armgardt.** 45 Grieselstrasse, Bensheim 6140, Hessen, Germany.

**Artelano.** 4 rue Schoelcher, Paris 75014, France. *Outlets* Belgium: Lydia Maughan, 75 avenue de l'université, Brussels 1050. Germany: Harald Noede KG, 3 Oderveg, Zirenberg 3501. UK: Walter International, 42 High Street, Daventry, Northants NN1 1HU. USA: Luminaire, 7300 South West 45th Street, Miami, Florida 33155.

**Artipresent-Autentics.** Rohrerstrasse, Leinfelden 7022, Germany. *Outlets* Austria: Prodomo, Flachgasse 35–37, 1152 Vienna. France: Jean-Marie Ritterbeck, 1 Allée Taine, 77340 Pontautt-Combantt. Japan: Shimada Int. Ass. Inc., Canal Tower

10F, 9-3 Koamicho, Nihonbashi, Chuo-ku, Tokyo 103. Spain: Pilma Valenica 1, Barcelona 08015.

**Atelier International Ltd.** 30–20 Thomson Avenue, Long Island City, New York 11101, USA.

**Atoll Möbelideen GmbH.** Heckerswiesen-strasse 6, 3500 Kassel, Germany. *Outlets* Austria: Möbelgalerie Alexander Vrubl, Renngasse 7, 1010 Vienna. Italy/ Switzerland: L'Oggetto-Rosario Rao, Holunderweg 20, 4552 Derendingen, Switzerland. The Netherlands/Belgium/ Luxembourg: Friday - Jan A. van't Riet, rue Emile Claus Straat 5, 1050 Brussels, Belgium.

**AV Mazzega Srl.** Via Vivarini 3, 30141 Murano, Venice, Italy. *Outlets* Belgium: Ardeco International Belgium sprl, Avenue Général de Gaulle 39, 1050 Brussels. France: Horas International SARL, rue Copernic 22, 1180 Brussels, Belgium. Germany: Afid GmbH, Gerner Strasse 24, 8000 Munich 19. Holland: Artimeta BV, De Koumen 86, 6436 Ke Heerlen. Mexico: Points Mazarik SA de CV, Avenida Pdte Mazarik 515, Col. Polanco, Mexico D.F. 11560. Spain: Kambi Iluminacion, Blay Net 35, 08830 Sant Boi de LLobregat, Barcelona. Switzerland: Vetrarti, Gajon A. & Co., Robweg 2, 5507 Mellingen.

**Baleri Italia.** Via S. Bernardino 39, Lallio 24040, Bergamo, Italy. *Outlets* France: Francis Helven, 21 Côte des Chapeliers, Valence 2000. Germany: Walter Schiedermeier, Marienbergerweg 12, Cologne 5000. Japan: Casatec Ltd, 9-6 Higashi, 2-chome Shibuya-ku, Tokyo 150. The Netherlands: Kreymborg, 66 avenue Molière, Brussels 1180, Belgium. Scandinavia: Lysygn, 1 Horseager, Greve 2670, Denmark. UK: Viaduct Furniture, 10 Spring Place, London NW5 3BH. USA: I.C.F. Inc., 305 East 63rd Street, New York 10021.

**Bang Design.** 62 Phillip St Balmain, NSW 2041, Australia.

**Barcino Disseny.** S.L. Roger de Lluria 95, 2–1, 08009 Barcelona, Spain. *Outlets* Austria/Benelux/Germany/Switzerland: Sabina Rademacher, Dos de Mayo 14, 2 - 08960 San Just Desvern, Spain. Latin America: Dani Maderas SA, J. M. Gutierrez 3989, Buenos Aires, Argentina. UK: The Conran Shop Ltd, Michelin House, 81 Fulham Road, London SW3 GRD.

**Bd. Ediciones de Diseño.** 291 Mallorca, 08037 Barcelona, Spain. *Outlets*

Austria/Germany: IMD Inter Marketing Distribution AG, Flöthbruchstrasse 11, 4156 Willich 2, Anrath, Germany. Belgium: Quattro, 25 rue de la Regence, 1000 Brussels. Canada: Triede, 460 McGill, Montreal, Quebec H2Y 2H2. France: 8 rue des Quatre Fils, 75003 Paris. Greece: Varangis Avepe SA, 40 M. Botsari, GR 15121 Pefki. Holland: IMD Inter Marketing Distribution AG, Beverweerdlaan 22, 6825 AE Arnhem. Hong Kong: Le Cadre Gallery, 8 Sunning Road G/F, Causeway Bay. Italy: Zoltan, Via Alesandria 5, 20144 Milan. Japan: Art Front Gallery, Daikanyama Edge 3F, 28-10 Sarugaku-cho, Shibuya-ku, Tokyo 105; Mimori Trading Co. Ltd, Toc. Bldg, 7-22-17 Nishigatanda, Shinagawa-ku, Tokyo. Portugal: Arquitectonica, Rua da Escola Politécnica 94, 1200 Lisbon. Singapore: Galerie Ecletique, 58 Tanjong Pagar Road. Switzerland: IMD Inter Marketing Distribution AG, Eebrunnestrasse 26, 5212 Hausen (AG). UK: Interior Marketing, 2 Woods Cottages, Hartfield Broad Oak, Bishop's Stortford, Herts CM22 7BU. USA: Luminaire, 7300 Southwest 45th Street, Miami, Florida 33155; Current, 1201 Wester Avenue, Seattle, WA 98101; Di-zin, 1320 Main Street, Venice, CA 90291.

**Belux AG.** Bremgarterstrasse 109, 5610 Wohlen, Switzerland. *Outlets* Australia: Création Baumann, 87 King William Street, Fitzroy, Victoria 3065. Canada: Création Baumann, 302 King Street, East Toronto, Ontario M5A 1K6. France: Belux France, Technopolis 4, ZAC de Mercières, 60200 Compiègne. Germany: Nils Holger Moormann, Kirchplatz, 8213 Aschau im Chiemgau. Italy: Twin Srl, Via conservatorio N. 22, 20122 Milan. Japan: Création Baumann Japan Ltd, Tokyo Design Center, 5-25-19 Higashi-Gotanda, Shinagawa-ku, Tokyo 141. The Netherlands: Belux Benelux Hans N. Zwart, De Zwaan 23, 2266 NN Leidschendam. Scandinavia: Osterby Christian, Birkewaenget 21, 3520 Farum, Denmark. Spain: Biok SA, Barrio de Amute S/N, Hondarriba/Guipuzcoa. UK: Lumino Limited, Lovet Road, Harlow, Essex CM19 5T8. USA: Ernest Stöcklin, 135 Fort Lee Road, Leonia, NJ 07605.

**Boym Design Studio.** 56 West 11th Street, New York, NY 10011, USA. *Outlet* France: Néotù, 25 rue du Renard, Paris 75004.

**BRF.** Loc. S. Marziale, colle Val d'Elsa 53034, Siena, Italy. *Outlets* Belgium: UBIK Sprl, 18 Galerie du Roi, 1000 Brussels. France: Artefact, 10 rue du Temple, 2100 Dijon. Germany: Kleine Wohntechnik, Friedrichstrasse 129, 75072 Siegen. The

Netherlands: Visio, Znid Willemsvaart 19, 05211 s'Hertogenbosch.

**Candle Srl.** Alzaia Trieste 49, 20094 Corsico, Italy. *Outlets* France: Rousselin E. Pecnard, 66 avenue des Ternes, 75017 Paris. Germany: Fulvio Folci, Niederkasselerstrasse 61, 4000 Düsseldorf 11. Japan: Arflex Japan Ltd, 1350 Nagahama, Ashiwada-mura, Minamitsuru-gun, Yamanashi Prefecture. The Netherlands: Andrea Kok, Pilatus 4, 1186 EK Amstelveen. Spain: Casimiro Fernandez, Urbanisacion Soto de Llaner, casa 5, 33193 Pruvia, Principado de Asturias. UK: Clemente Cavigioli, 86 Ladbroke Grove, London W11 2HE. USA: Ivan Luini I.L. Euro . Inc., 900 Broadway 902, New York, NY 10003.

**Cappellini Arte.** Via Marconi 35, 22060 Arosio, Italy. *Outlets* Austria: Wolfgang Bischof OHG, Judenplatz 6, 1010 Vienna. Belgium: Rika Andries, Turnhoutsebaan 144b, 2200 Borgerhout. France: Cerutti Giuseppe, Loc. Grand Chemin 1, 11020 Saint Christophe. Germany: Novus, Gartenstrasse 26, 7959 Achstetten Bronnen 3. The Netherlands: Hansje Kalff Meubelagenturen, Puttensestraat 8, 1181 Je Amstelveen. Sweden: Mobile Box AB, Nybrogatan 11, 11439 Stockholm. Switzerland: Yves Humbrecht Diffusion, Mon Repos 3, 1066 Epalinges. UK: SCP Ltd, 135–139 Curtain Road, London EC2. USA/Canada: Ivan Luini, 453 West 19th Street, App. 6A, New York, NY 10011.

**Cassina SpA.** Via Luigi Busnelli 1, Meda 20036, Milan, Italy. *Outlets* France: Sanda, 168 rue du Faubourg Saint Honoré, Paris 75008. Germany: Pesch GmbH & Co. KG, Kaiser Wilhelm Ring 22, 5000 Cologne 1. Japan: Cassina Japan Inc., 2-9-6 Higashi, Shibuya-ku, Tokyo 150. The Netherlands: Mobica, 31 Middenweg, 3401 Ijsselstein. Spain: Mobilplast, 40 calle Milagro, 08028 Barcelona. UK: Marcatré, 179 Shaftesbury Avenue, London WC2H 8AR. USA: Atelier International Inc., The International Design Center, 30–20 Thomson Avenue, Long Island City, NY 11101.

**Chairs.** Axis Bldg 4F, 5-17-1-413 Roppongi, Minato-ku, Tokyo, Japan.

**Chairwork.** 26 Huntingdon Street, London N1 1BS, UK.

**Chueca.** Carretera Valencia-Barcelona, KM.9, Museros 46136 Valencia, Spain. *Outlet* UK: Walter International, 42 High Street, Daventry, Northants NN11 4HU.

**ClassiCon GmbH.** Perchtinger Strasse 8, 81379 Munich, Germany. *Outlets* Austria: Agentur Gordis, Porzellangasse 9, 1090 Vienna. Belgium/Luxembourg: Dépeche, Diestseestraat 8, 3220 Aarschot. Denmark: Tegnestuen, Norre Sogade 37 C. 6.2, 1370 Copenhagen. France: Claude Cénet, Héry-sur-Alby, 74540 Alby-Sur-Chéran. Italy: FAI, Frigerio Architetture d'Interni Srl, 124 corso Italia, 20033 Desio, Milan. Japan: Yamada Shomei Lighting Co., 3-16-12 Sotokanda, Chiyoda-ku, Tokyo 101. The Netherlands: Topic BV/Agencies, Graaf Florisweg 71, 2805 AH Gouda. Switzerland: Peter Müller, Kirchmattenweg 7, 79618 Rheinfelden. UK: Aram Designs Ltd, 3 Kean Street, Covent Garden, London WC2B 4AT.

**Concord Lighting Ltd.** 174 High Holborn, London, UK. Export Dept.: Concord Lighting Ltd, Avis Way, Newhaven, East Sussex BN9 0HX, UK.

**Laslo Conek.** 90 Poletti, Modena 41100, Italy.

**Gaetan Coolen.** 70 Aardbruggestraat, Alken 3570, Limburg, Belgium.

**Bruno Danese Srl.** Viale Francia 61, 20036 Meda, Italy.

**Deko Collezioni Srl.** Via Pattigna 5, Felegara 43040, Parma, Italy.

**Deko France SARL.** 12 avenue de la Grande Armée, Paris 75017, France. *Outlets* Germany: Christian Robert GmbH, Bunsenstrasse 5, Martinsried 8033. Greece: Research Ltd, 21 Vas Dipla Str., Athens. Japan: Toyota Tsusho Corporation, 7-23 Meieki 4-chome, Nakamura, Nagoya 450. The Netherlands: Faram Nederland B.V., 50 Wageningselaan, La Veenendaal 3903. Spain: Intersilla Y Kode SA, 2 Poligono Collsabadell Parcela G Nave, Llinars del Valles 8450. UK: Balido Ltd, 44 Grove Road, Tring, Herts HP23 5PD.

**Design House AWA,** 1-21-1 Jingumae, Shibuya-ku, Tokyo 150, Japan.

**Dietz Design Management GmbH.** Scheffelstrasse 5, Frankfurt 6000, Postfach 100736, Germany.

**David D'Imperio.** 2961 Aviation House, Miami, Florida 33133, USA. *Outlet* USA: Modernage Galleries, 121 Greene Street, New York, NY 10012.

**Dissing + Weitling Arkitektfirma A/S.** Overgaden neden Vandet 45, Copenhagen 1414, Denmark.

**Nanna Ditzel.** 4 Klareboderne, Copenhagen 1115, Denmark.

**Divano SA.** Proyecto, 9 - Pol. Ind. "San Francisco", Beniparrell 46469, Valencia, Spain.

**Andreas Dober.** Alexanderstrasse 136, 7000 Stuttgart 1, Germany.

**Doesinger/Doesinger.** 21B Graben, Linz 4020, Austria.

**Domodinamica Srl.** Alzaia Naviglio Pavese 118, 20142 Milan, Italy.

**Driade SpA.** Via Padana Inferiore 12, Fossadello di Caorso 29012, Piacenza, Italy. *Outlets* France: Arturo Del Punta, 7 rue Simon Le Franc, 75004 Paris. Germany: Stefan Müller, Bereiteranger 7, 8000 Munich 90. Japan: Ambiente International Inc., Sumitomo Semei Bldg, 3-1-30 Minami-Aoyama, Minato-ku, Tokyo. The Netherlands: Espaces & Lignes, Nassaulaan 2A, 2514 The Hague. Scandinavia: Design Distribution, Doebelnsgatan 38A 1, 11352 Stockholm, Sweden. Spain: Bd. Ediciones de Diseño, 291 Mallorca, 08037 Barcelona. UK: Viaduct Furniture Ltd, Spring House, 10 Spring Place, London NW5 3BH.

**Droog Design. (un)Limited editions.** Noorrdeinde 19–21, 2611 KE Delft, The Netherlands. *Outlet* Italy: Ziggurat Design Group, Va del Pozzo Toscanelli 3, 20132 Milan.

**D-Tec Industriedesign GmbH.** Telleringstrasse 5, 4000 Düsseldorf 13, Germany. *Outlets* Austria: D-Tec Industriedesign GmbH, Telleringstrasse 5, 4000 Düsseldorf 13. Belgium/The Netherlands: D-Tec Nederland, Fuutstraat 35, 6921 WG Duiven, Holland. France: Marc Loubet, 31 avenue Parmentier, 75011 Paris. Japan: Eternal Inc., 3F Nakajima Bldg, 3 17-15 Nishiozabou, Minato-ku, Tokyo 106. Scandinavia: Nordic Design Group, Roholmsvej 10a, 2620 Albertslund, Denmark. Switzerland: Mobilform, Sagegasse 2, 3110 Munsingen.

**Dyson Appliances Ltd.** Bathford, Bath BA1 7RS, UK.

**Ecart International SA.** 111 rue St Antoine, 75004 Paris, France. *Outlet* Japan: H.A. deux Inc., Hiroo Garden Hills A-703, 4-1-6 Hiroo, Shibuya-ku, Tokyo 150.

**EFM.** 588 Broadway, New York, NY 10012, USA; Via G. Morone 6, 20121 Milan, Italy.

**Thomas Eisl.** 3 Nimrod Passage, London N1 4BU, UK.

**ERCO Leuchten GmbH.** 5880 Lüdenscheid, Germany. *Outlets* Austria: ERCO Leuchten GmbH, Modecenterstrasse 14, 1030

Vienna. Belgium: ERCO Lighting Belgium Bvba/spri, avenue Molière 211, 1060 Brussels. France: ERCO Lumières SARL, 6ter rue des Saints-Pères, 75007 Paris. Italy: ERCO Illuminazione Srl, Via Cassanese 224, Palazzo Leonardo, 20090 Segrate, Milan. The Netherlands: ERCO Lighting Nederland BV, Goolmeer 13, 1411 De Naarden. Norway: ERCO Belysning AS, Industriveien 8 B, 1473 Skarer; Postboks 83, Ellingsrudasen, 1006 Oslo 10. Spain: Erco Illuminacion SA, Oficinas y almacén central, Avenida Barcelona, s/n, esq. Virgen de Montserrat, 08970 Sant Joan Despi, Barcelona. UK: ERCO Lighting Ltd, 38 Dover Street, London W1X 3RB.

**Flores Design Edition.** Benrather Strasse 6, 0213 Düsseldorf, Germany.

**Flos SpA.** Via Angelo Faini 2, Bovezzo 25073, Brescia, Italy. *Outlets* Belgium: Flos SA, Gossetlaan 50, 1702 Groot-Bijgaarden. France: Flos SARL, 23 rue de Bourgogne, 75007 Paris. Germany: Flos GmbH, Am Probsthof 94, 5300 Bonn 1. Japan: Flos Co. Ltd, PMC Building, 1-23-5 Higashi-Azabu, Minato-ku, Tokyo 106. Spain: Flos SA, c/Bovedillas 16, San Just Desvern, 08960 Barcelona. Switzerland: Flos SA, 75 Blvd St-Georges, 1205 Geneva. UK: Flos Ltd, The Studio, 120 High Street, South Milford, Leeds LS25 5AQ Yorks. USA: Flos Inc., 200 McKay Road, Huntingdon Station, New York, NY 11746.

**FM Design.** 1a Lonsdale Square, London N1 1EN, UK.

**Formfürsorge.** 12 Grosse Pfahlstrasse, Hanover 30161, Germany.

**Foscarini Murano SpA.** 1 Fondamenta Manin, Murano, Venice 30141, Italy. *Outlets* France: Horas International, 150 rue Championnet, Paris. Germany: Alta Linea GmbH, 6 Sandhof, 4040 Neuss 21 Norff. The Netherlands: Horas International, Beemdstraat 25, Ruisbroek 1610. UK: Liaison, 917–919 Fulham Road, London SW6 5HU.

**Fountainhead Computers,** 8 Pasteur Ste 170, Irvine, California 92718, USA.

**France Telecom.** 26 rue du Commandant Mouchette, Paris 75014, France.

**Fratelli Fantini SpA,** Via M. Buonarroti 4, 28010 Pella, Italy. *Outlets* France: Parazines Daniel, "La Calmeraie", avenue de la Colline, 06270 Villeneuve, Loubet. Germany: Vorberg GmbH, Bahnhofstrasse 2, 0838 Groebenzell. Japan: Mitsui & Co. Ltd, 16–21 Meieki Minami 1-chome, Nakamura-ku, Nagoya. USA: Hastings Tile

& Il Bagno Collection, 30 Commercial Street, Freeport 11520, New York.

**Fredericia Stolefabrik.** 183 Treldevej, Fredericia 7000, Denmark.

**Gallery 91,** 91 Grand Street, New York, NY 10013, USA.

**Gebrüder Thonet GmbH.** Michael-Thonet Strasse 1, Postfach 1520, 35059 Frankenberg/Eder, Germany. *Outlets* Austria: Leyss classic, Tiergartenstrasse 127, 6020 Innsbruck. Belgium: N.V. Trade Center Belgium, Junolaan 1, 2900 Schoten. Denmark: Haslund International Interior A/S, Esplanaden 6–8, 1263 Copenhagen. Finland: Asra Oy, Pohjoisranta 14A, 00170 Helsinki. France: Claude Cénet, Les Monts, Héry-sur-Alby, 74540 Alby-sur-Chéran. Hong Kong: Vaford Technology Ltd, 23/F Dah Sing Financial Centre, 108 Gloucester Road, Wanchai. Ireland: O'Hagan Design Ltd, 99–101 Capel Street, Dublin 1. Italy: Frigerio Architettura d'Interni, Divisione FAI, C.so Italia 124, Casella Postale 70, 20033 Desio, Milan. Japan: Aidec Co. Ltd, No. 28 Mori Bldg, 6 F, 16-13 Nishiazabu 4, Minato-ku, Tokyo 106. The Netherlands: Bitter Culemborg BV, Industrieweg 18, 4153 BW Beesd. Norway: Martens Interior AS, Bygdoy Alle 58 B, 0265 Oslo. Spain: Santa Cole, Santisima Trinidad del Monte 10, 08017 Barcelona. Sweden: Mobile Box AB, Nybrogatan 11, 11439 Stockholm. Switzerland: Seleform AG, Im Gewerbezentrum, Gustav-Maurer-Strasse 8, Postfach 184, 8702 Zollikon-Zh. UK: Aram Designs Ltd, 3 Kean Street, Covent Garden, London WC2B 4AT.

**GK Sekkei Inc.** Horizon-1 Bldg, 30-16 Nishi Waseda 3-chome, Shinjuku-ku, Tokyo, Japan 169.

**Go Video.** 14455 N. Hayden Road Ste 219, Scottsdale, Arizona 85260, USA.

**Grid Systems.** 46501 Landing Parkway, Fremont, CA 94537, USA. *Outlets* Austria: Grid Systems (Federal Headquarters), 2070 Chain Bridge Road, Suite 150, Vienna 22182. France: Tandy Grid France SNC, BP 209, 92502 rue il Malmaison, Cedex. Germany: Tandy Grid Deutschland, 4030 Ratingen. Italy: Victor Technologies Srl, Via Acerbi 23, 16148 Genoa. The Netherlands: Tandy Grid Netherlands BV, PO Box 4619, 4803 EP Breda. Scandinavia: Tandy Grid Europe (European Headquarters), 19486 Upplands, Väsby, Sweden. Spain: Tandy Grid España SA, Edificio Bronce, Avenida de Burgos 8a, pta 16–17, 28036 Madrid. UK: Tandy Grid UK, The Summit Centre, Skyport Drive, West Drayton UB7 OLJ.

**Koji Hamai.** Daisanishigen-Haim B33, 1-5-10 Kamitakaido, Suginami-ku, Tokyo 168, Japan.

**Jochen Henkels Büro für Produkt-gestaltung.** Gausstrasse 15, 2000 Hamburg 50, Germany.

**Hishinuma Associates.** 5-41-2 Jingumae, Shibuya-ku, Tokyo 150, Japan.

**Idée.** 5-4-44 Minami-Aoyama, Minato-ku, Tokyo 107, Japan. *Outlet* France: Idée Europe, 21 rue Danielle Casanova, Paris 75001.

**Inno.** Merikatu 1, 00140 Helsinki, Finland. *Outlets* Australia: Dedece, 30 Boronia Street, Redfern 2016, NSW. Austria: Centroform, Lasserstrasse 10, 5021 Salzburg. Belgium: Tradix, rue du Mail 90-92, 1050 Brussels. Denmark: Søren Sørensen, Hostrups Have 19, 1954 Frederiksberg. France: Agence Frederic Cabantous, 4 Square Nungasser, 94160 Saint Manadé. Germany: Omniform, Postfach 1408, Dr Pieke Strasse 8, 4834 Harsewinkel. Japan: Archi's Corporation, Gable Bldg 3-5, Shiba Daimon 1-chome, Minato-ku, Tokyo 105. The Netherlands: Meubin, Amerfoortseweg 40, 3951 LC Maarn. New Zealand: Dedece, 6 Fox Street, Parnell, Auckland. Norway: Artinterior A/S, Boks 57, Skøyen, 0212 Oslo 2. Sweden: Inno Interior Svenska AB, Käkbrinken 5, Box 2039, 10311 Stockholm. Switzerland: Inno Switzerland, Gehrenholzpark, 8055 Zurich. Thailand: Architectural Products, 29/4 Sukhumvit 31, Phrakanong, Bangkok 10110. UK: Dutch Design Centre, Royalty Studios, 105 Lancaster Road, London W11 1UG.

**Insight Telecast.** 39650 Liberty Street, Fremont, CA 44538, USA.

**Institute of Technology.** Gregersengvej, Tastrup 2630, Copenhagen, Denmark.

**ISM Objects.** 570 Chapel Street, South Yarra 3141, Victoria, Australia.

**Italiana Luce Srl.** 118 Via Edison, Settimo Milanese, Milan 20019, Italy. *Outlets* Austria: Konsequent Möbelagentur Dagmar Neuger, 87 Kampenwandstrasse, Aschau im Chiemgau 8213. Belgium: Kreymborg, 66 Avenue Molière, Brussels 1180. France: Pierre Nourissat, 14 avenue de la Gare, Bièvres 91570, Paris. Germany: Interprofil GmbH, 9 Ruhberg, 6301 Fernwald 1. Japan: Matsushita Electric Works Italia, 18 Viale Elvezia, Milan 20154. The Netherlands: Kreymborg, 63 Minervalaan, Amsterdam 1077. Scandinavia: Atelje Lyktan, Ahus 29600. Spain: Carpyen sa

Iluminacion, 29 Duran i Borrel, Barcelona 08023. UK: Ambience, 273 Brighton Road, Belmont-Sutton, Surrey SM2 5SU. USA: IL USA Inc., 400 Long Beach Blvd, Stratford 06497, Connecticut.

**Hannu Kähönen.** 5 Laivanvarustajankatu, Helsinki, SF-00140, Finland.

**Källemo AB.** Box 605, 331 26 Varnamo, Sweden. *Outlets* Germany: MGM Möbel GmbH, Burg Modrath, Kölnerstrasse 151, 5014 Kerpen, Germany. Italy: T-Group. Via Roma 144, 33033 Codroipo, Udine. Japan: Swedish Furniture Group, Sweden Center Building, 6-11-9 Roppongi, Minato-ku, Tokyo 106. USA: Limn, 290 Townsend Street, San Francisco, CA 94107, USA.

**Kartell SpA.** Via delle Industrie 1, 20082 Noviglio, Milan, Italy. *Outlets* Australia: Plastex, 85 Fairbank Road, 3168 Clayton, Victoria. Austria: Eugen Leopold, Fielderstrasse 2–4, 4020 Linz. Belgium: Tradix SA, 90–92 rue du Mail, 1050 Brussels. Denmark: Collection Creative, Danas Plads 15, 2000 Frederiksberg. France: C & D Diffusion SARL, 3 avenue du Bois Vert, 77240 Vert-Saint-Denis. Germany: Gotthilf Riexinger, Vorstadt 7, 7034 Gärtringen. Hong Kong: William Artists International Ltd, 232 Aberdeen Main Road, 3/F Shing Dao, Aberdeen. Israel: Goldberg and Co., 21/10 Haorgim Street, 58857 Holon. Japan: Interdecor Inc., 2-9-6 Higashi, Shibuya-ku, Tokyo 150. Lebanon: Vent Nouveau SARL, PO Box 233, Jal El Dib, Beirut. The Netherlands: Modular Systems, Bosboom Toussaintstraat 24, 1054 Amsterdam. Portugal: Grup Dimensao SA, Av. Eng. Arantes E Oliveira 5, 1900 Lisbon. Spain: Jordi Rotger, Zaragoza 62, 8008 Barcelona. Sweden: Claes Brechensbauer, Möbelagentur, Kyrkoköpinge Pl. 26, 23191 Trelleborg. Switzerland: Gatto Diffusion, 30 rue Des Chavannes, 2016 Cortaillod. Turkey: Mood, Akkavak Sok. 47/2 Nisantasi, 80220 Istanbul. UK: Environment, The Studio, 120 High Street, South Milford, Leeds LS25 5AQ, Yorks. USA: I.L.Euro Inc., 900 Broadway 902, New York, NY 10003.

**Katz-Flechtmöbel.** 13 Hoher-Baum-Weg, Hagold 7270, Württemberg, Germany. *Outlets* Austria: "Die Zwet" Wohmel, 37 Eimfang, Schwaz 6130. Luxembourg: Epoque-Einrichtungen, 15 rue Philippe, Luxembourg 2340. Switzerland: Domizil Möbel, 90 Lehmer Strasse, Stigallen 9014.

**Yaacov Kaufman.** 17 Alexander Yanai, Tel Aviv, Israel 62498.

**Kenwood Ltd.** New Lane, Havant, Hants PO9 2NH, UK. *Outlets* France: Société Kenwood France, Immeuble Strategic Orly, 13 rue du Pont des Halles, 94150 Rungis. Germany: Pfeiffer Marketing GmbH, Halleschestrasse 12–14, 6800 Mannheim 31. Italy: EHP Italia SpA, Via Trento 59, 20021 Ospiate i Bollate, Milan. Japan: Aikosha Manufacturing Co. Ltd, 7-10-8 Chuo, Waribi-Schi, Saitama 335. The Netherlands/Antilles: Muskus Trading NV, PO Box 580, Curacao. USA: Kenwood Appliances, 156 Halsey Road, Parsippany, New Jersey 07054.

**KI.** 1330 Bellevue Street, Green Bay, Wisconsin 54308-8100, USA.

**Kirk Telecom.** 21 Ane Stauningsvej, Horsens 8700, Denmark. *Outlets* The Netherlands: Alcatel Business System BV, 10-20 Platinaweg, Postbus 40660, The Hague 2504 LR.

**Setsuo Kitaoka.** 17-18 Sarugaku-cho, Shibuya-ku, Tokyo, Japan.

**Komplot Design.** 16 Faelledvej, Copenhagen, DK 2200N, Denmark.

**Kyushu Matsushita Electric Co. Ltd.** Business Equipment Division, 4-1-62 Minoshima, Hakata-ku, Fukuoka City, Fukuoka 812, Japan.

**Lara Designs Inc.** 7355 N. W. 54 Court, Fort Lauderdale, Florida 33319, USA. *Outlet* Germany: Ruf Design GmbH, Gewerbealle 4, 4330 Mulheim a.d. Ruhr.

**Leucos Srl.** Via Treviso 777, Scorze, Venice, Italy. *Outlets* France: Artemide SARL, 6–8 rue Basfroi, Paris 75011. Germany: Leucos Deutschland GmbH, Bunsenstrasse 5, Martinsried, B. Munich 8033. Japan: Arflex Japan Ltd, 4565 Kodachi Kawaguchiko-cho, Minimisuru-gun-Yamanashi. The Netherlands: Kreymborg BV, Minervalaan 63, 1077 Amsterdam. Spain: Forum International, Venida de Salvert 25, 46018 Valencia. UK: MW United, 3 Willow Business, London SE26 4QP. USA: Leucos USA Inc., 70 Campus Plaza, Edison, NJ 08837.

**M & Co.** 50 West 17th Street, New York, NY 10011, USA. *Outlet* Germany: Teunen & Teunen, Schloss Johannisberg, 6222 Geisengeim 2.

**Maki Textile Studio.** Chiaki Maki, 899–7 Tothara, Itsukaichi-machi, Nishitamagun, Tokyo 109-01, Japan.

**MAP.** 570 Chapel Street, South Yarra, Melbourne, Victoria, Australia.

**Nani Marquina.** 3 Bonavista, Barcelona 08012, Spain.

**Matsushita Electric Works Ltd.** 1048 Kodama, Osaka 571, Japan. *Outlets* Australia: Panasonic (Australia) Pty Ltd, PO Box 319, 95–99 Epping Road, North Ryde, NSW 2113. Germany: Panasonic Deutschland GmbH, Winsbergring 15, 2000 Hamburg 54. Italy: Fratelli Milani Srl, Via Valsolda 20143, Milan 13. The Netherlands: Haagtechno BV, Rietveldenweg 60, Postbus 236, Den Bosch. Scandinavia: Panasonic Svenska AB, Instrumentagen 29–31, PO Box 47327, 10074 Stockholm, Sweden. UK: Panasonic Business Systems UK, Panasonic House, Willoughby Road, Bracknell, Berks. RG12 4FP. USA: Panasonic Communication & Systems Company, Communication Systems Division, 2 Panasonic Way, Secaucus, NJ 07094.

**Matsushita Seiko Co. Ltd.** 62-2-6 Chome, Imafuku Nishi, Joto-ku, Osaka 536, Japan.

**Ingo Maurer.** 47 Kaiserstrasse, 8000 Munich 40, Germany. *Outlets* France: Altras SARL, 24 rue Lafitte, Paris, 75009. Italy: Pierre Daverio & C. SAS, Via del Colle 3, Casciago 21020. The Netherlands: Peter A. Hesselmans, 284 P. J. Oudstraat, Papendrecht 3354 V.J. Scandinavia (except Sweden): Finn Sloth, 2 Heilsmindevej, Charlottenlund, Denmark 2920. Switzerland: Domani AG, 231 Seefeldstrasse, Zurich 8008. USA: Ivan Luini, 453 West 19th Street, Apt 6a, New York, NY 10011.

**Metalarte SA.** Avda de Barcelona 4, 08970 Saint Joan Despi, Barcelona, Spain. *Outlets* Argentina: Tecnoilar SA, Nicolás A. Caputo, Paraguay 792 5, 1057 Buenos Aires. Australia: Tangent, 6–36 Boronia Street, Redfern NSW 2016. Austria: Molto Luce, Europastrasse 45, 4600 Wels. Belgium: Light SA, Boulevard M. Lemonnier 99, 1000 Brussels. Brazil: Design Alternativo, Rua Marques do Herval 66, CEP 90570-Porto Alegre RS. Canada: Angle International, 460A rue McGill, Montreal, Quebec H2Y 2A3. Chile: Interdesign, Isidora Goyenechea 3200, Santiago de Chile. France: Electrorama, 11 boulevard Saint Germain, 75005 Paris. Germany: Altalinea, 6 Sandhof, 41469 Neuss 21 Norf. Hong Kong: Teamwork Design Studio Ltd, 6A Kiu Yin Commercial Building, 361-363 Lockhart Road, Wanchai. The Netherlands: Hooge Products Verlichting, Moeskampweg 10, 5222 s' Hertogenbosch. Italy: Barovier & Toso Srl,

Fondamenta Vetrai 28, 30141 Murano, Venice. Mexico: Marca Interiores SA de C.V., Insurgentes Sur 1180, Col. del Valle, 03210 Mexico D.F. Portugal: Electro Ravd, Rua da Trindade 1–29, 4002-Porto. Singapore: Relex Electric (F.E.) PTE Ltd, 605b MacPherson Road, 07-14 Citimac Industrial Complex. Switzerland: U.S.W. SA, Château D'Affry, Route de Château D'Affry 33, 1762 Givisiez, Fribourg. UK: Mr Light HMP Group Ltd, 275 Fulham Road, London SW10 9PZ. Uruguay: Artesanos Unidos SA, José E. Rodo 2174, Montevideo. USA: Hinson Lamps, 27–35 Jackson Avenue, Long Island City, NY 11101-2817. Venezuela: Iluminación Helios CA, Parque Central, Edif. Anauco, Sotano 1, Local DS-42, Caracas 1015-A.

**METAmoderne.** Kniestrasse 22, 3000 Hanover 1, Germany.

**Meubels en daavomheen.** 8A11 1e Looiersdwarsstraat, Amsterdam 1016, The Netherlands.

**Mitsubishi USA.** 5665 Plaza Drive, Cypress, California 90630, USA.

**Molteni & Co. SpA.** Via Rossini 50, 20034 Gittisano, Milan, Italy. *Outlet* UK: Orchard Associates, Box No.65, Teddington, Middx TW11 9ED.

**Montis BV.** Steenstraat 2, Postbus 153, Dongen 5100 AD, Holland. *Outlets* Germany: Montis Deutschland GmbH, Adolf Kolpingstrasse 13, 4514 Ostercappeln. USA: Montis America Inc., PO Box 7591, High Point, NC 27264.

**Moormann Möbel-Produktions- und Handels GmbH.** Kirchplatz, Aschau im Chiemgau 8213, Germany. *Outlet* Switzerland: Andome engros, Pfungener Strasse 77, Oberembrach 8425.

**Morphos.** See *Acerbis International*

**National Panasonic, Japan.** Matsushita Electric Works Ltd, 1048 Kadoma, Osaka 571, Japan.

**Nemo Srl (Group Cassina).** 69 Via Piave, Rovellasca 22069, Como, Italy.

**Néotù.** 25 rue du Renard, 75004 Paris, France. *Outlet* USA: 133 Greene Street, New York, NY 10012.

**Neto Furniture Design Ltd.** 74 Hei Beivar St., Tel Aviv, Israel.

**Nihon Sheet Glass Co. Ltd.** 2-1-7 Kaigan, Minato-ku, Tokyo 106, Japan.

**Nihon Touheki Ltd.** Nendozaka Tokithu Zuchi, Tokitu-choh, Toki-shi, Gifu-ken, Japan.

**North Studio Inc.** 58 Stewart Street, Toronto, Ontario, Canada.

**Noto – Zeus.** Via Vigevano 8, 20144 Milan, Italy. *Outlets* France: Jean Gabriel Robin, Chemin des Sables, 69970 Chaponnay. Germany: Sabine Hainlen, Hermann Kurz Strasse 14, 7000 Stuttgart 1. Japan: Ambiente International, Sumitomo Seimei Bldg, 3-1-30, Minami-Aoyama, Minato-ku, Tokyo 107. The Netherlands: Andrea Kok Agenturen, Pilatus 4, 1186 EK Amstelveen. Scandinavia/Spain: Noto Srl, Via Vigevano 8, 20144 Milan, Italy. UK: Viaduct, 1–10 Summer's Street, London SE1R 5BD. USA: Modern Age, 795 Broadway, New York, NY 10003.

**Novo Nordisk A/S.** Novo Allé, Bagsvaerd 2880, Denmark.

**Nuno Corporation.** Axis Bldg, 5-17-1 Roppongi, Minato-ku, Tokyo 106, Japan.

**Objets Pompadour.** 74 Bis rue de Paris, Meudon 92190, France.

**Olivari B. SpA.** Via G. Matteotti 140, Borgomanero 28021, Italy. *Outlets* Belgium: Van Osta Olav, Hofstraat 76, 21090 Essen. Canada: Ferleo Hardware, 72 Kincort Street, Toronto, Ontario M6M 3E3. France: LA Quincaillerie, 4 Blvd St Germain, Paris 75005. Japan: Shukoh Co. Ltd, 2-10-2-chome, Yaguchi, Ohta-ku, Tokyo 146. The Netherlands: Van Osta Frank, 92 Bredaseweg, 4702 KV Roosendaal.

**Olivetti Italia SpA.** Via Lorenteggio 257, 20152 Milan, Italy. *Outlets* France: Olivetti France, Cedex 69, 92047 La Défense, Paris. Germany: Olivetti GmbH, 34 Lyoner Strasse, 6000 Frankfurt am Main. The Netherlands: Olivetti Nederland, 19–21 Verbeekstraat, PO Box 111-72, 2332 CA Leiden. Scandinavia: Olivetti A/S, 107–111 Lersø Parkalle, 2100 Copenhagen, Denmark. Spain: Olivetti España SA, Conde de Peñalver 84, 28006 Madrid. UK: Olivetti UK, Olivetti House, 86–88 Upper Richmond Road, London SW15 2VR. USA: Olivetti North America, E 22425 Appleway, Liberty Lake, WA 99019-9534.

**OWO.** 1 rue Anaury, Montfort l'Anaury 78410, France. *Outlets* Germany: Schroer KG, Alte Liner Strasse 135, Postfach 2627, Krefeld 4150. Italy: Stile Mobili Moderni, Via Brozzoni 9, Brescia 25100. Japan: Philippe Terrien Kig, Kobari Building SF, Nishi Azabu, 4-11-30 Minato-ku, Tokyo 106. The Netherlands: Espaces et Lignes, rue Uvens Straat, 1210 Brussels, Belgium. Scandinavia: Design Distribution, Doebelnsgatan 38A, 11352 Stockholm,

Sweden. Spain: Vincon, Paseo de Gracia 96, 08008 Barcelona. UK: Design Museum, Butler's Wharf, London SE1 2YD. USA: Modern Age/DVDH, 121 Greene Street, New York, NY 10012.

**Oxo International.** 230 Fifth Avenue, New York, NY 10001, USA. *Outlet* UK: Jim Wilkinson Promotions, Burnley BB11 5SK, Lancs.

**Palazzetti.** 515 Madison Avenue, 2nd Floor, New York, NY 10022, USA.

**Patton Design.** 8 Pasteur Ste 170, Irvine, CA 92718, USA.

**Pentagon.** Dreieichstrasse 39, 6000 Frankfurt am Main 70, Germany.

**Perobell.** Avenida Arraona 23, 08206 Sabadell, Barcelona, Spain. *Outlets* Austria: Otto Dunkelblum, Vienna. Belgium: Frank Billiet, Kortrijk. Canada: Tendex Silko, Toronto. Denmark: Frank Rasmussen, Virum. France: Francisco Chamizo, Tarbes. Greece: Avax, Athens. Holland: Amda. Frans Stroosnijder, Amstelveen. Italy: Res-Nova, Turin. Portugal: Paragrama, Porto. Singapore: X-Tra Designs, 86–87 East Coast Road, Singapore 1542. Taiwan: Anivant International (VIVO), No. 107-1 Section 4, Hsin. YI Road, Taipei. UK: Maison Designs Retail, London.

**Philips Consumer Electronics.** Alexanderstrasse 2, 2000 Hamburg 1, Germany.

**Philips International BV.** PO Box 218, 5600 MD Eindhoven, The Netherlands. *Outlets* Austria: Österreichische Philips Industrie GmbH, 64 Triester Strasse, 1100 Vienna. Belgium: NV Philips, 2 De Brouckereplein, PO Box 218, 1000 Brussels. Denmark: Philips Elapparat AS, 80 Pragsboulevard, 2300 Copenhagen. Finland: OY Philips AB, 8 Kaivokatu, Helsinki. France: SA Philips Industriale et Commerciale, 50 avenue Montaigne, 75380 Paris. Germany: Philips GmbH, Unternehmensbereich Haustechnik, Kilanstrasse 19, 8500 Nuremberg; Allgemeine Deutsche Philips Ind. GmbH, Steindamm 94, 2000 Hamburg. Italy: Philips Italia SA, Piazza IV Novembre 3, 20100 Milan. Japan: Philips Industrial Development and Consultants Co. Ltd, Shuwa, Shinagawa Bldg, 26-33 Takanawa 3-chome, Minato-ku, Tokyo 108. Norway: Norsk AS Philips, PO Box 5040, 6 Soerkedaksveien, Oslo 3. Spain: Philips Iberica SAE, 2 Martinez Villergas, Apertado 2065, 28027 Madrid. Sweden: Philips Norden AB, 11584 Stockholm. UK:

Philips Electrical and Associated Industries Ltd, Arundel Great Court, 8 Arundel Street, London WC2 3DT. USA: North American Philips Corporation, 100 East 42nd Street, New York, NY 10017.

**Paolo Piva.** 2765 San Polo, Venice 30100, Italy.

**PK Electronics.** 575 Anton Blvd, Suite 300, Costa Mesa, CA 92626, USA.

**Plan Créatif/Crabtree Hall.** 10 rue Mercoeur, Paris 75011, France. *Outlet* UK: Plan Créatif/Crabtree Hall, 70 Crabtree Lane, London SW6 6LT.

**Pol International Design Company.** 123 Chaussée de Mons, 1070 Brussels, Belgium. *Outlets* Belgium/Luxembourg: Tradix SA, 90–92 rue du Mail, 1050 Brussels. France: The Conran Shop, rue du Bac 117, 75007 Paris. Germany/Austria/Switzerland: D-Tec, Telleringstrasse 5, 4000 Düsseldorf 13, Germany. Italy/USA: Montina, Via Palmarina 4, 33048 San Giovanni al Natisone, Udine, Italy.

**Product M.** 500-2 Gyìda-shi, Saitama, Japan.

**Punt Mobles SL.** Islas Baleares 48, Pol. Ind. Fuente del Jarro, 46980 Paterna, Valenica, Spain. *Outlets* France: Dominique Devot, 11 rue Azais Barthes, Beziers 34500. Germany: Designfocus GmbH, 1 Konrad Adeanauer, Erftstadt 5042. Italy: C & C Distribuzione, Loc. Grand Chemin 1, Saint Christophe, Aosta 11020. The Netherlands: Heneka & Goldschmidt, 10401 Eerste Constantijn Huygensstraat, Amsterdam 1054 BZ. Switzerland: Claudia Marlier Pollo, 40 Rebbergstrasse, Oberengstringen 8102.

**Renault Italia SpA.** 1159 Via Tiburtina, Rome 00156, Italy.

**Casimir Reynders.** 16 Pieter van Houdtstraat, Berlingen 3580, Limburg, Belgium.

**Royal College of Art.** Kensington Gore, London SW7 2EU, UK.

**Royal Copenhagen A/S.** 45 Smallegade, Copenhagen 2000, Denmark. *Outlets* France: Georg Jensen SARL, 239 rue Saint-Honoré, Paris 75001. Germany: Royal Copenhagen GmbH, Musterhaus am Messekreisel, 30 Deutz-Mülheimer Strasse, Cologne 21 5000. Italy: Royal Copenhagen (Italy) Srl, Via Rovigno 13, Milan 20125. Japan: Royal Copenhagen (Japan) Ltd, 10th Floor Mita Kokusai Building, 1-4-28 Mita, Minato-ku, Tokyo 108. UK:

Royal Copenhagen Porcelain & Georg Jensen Ltd, 70 St John Street, London EC1M 4DT. USA: Royal Copenhagen Incorporated, 27 Holland Avenue, White Plains, New York, NY 10603.

**Ruine Design Associates, Inc.** Suite 6A, 250 West 27th Street, New York, NY 10001, USA. *Outlets* Canada: Telio and Cie, 1407 rue de la Montagne, Montreal H3G 1Z3, Canada. Germany: iD GmbH, Gilleshutte 99, 4052 Korschenbroich 1. Spain: Scarabat, Ctra de Benifasar 11, 43560 La Senia, Tarragona.

**Toby Russell.** 1 Arlington Cottages, Sutton Lane, London W4 4HB, UK.

**Sakaegi Design Studio.** 1-74, Nakamizuno-cho, Aichi-ken, Japan.

**Sambonet SpA.** 62 Via XXVI Aprile, Vercelli 13100, Italy. *Outlets* Germany: Rosenthal Aktiengesellschaft, Gastronomie Service, Havilandstrasse 62, Postfach 1, W-8598 Waldershof. Japan: Shimizu Tableware Co. Ltd, 6-4-2 Kokubo, Kofu City, Yamanashi Prefecture. UK: Chinacraft Hotelware, Parke House, 130 Barbly Road, London W10 6BW. USA: Sambonet USA Inc., 355 Murrayhill Parkway, East Rutherford, NJ07073.

**Sawaya & Moroni SpA.** Via Manzoni 11, 20121 Milan, Italy. *Outlet* UK: The Ikon Corporation, B5L Metropolitan Wharf, Wapping Wall, London E1 9SS.

**Winfried Scheuer.** 53 Leinster Square, London W2 4PU, UK.

**Jurgen Schmid,** Zeppelinstrasse 53, Ammerbuchl 7403, Germany.

**SCP Ltd.** 135–139 Curtain Road, London EC2A 3BX, UK. *Outlets* Germany: Teunen & Teunen, Postfach 36, 6222 Geisenheim 2. Japan: Kiya Gallery, Office 9-2 Sarugaku-cho, Shibuya-ku, Tokyo. The Netherlands: Jones Import, Ch de Ruisbroek 290, 1620 Drogenbos, Belgium. Scandinavia: C & B1 Interior, Birgerjarlsg 34, Box 26126, Stockholm, Sweden. Spain: Pilma, Llanca 33, Barcelona 08015. Taiwan: Vivo 107-1, Section 4, Hsin Yi Road 10657, Taiei. USA: Palazzetti Inc., 515 Madison Avenue, New York, NY 10022.

**Seiko Instruments USA, Inc.** 1130 Ringwood Court, San Jose, California 95131, USA.

**Masafumi Sekine.** 1505-3, Oya-cho, Omiya-city, Saitamaken 330, Japan.

**Sharp Corporation.** 22-22 Nagaike-cho, Abeno-ku, Osaka 545, Japan.

**SIG Workshop Co. Ltd.** 3-4 Asahigaoka, Matsto-Ishikawa 924, Japan.

**Silit Werke GmbH & Co. KG.** Neufraer Strasse 2–8, 7940 Riedlingen, Germany. *Outlets* France: Silit France, B.P. 175, 71100 Chalon/Saone. Italy: Silit-Italiana Srl, Via Pacinotti 6, 39100 Bolzano. Switzerland: Silit-Schweiz AG, Tagernanstrasse 16, 8645 Jona.

**Siom Inc.** 5-10-10 Harue-cho, Edogawa-ku, Tokyo 134, Japan.

**Sony Corporation.** 6-7-35 Kitashinagawa, Shinagawa-ku, Tokyo 141, Japan.

**Space.** 12 Dolland Street, London SE11 5LN. *Outlet* France: Gladys Mougin, 30 rue de Lille, Paris 75007.

**Structure Design.** 188 Josefstrasse, 8005 Zurich, Switzerland. *Outlets* Germany: Anthologie Quartett, Schloss Huennefeld, Haus Sorgenfrei, 4515 Bad Essen 1. Italy: Dilmos Galerie, Piazza San Marco 1, 20121 Milan.

**Stua SA.** Polifono 26, Astifarrafa, 20115 San Sebastian, Guipúzcoa, Spain.

**Sunsha Comm. & Marketing.** G-19 Suyog Ind. Estate, LBS Marg. Vikhroli, Bombay 400083, Maharashtra, India.

**Swatch Telecom.** Jakob Stämpflistrasse 94, 2504 Biel-Bienne, Switzerland. *Outlets* Italy: SMH Italia SpA, Milanofiori, Strada 7, Palazzo R1, 20089 Rozzano, Milan. UK: SMH (UK) Ltd, Empress Road, Bevois Valley, Southampton, Hants SO9 7BW.

**Takata Lemnos Inc.** 511 Hayakawa, Toyama, Japan.

**Takefu Knife Village.** Hamono-Kogyodanchi, Ikenokami, Takefu-Fukui 915, Japan.

**Takenaka Works Co. Ltd.** 2-1-16 Miyuki-cho, Takaoka-City, Toyama, Japan.

**Taylor Made Golf Co.** 2271 Cosmos Court, Carlsbad, CA 92009, USA.

**The Glasshouse.** 65 Long Acre, London WC2E 9JH, UK.

**Walter Thut AG.** 5115 Möriken, Switzerland. *Outlet* Germany: Moormann Möbel Produktions- und Handels GmbH, Kirchplatz, 8213 Aschau im Chiemgau.

**Toshiba Corporation.** 1-1 Shibaura 1-chome, Minato-ku, Tokyo 105-01, Japan.

**Toto Ltd.** 7-3-37 Akasaka, Minato-ku, Tokyo 107, Japan.

**Gerard van der Berg.** 9d Prinsenkade, Breda 4811 VB, Holland.

**Vanlux SA.** Poligono Eitua s/n, 48240 Berriz, Spain. *Outlets* Australia: Inlite Pty Ltd, 76–78 Balmain Street, Richmond 3121 Victoria. Austria: Plan Licht, Vomperbach 187a, 6130 Schwaz. Benelux: Hilite NV, Leopold II Laan 35, 8000 Bruges, Belgium. Canada: Eurofase Canada Inc., 6900 Airport Road Unit 239B, Box 62, Mississauga, Ontario L4V 1EB. Denmark: Pasta Lab International, Duevej 54, 2000 Copenhagen. Finland: Inno Interior KY, Merikatu 1, 00140 Helsinki. France: Luci France, 96 Boulevard Auguste Blanqui, 75013 Paris. Germany: B Lux Deutschland GmbH, Tülbeckstrasse 55, 8000 Munich 2. Hong Kong: Krohn Ltd, 69 Jervois Street. Italy: Contempora di Zannier Luigi, Piazza Rizzolatti 4, 33090 Clauzetto. Japan: Akane Inc., 5-10 Higashinkano, 5-chome, Nakaho-ku, Tokyo. Portugal: Parisete Moveis e Decoracoes, Avenida de Paris 7A, 1000 Lisbon. Singapore: X.Tra Designs Private Ltd, 336 Tanjong Katong Road. South Africa: Peter Stuart, PO Box 782962, 02146 Sandton. Switzerland: Dedalus, C/Via Gismonda No. 17, 6850 Mendrisio. Taiwan: Pinhole International, No. 11, Lane 639 Min Sheng E Road, Taipei 10447. UK: Candell Ltd, Carrera House, 33 Sutherland Road, Walthamstow, London E17 6BH. USA: Artup Corporation, Alex Lodge, 3101 Shannon Street, Santa Ana, CA 92704.

**Venini SpA.** 50 Fond.ta Vetrai, Murano, Venice 30141, Italy. *Outlets* France: Collectania, 168 rue de Rivoli, Paris 75001. Germany: Graf Bethusy - Huc Vertriebs, 1 Hans-Sachs-Strasse, Krailling 8033. Hong Kong/Singapore: Lane Crawford Ltd, 28 Tong Chong Street, 8/F Somerset House, Hong Kong (Quarry Bay). Japan: Kitaichi Glass Co. Ltd, 1-6-10 Hanazono, Otaru, Hokkaido 047. Monaco: L'Art Venitien, 4 Avenue de la Madone, Monaco 98000. The Netherlands: Desideri, 50 Gossetlaan, Groot-Bijgaarden 1702, Belgium. Saudi Arabia: Khair M. Al-Khadra Trading Estate, PO Box 1376, Jeddah 21431. UK: Liberty Retail Ltd, Regent Street, London W1R 6AH. USA: Hampstead Lighting & Accessories, Suite 100, 1150 Alpha Drive, Alpharetta, GA 30201.

**Vericom GmbH.** Hauptstrasse 8, W-8901 Adelsried, Germany.

**Verrerie de Nonfoux.** 1417 Nonfoux, Switzerland. *Outlets* France: Quartz Diffusion, 12 rue des Quatre Vents, 75006 Paris. Germany: Lichtenberg Studio Glass, Christel-Schmidt Allee 25, 2070 Ahrensburg. USA: New Glass, 345 West Broadway, New York, NY 10013.

**Vest Leuchten GmbH.** Piaristengasse 21, Vienna 1080, Austria.

**Via Inc.** 1480 Kleppe Lane, Sparks, Nevada 89431, USA.

**Vitra (International) AG.** Klünenfeldstrasse 20, 4127 Birsfelden, Switzerland. *Outlets* Austria: Vitra Ges.m.b.H., Pfeilgasse 35, 1080 Vienna. Belgium: N.V. Vitra Belgium SA, Woluwelaan 140A, 1831 Diegem. France: Vitra Sarl, 40 rue Violet, 75015 Paris. Germany: Vitra GmbH, Charles Eames-Strasse 2, 7858 Weil am Rhein. Italy: Vitra Italia Srl, Corso di Porta Romana 6, 20122 Milan. Japan: Haller Japan Ltd, Canal Tower, 9-3 Koamicho Nihonbashi, Chuo-ku, Tokyo 103. The Netherlands: Vitra Nederland BV, Assumburg 73, 1081 GB, Amsterdam. Saudi Arabia: Vitra Middle East Ltd, PO Box 64 80, Dammam 31442. Spain: Vitra Hispania SA, Serrano No. 5, 4o, 4a, 28001 Madrid. UK: Vitra Ltd, 13 Grosvenor Street, London W1X 9FB. USA: Vitra Seating Inc., 30–20 Thomson Avenue, Long Island City, New York, NY 11101.

**Wales and Wales.** The Longbarn Workshop, Muddles Green, Chiddingly BN8 6HU, East Sussex, UK.

**Wilkinson Sword GmbH.** Schützenstrasse 110, 42659 Solingen, Germany.

**Franz Wittmann Möbelwerkstätten.** 3492 Etsdorf, Kamp, Austria.

**Woka Lamps Vienna.** Singerstrasse 16, 1010 Vienna, Austria. *Outlets* France: Altras, rue Lafitte 24, 75009 Paris. Germany: HJ Rottwinkel, Schwarzbacher-strasse 7, 1000 Berlin 31. Hong Kong: Le Cadre Gallery, 4B Causeway Bay, 8 Sunning Road. Italy: Gabrielle Galimberti, Via Ponchielli 44, 20052 Monza. Japan: Seibu Department Stores Ltd, Sunshine 60, 1-1 Higashi-Ikebukuro 3-chome, Toshima-ku, Tokyo. The Netherlands: Art Collection, Win Hermeler, Weijland 63, 2415 BD Nieuwerburg. Spain: Bd. Ediciones de Diseño, Mallorca 291, Barcelona 37. Sweden/Norway: Idé Individuell, Kungsholmstrand 185, 11248 Stockholm. Switzerland: FA Anliker, Vitrine AG, Gerechtigkeitsgasse 73, 3011 Bern. USA: George Kovacs Inc., 24 West 40th Street, 12th Floor, New York, NY 10018.

**X99.** Xantenerstrasse 99, Köln Nippes 50733, Germany. *Outlets* Switzerland: Mobitare AG, Tramstrasse 7, 5034 Suhr. USA: TE-MA, 14 Maple Lane, Woodstock, NY 12498.

**Yamada Shomei Lighting Co. Inc.** 3-16-12 Sotokanda, Chiyoda-ku, Tokyo 101, Japan.

*Outlet* Italy: I Guzzini Illuminazione Srl, 62019 Recanati, PO Box 39-59.

**Yamagiwa Corporation.** 4-1-1 Soto Kamda, Chiyoda-ku, Tokyo, Japan.

**Yamaha Corporation.** 1-7-1 Yuraku-cho, Chiyoda-ku, Tokyo 100, Japan.

**Yamaha Design Laboratory.** 10-1 Nakazawa-cho, Hamamatsu-shi, Shizuoka, Japan.

**Zanotta SpA.** Via Vittorio Veneto 57, 20054 Nova Milanese, Italy. *Outlets* Australia: Arredorama International Pty Ltd, 1 Ross Street, Glebe, NSW No. 2037. Austria: Prodomo, 35–37 Flachgasse, 1060 Vienna. Belgium: Zaira Mis, 35 Boulevard Saint Michel, 1040 Brussels. Denmark: Paustian, 2 Kalkbraendrilbskaj, 2100 Copenhagen. Germany: Fulvio Folci, 14 Dahlienweg, 4000 Düsseldorf 30. Japan: Nova Oshima Co. Ltd, Sakakura Bldg, Akasaka, Minato-ku, Tokyo. The Netherlands: Hansje Kalff, 8 Puttensestraat, 1181 Je Amstelveen, Holland. Norway: Bente Holm, 64 Parkveien, Oslo 2. Spain: Bd. Ediciones de Diseño, 291 Mallorca, 08037 Barcelona. Sweden: Inside, 37 Hamngatan, 11147 Stockholm. Switzerland: Peter Kaufmann, 123 Rychenbergstrasse, 8400 Winterhur. UK: The Architectural Trading Co. Ltd, 219–29 Shaftesbury Avenue, London WC2H 8AR. USA: International Contract Furnishings, 305 East 63rd Street, New York, NY 10021.

**Zerodisegno (Division of Quattrocchio).** Via Isonzo 51, Alessandria 15100, Italy. *Outlets* Germany: Present Perfect, 95 Frauenlobstrasse, Mainz 6500. The Netherlands: Evat-Thea Verhoeven Design, 5/a Lambertusstraat, TB Hedikhuizen 5256. Spain: José Cunill Bonmam, San Juan B./ La Salle 1, Esca 3o, 29, Premia de Mar 08330, Barcelona. Switzerland: Pur Sitzmobel, 33 Gaswerkstrasse, Langenthal 4900. USA: Zero US Corporation, Industrial Circle, Lincoln, RI 02865.

Acquisitions by design collections in 1993. Dates given in parentheses refer to the dates of the designs (from 1960 to the present day).

# Acquisitions

## Austria

Austrian Museum of Applied Arts, Vienna

**Ralmund Abraham** architectural model, *Wohn-und Geschäftshaus Friedrichstrasse Berlin* (1983–87)

**Ralmund Abraham** architectural model, *Haus Traviattagasse*

**Vito Acconci** two sculptures, *Name Calling* (1984–90) and *Multi Bed* (1992)

**Evelyne Egerer** sculpture, *Ewig Dein* (1988)

**Frank Gehry** architectural model, *House Santa Monica*

**Jenny Holzer** electronic signs, *13 Signs* (1992)

**Jenny Holzer** cast of a Biedermeier sofa, *Aluminium Sofa* (1992)

**Ulrike Johannsen** object, *Reise Reliqular*

**Donald Judd** *Show Case* (1993)

**Peter Kogler** curtain, *Ameise* (1993)

**Jasper Morrison** installation

**Margarethe Schütte-Lihotzky** *Furniture for Room*

**Philippe Starck** three armchairs, *Richard II* (1984)

**Rosemarie Trockel** carpet

## Brazil

Museu de Arte de São Paulo

**José Carlos Bornancini** camping equipment, manufactured by Mundial Brazil

**José Carlos Bornancini** letter opener with gold inlay, manufactured by Zivi SA

**Gaspar Glusberg** two lamps, manufactured by Modulor

**Nathan George Horwitt** *Museum Watch*, manufactured by Movado Watch Corporation

**Lufthansa** luggage labels

**Erik Magnussen** three thermos flasks (1976), manufactured by Stelton A/S

**Pelikan Designer** Tricycle, *Rabo*, manufactured by Rabo A/S

**Philippe Starck** toothbrush

**Thygessen and Sorensen** Chair, *MO 8000*, manufactured by Magnus Olesen A/S

**Andy Warhol** watch, *Times Five* (1987), manufactured by Movado Watch Corporation

## Canada

Musée des Arts Décoratifs de Montréal

**Junichi Arai** textile, *Basket Weave Big Pocket*

**Constantin Boym** clock, *Mona Lisa*

**Constantin Boym** vase, *Recycle* (1988)

**Andrea Branzi** coffee tables, *Euclidi* (1988)

**Andrea Branzi** bookshelf, *Piccolo albero* (1991)

**Antonio Cagianelli** mirror, *Narcisse-cream* (1991)

**Masahiro Chatani** Q Card

**Frank Gehry** chair, *High Sticking* (prototype) (1990)

**Frank Gehry** side chair, *High Sticking* (1991)

**Frank Gehry** armchair, *Hat Trick* (1991)

**Fujiwo Ishimoto** textile, *Kalliomaa* (1988)

**Kyoko Kumai** fibre work, *Blowing in the wind* (1988)

**Shiro Kuramata** vase

**Shiro Kuramata** stool

**Masayuki Kurokawa** desk accessories

**Masayuki Kurokawa** stacking trays, *Pyramid* (1991)

**Vannetta Le Coadic** necklace

**Locadia** speaker

**Bruno Martinazzi** bracelet, *Goldfinger*

**Shin Matsunaga** posters

**Howard Meister** table, *Signal* (1984)

**Alessandro Mendini** vase (1986)

**Bruce Metcalf** brooch, *Cactus Head in a Frame of Missiles* (1987)

**Forrest Myers** *Thicket* (1991)

**Sinya Okayama** posters

**U.G. Sato** *Worm Eaten Box* (1991)

**Serengeti** sunglasses with case

**Ettore Sottsass** textile, *Schizzo* (1983)

**Reiko Sudo** textile, *Stainless Embossed*

**Shigeru Uchida** clock, *Dear Morris*

**Masanori Umeda** coffee set, *Mutsugoro* (c. 1980)

**Vent Design Associates** wetsuit, *Animal* (1988–89)

**Todd Wood** gardening tools, *Plus Four*

## Denmark

Museum of Decorative Art, Copenhagen

**Hans Amos Christensen** chair (1991)

**Riccardo Dalisi** Neapolitanian coffee maker (1979), manufactured by Alessi

**Danese** 25 objects, mostly by Enzo Mari and Bruno Danese (1960–87)

**Gunvor and Niels Jørgen Haugesen** bookcases (1991), manufactured by Maibølle Møbler

**Helly Hensen A/S** vinyl clothing (1970s)

**Finn Juhl** table lamp (1963), manufactured by Lyfa

**Birger Kaipiainen** dinner service, *Eeva* (1970), manufactured by Arabia Finland

**Vico Magistretti** table lamp, *Eclisse* (1967), manufactured by Artemide

**Eric Magnussen** child's chair (1968)

**Lars Mathiesen/Komplot Design** TransitCarrier (1989–91)

**Verner Panton** Cone chair (1961)

**Philippe Starck** table, *Tippy Jackson* (1982), manufactured by Aleph

**Philippe Starck** four different chairs

**Reinhold Weiss** table ventilator, *HL1* (1961), manufactured by Braun

**Bjørn Wiinblad** coffee service, *Romanze* (1960–61), manufactured by Rosenthal

**Bjørn Wiinblad** coffee service, *Assimitria* (1985), manufactured by Rosenthal

**Bjørn Wiinblad** coffee service, *Zauberflöte* (1968), manufactured by Rosenthal

## France

**Musée des Arts Décoratifs, Paris**

**Alessi** draining board, manufactured by Alessi

**Alessi** teapot, manufactured by Alessi

**André Arbus** armchair

**François Arnal** table, manufactured by Atelier A

**François Arnal** stool (1970), manufactured by Atelier A

**Artcodif** decanter, manufactured by Artcodif

**Artcodif** glass, manufactured by Artcodif

**Gian Paolo Babetto** bracelet (1992)

**Mario Barbaglia and Marco Colombo** table lamp (1985), manufactured by Italiana Luce

**Cini Boeri** armchair, manufactured by FIAM

**Bülow-Hübe** cup and saucer (1987), manufactured by Royal Copenhagen

**Bülow-Hübe** spoon (1989), manufactured by Royal Copenhagen

**César** desk (1966)

**Joe Colombo** armchair (1964)

**Claude Courtecuisse** seat and table, *Ondulys*, manufactured by Printemps

**Claude Courtecuisse** seat, manufactured by Mobel Italia

**Claude Courtecuisse** two seats, manufactured by Cattaneo

**Dan Dailey** vase (1988)

**Danese** collection of desks and tableware, manufactured by Danese

**Albert Duraz** a range of jewellery including rings, brooches, pendants and necklaces (1960–90)

**Mokoto Fujiwara** sculpture (1991)

**Ingjerd Havenevold** bracelet (1992)

**Massimo Iosa Ghini** decanter

**Hisatoshi Iwata** vase (1991)

**Itoko Iwata** dish (1990)

**Danny Lane** table, manufactured by FIAM

**Etienne Leperlier** goblet (1991)

**Jean Leppien** *Duisburg* (1968)

**Stanislas Libensky** *Arcus II*

**Alberto Meda** chair (1989), manufactured by Alias

**Alberto Meda** ceiling light (1990)

**Ursula Morley-Price** goblet (1991)

**Pascal Mourgue** armchair, *Bridge* (1990), manufactured by Fermob

**Rémy Muratore** glassware (1990)

**Verner Panton** screen (late 1960s)

**Mario Pinton** ring (1992)

**Oldrich Pliva** sculpture (1986)

**Paolo Rizatto** ceiling light (1990), manufactured by Luceplan

**Paolo Rizatto** standard lamp (1988), manufactured by Luceplan

**Zofia Rostad** collection of crockery, manufactured by Philippe Deshoulières

**Pete Sans** seat (1987), manufactured by Bd. Ediciones

**Richard Sapper** armchair, manufactured by B & B Italia

**Afra Scarpa** seat (1989), manufactured by Meritalia

**Tobia Scarpa** seat (1989), manufactured by Meritalia

**Philippe Starck** lamp (1988), manufactured by Flos

**Philippe Starck** armchair (1981), manufactured by Baleri

**Roger Tallon** armchair (1966)

**Detlef Thomas** ring (1992)

**Oscar Tusquets** armchair (1986)

**Yukio Veno** sculpture (1990)

**Massimo Vignelli** table, manufactured by Casigliani

**Frantisek Vizner** goblet (1972/1986)

## Germany

**Kunstmuseum Düsseldorf im Ehrenhof**

**Christian Borngraber** collection of furniture and lamps (1993)

**Henning Koppel** jug (1962), manufactured by Torben Orskov

**Jasper Morrison** chair (1984)

**Richard Sapper and Marco Zanuso** telephone (1966), manufactured by Fa. Siemens

**Jean-Pierre Vitrac** picnic set (1977), manufactured by Diam

**Zanotta** sofa (c. 1968), manufactured by Zanotta

**Vitra Design Museum, Weil am Rhein**
The collection is devoted primarily to the development of the chair over the last 140 years. It was opened in November 1989 and is intended to serve as an exhibition space as well as a permanent collection. Some major acquisitions of last year include:

**Richard Artschwager** three chairs

**Mario Bellini** *Teneride* (prototype)

**Pierre Chareau** table and desk

**Frank Gehry** two x *Little Beaver*

**René Herbst** chair, *Sandows*

**Coop Himmelblau** *Vodöl*

**Shiro Kuramata** *Hommage à Hoffmann*

**Serge Mouille** several lamps

**Marc Newson** chaise-longue, *Lokheed*

**Isamu Noguchi** table

**Schinkel** cast-iron chair

**Wilhelm Wagenfeld** *Kubus*

## Japan

There are no public design museums in Japan at the present time. However, there are approximately 15 in the planning stage with no fixed date for completion. The Suntory Design Museum is privately run and is scheduled to open next year. As for permanent collections in museums and galleries in Japan, there are a few for posters only, but not for products. There are no concrete plans for permanent collections for other items, but there is a possibility that such a collection could be founded within the next three years.

## The Netherlands

### Museum Boymans-van Beuningen, Rotterdam

**Gerry Baptist** cupboard, *Metafour* (1991), manufactured by Gerry Baptist

**Theo Remy** cupboard with drawers (1991), manufactured by Theo Remy

**Jan Siebers** mirror, *Timide* (1991), manufactured by Mirrorglass

**Bořek Šípek** coat stand (1989), manufactured by Vitra

**Bořek Šípek** three vases, *Isotta, 407* and *212* (1991), manufactured by Alterego and Driade

**Ettore Sottsass** two vases (c. 1975), manufactured by Vistosi

**Ettore Sottsass** two vases, *Me Stesso* and *Mai e Mai pui* (1992), manufactured by Bitossi

### Stedelijk Museum, Amsterdam

**Ron Arad** chair, *Eight by One* (1993)

**Ron Arad** bookshelf, *Mini Bookworm* (1993)

**Rob Birza** service (1990)

**Barbara Broekman** carpet (1993)

**Aldo Cibic** writing table, *Sophia* (1985)

**Aldo Cibic and C. Ongaro** lamp, *Buenos Aires* (1986)

**Danese** index (1993)

**Daquin** tapestry, *Pli horizontal* (1974)

**M. Dumas** service (1988)

**Niels Haugesen** chair, *X-line* (1970)

**Richard Hutten** table-chair (1991)

**Enzo Mari** box (1992)

**Ingo Maurer** lamp, *Tijuca* (1989)

**Ulf Moritz** fabric, *Saturn* (1992)

**Ulf Moritz** fabric, *Paradisis* (1992)

**Barbara Nanning** schaalvorm (1992)

**Barbara Nanning** ceramic object (1992)

**Claudio Nardi** chair, *Alice* (1991)

**Ninaber/Peters/Krouwel** memo-holder (1993)

**Ninaber/Peters/Krouwel** Siemens spotlights (1990)

**Dieter Rams** chair (1970)

**Richard Sapper** lamps (1992)

**M. Schouten** service (1989)

**H. Schuil** service (1988)

**Peter Shire** armchair, *Bel Air* (1982)

**Bořek Šípek** Sèvres porcelain (1991)

**Bořek Šípek** cutlery, *Alix* (1988)

**Ettore Sottsass** bookcase, *Malabar* (1982)

**Ettore Sottsass** bookcase, *Metro* (1983)

**Ettore Sottsass** vase, *Voglio Dire* (1992)

**Ettore Sottsass** vase, *Mi accorgo* (1992)

**George Sowden** chair, *Gloucester* (1986)

**Henk Stallinga** lamp, *Watt* (1993)

**Philippe Starck** prototype lamp (1992)

**Philippe Starck** vase (1988)

**Peter Struyken** service (1989)

**Masanori Umeda** cabinet, *Ginza* (1982)

**R. van Koningsbruggen** service (1989)

**F. van Nieuwenborg** lamp, *Lazurro* (1992)

**A. and H. van Onck** cutlery, *Serafino* (1992)

## Sweden

### Nationalmuseum, Stockholm

**Charlotte Alexanderson** unglazed earthenware candlesticks (1992)

**Love Arbén** cupboard, manufactured by Lammhults AB

**Maria Bengtzon/Ergonomi Design Gruppen AB** cutlery for the disabled (1992), manufactured by RFSU Rehab

**Acton Bjørn** typewriter, *Facit Model 1820* (1969), manufactured by Facit AB

**Karin Björquist** pieces from the Nobel service (1991), made in celebration of the 90th anniversary of the Nobel prize; manufactured by Gustavsberg/Rörstrand

**Anna Carlgren** object, *Guldstav* (1990)

**Gunnar Cyrén** pieces from the Nobel service, glass (1991), made in celebration of the 90th anniversary of the Nobel prize; manufactured by Sandviks glassworks

**Gunnar Cyrén** cutlery (1992), made in celebration of the 90th anniversary of the Nobel prize; manufactured by Älghults glassworks

**Ingrid Dessau** tablecloth and napkin (1991), made in celebration of the 90th anniversary of the Nobel prize; manufactured by Klässbols Linneväveri AB

**Rudolf Gärdemann** table mat (1987)

**Ulla Grytt** tapestry, *Pelare* (1991)

**AB Elsa Gullberg Textilier och Inredning** tablecloths, linen damask and samples of printed fabrics by different designers (1992)

**Ingela Håkgansson** printed fabric, *Luanda* (1986), manufactured by Borås Wäfveri AB

**Tom Hedqvist** printed fabric, *Bongo* (1985), manufactured by Borås Wäfveri AB

**Åsa Hellman** jug, *Knossos I* (1992)

**Hertha Hillfon** object, *Herthas ansikte* (1975)

**Björn Hultén** chair, *Sally Brown* (1988), manufactured by Gärsnäs AB

**Sven-Eric Juhlin and Maria Bengtzon/Ergonomi Design Gruppen AB** cream jug, sugar bowl and tray (1991), manufactured by Dynoplast A/S

**Jennifer Lee** stoneware pot (1992)

**Gunilla Kihlgren** glass vase (1991), manufactured by Peter Kuchinke, Målerås glassworks

**Anja Kjaer and Darryle Hinz** glasses for champagne, red and white wine, dessert wine and water (1992), made in celebration of the silver wedding of Queen Margrethe and Prince Henrik; manufactured by Holmegaards glassworks

**Bo Klevert** dish, *Hällekar* (1988)

**Eva Maria Kothe** earthenware vase (1992)

**Jonas Palmius** chair, *Excent* (1992), manufactured by Gärsnäs AB

**Gerd Hiort Petersen** porcelain bowl (1991)

**Rigmor Roxner** bowl, *Stjärnform* (1990)

**Thomas Sandell and Bjästa Snickeri** cupboard, *Panik* (1990)

**Astrid Sampe** table mats, *Sigilltablett* (1964), manufactured by Almedahl Dalsjöfors AB

**Richard Sapper** pot (1983), manufactured by Alessi

**Kennet Williamsson** earthenware object (1991)

### Röhsska Konstlöjdmuseet, Gothenburg

**Charlotte Alexandersson** candle-holder (1992)

**Love Arbén** cupboard, *Ono* (1991), manufactured by Lammhults Möbel

**Love Arbén** cabinet, *Parad* (1990), manufactured by Lammhults Möbel

**Kerstin Asling-Sundberg** carpet, *Snowflakes* (1991)

**Hertha Bengtson** vase (1992)

**Karin Bjørquist** design for nine pieces of porcelain for the Nobel Jubilee (1991), manufactured by Gustavsberg/Rörstrand

**Gunnar Cyrén** glassware (11 pieces), manufactured by Orrefors Glasbruk

**Gunnar Cyrén** cutlery, manufactured by Älghult

**Ingrid Dessau** textile, manufactured by Klässbol Linen Factory

**Ingrid Dessau** linen tablecloth designed for the Nobel Jubilee (1991), woven by Klässbol Linen Factory

**Ingrid Dessau** linen damask napkin from the ceremonial equipment of the Nobel Jubilee (1991), woven by Klässbol Linen Factory

**Anna Ehrner** service, *Felicia* (1991), manufactured by Kosta-Boda Glasbruk

**Kjell Engman** service, *Filippa* (1990), manufactured by Kosta-Boda Glasbruk

**Nora Feruzzi** printed silk velvet, *Lolipop* (1991)

**Kaj Franck** vase (1960s), manufactured by Nuutajärvi

**Sven Fristedt** fabric, *Airport* (1988), *Check-in* (1988) and *Gale 1–4* (1988), printed by Borås Wafveri

**Ann-Sofie Gelfius** stoneware bowl (1991)

**Viola Grästen** fabric, *Festivo* (1980s)

**Marie-Louise Hellgren** teacups and saucers (1990), manufactured by Höganäs Keramik AB

**Darryle Hinz and Anja Kjaer** dish (1991)

**Anders Högberg** caddy (1989), manufactured by Alessi SpA

**Bjørn Hultén** chair, *Sally Brown* (1989), manufactured by Gärsnäs AB

**John Kandell** chair, *Camilla* (1990), manufactured by Källemo

**Ingela Karlsson** earthenware dish (1991)

**Jennifer Lee** stoneware pot (1993)

**Ralf Lindberg** chair, *Tati* (1988), manufactured by Gärsnäs AB

**Ralf Lindberg** Chair, *Elle* (1990), manufactured by Gärsnäs AB

**Annika Malmström-Bladini** fabrics, *Avanti* (1983), *Tahiti* (1990) and *Rakel* (1984), manufactured by Strömma; *Allegro* (1960) and *Forte* (1960), manufactured by Mølnlycke

**Anne Nilsson** candlesticks, *Polka* (1992), manufactured by Orrefors Glasbruk

**Signe Persson-Mellin** teabottle and jugs (1990), manufactured by Höganäs Keramik AB

**Ingegerd Råman** stoneware saucer and jug (1992)

**Ingegerd Råman** wine-glasses and vase (1992), manufactured by Skrufs Glasbruk AB

**Thomas Sandell** dining-table/writing-table (1991), manufactured by Element Design AB

**Richard Sapper** kettle with melodic whistle (1983), manufactured by Alessi SpA

**Philippe Starck** lemon squeezer (1990), manufactured by Alessi SpA

**Mats Theselius** porcelain mini-cabinet (1991), manufactured by Agador

**Vivianna Torun Bülow-Hübe** cutlery, *Torun*, manufactured by Dansk International Designs Ltd

**Ann Wåhlstrøm** service, *Terazzo* (1992), manufactured by Kosta-Boda Glasbruk

## Switzerland

### Museum für Gestaltung, Zurich
At present the design collection is not accessible to the public, although a permanent exhibition space is being planned.

**Baltensweiler AG** lamp, *Manhattan*

**André W. Blandenier** fruit plate, mirror, chair, pedestal table and folding screen (1990–92)

**Marcel Breuer** lounge chair (1973), manufactured by Knoll International

**Andreas Christen** table (1980), manufactured by Lehni

**Fabric Frontline** various fabrics (1991–92)

**Sonnhild Kestler** two silk scarves (1992), manufactured by Georg

**Le Corbusier** two wall lamps

**Jo Niemeyer** table lamp, *Tubo* (1984), manufactured by Belux

**Ursula Rodel** various fabrics and sketchbooks (1970–90)

**Marianne Straub** various fabrics

**Karin Wälchli** various fabrics and plates (1991–92)

**Hanspeter Weidmann** plywood table (1991)

## UK

### The Design Museum, London
**G Plan** chairs (1964)

**Hoover** Rainbow Autoboil kettle (1973)

**Morphy Richards** "traditional" copper kettle (1992)

**Russell Hobbs** *Futura* kettle (1977)

**Sinclair** Cambridge calculator (1970s)

### Victoria and Albert Museum, London
**Barker Bros** side plate, *Fiesta*

**Barker Bros** plate (lines and leaf pattern)

**J. Broadhurst and Sons Ltd** side plate, *Pierrot*

**Martin Hunt** four coffee cups, *Technical Trials* (1984)

**Martin Hunt** three tumblers, *Technical Trials* (1984)

**Martin Hunt** oval dish and casserole with lid, *Pyroflam* (1991)

**Walter Keeler** salt-glazed stoneware jug (1990s)

**Robin Levien** teapot, cup, saucer and plate, *Sandie* (1985), manufactured by Johnston Bros

**Alfred Meakin** four side plates (c. 1960)

**Midwinter** coffee service, *Queensbury Stripe* (1963)

**Washington Pottery** side plate, *Polka Dot*

Textiles and Dress:

**Jenny Crisp** cane basket (1992)

**Maggie Henton** cane basket, *Triangular Bowl* (1992)

Pattern books or sample lengths from the following ranges:

**G.P. and J. Baker** *Jour d'Été* (1992)

**Kim Bentley and Sally Spens** *Cherubs*, *Angels* and others (1986–92)

**Neil Bottle and Timorous Beasties** *The Architextural Collection* (1993), manufactured by Warner Fabrics

**Michael Heindorff** *Still Life Collection* (1992), manufactured by Designers Guild

**Lilo** *Wedding Collection* (1992), manufactured by Borås Cotton

Hilton McConnico *Wedding Party* (1990), manufactured by Etamine (DG Distribution)

Hilton McConnico *Les Algues* (1990), manufactured by Etamine (DG Distribution)

Hilton McConnico *En Balade* (1991), manufactured by Etamine (DG Distribution)

John Stefanidis *The Iznik Collection* (1992)

John Stefanidis *Foibles* (1990)

Timorous Beasties hand-printed velvet hanging, *Large Eel* (1991), manufactured by Paul Simmons and Alastair McCauley

Wilton Royal Carpet Factory machine-woven carpet samples by leading designers including Lucienne Day, David Hicks and others (1950s–1980s)

Furniture Collection:

Joe Colombo trolley, *Boby Trolley* (1970), manufactured by Bieffeplast

Tom Dixon armchair, *Fat Chair* (1992), manufactured by Cappellini SpA

Tom Dixon chair, *S Chair* (1992), manufactured by Tom Dixon

Peter Murdoch two stools, *Stool Thing* (1964), manufactured by Eureka!

Rod Wales and Alison Wales cabinet (1993), manufactured by Rod Wales and Alison Wales

Audio systems and radios acquired for display in the Twentieth Century Gallery:

Hitachi portable component system, *TRK-W530E (BS)* (1989)

Inter Electronica SA radio, *TRP 408* (1968–71)

Mike Maloney stereo amplification system, *Aurora* and *Trillium* (1985), manufactured by Scientific Fidelity

Matsushita Electric Industrial Co. Ltd portable stereo/CD/tape and radio system, *RX-DS45* (1990)

Philips radio, *Philitina L2X 1OT* (1963)

Roberts' Radio transistor, *R500* (1964)

Sharp Corp. portable radio, *QT 50E* (1986)

Sharp Corp. radio, solid state AM transistor, *BP-156* (1970–72)

Sony Corp. radio cassette recorder, *My First Sony CFM-2500* (1992)

Sony Corp. radio, *Credit Card 1CR 501* (1985)

Sony Corp. personal stereo, *Stowaway TPS-L2* (1979–80)

Sony Corp. personal stereo, *Sony Sports Walkman FM* (1982–87)

Sony Corp. headphones, *MDR-3L2* (1979–80)

Daniel Weil *Radio in a Bag* (1980)

## USA

### The Brooklyn Museum, New York

Jaroslava Brychtová and Stanislav Libensky cast glass, *Spaces II* (1991–92)

Morison Cousins and Douglas Laib canister set, *Tupperware One Touch* (1990–91), manufactured by Tupperware

Eva Eisler brooch (1991)

Douglas G. Fitch armchair (1985), manufactured by Knoll (1985–86)

Frank Gehry chair and ottoman, *Power Play* (1991), manufactured by Knoll

Karen Karnes jar (1975)

Jung-Hoo Kim brooch, *Life in the Circus* (1987)

Jung-Hoo Kim brooch, *The Florid Wall* (1992)

Michael Lacktman chalice (c. 1965)

Warren MacKenzie tea bowl (c. 1980)

Nancy Meeker tea bowl (c. 1980)

Nancy Meeker bottle (c. 1980)

Nancy Meeker plate (c. 1980)

Peter Todd Mitchell printed wallpaper, wallpaper designs and textile designs (1949–62)

Peter Todd Mitchell chair, *Bean Bag* (c. 1965)

Frank Rebajes ring (c. 1975)

Frank Rebajes bracelet (c. 1975)

Frank Rebajes ring (c. 1975)

John Torreano vase (1991)

Peter Voulkos plate (1980)

Beatrice Wood chalice (c. 1975)

Arnold Zimmerman untitled sculpture, manufactured 1988

### Cooper-Hewitt Museum, New York

Gijs Bakker light, *Paraplulamp* (1973)

Miguel Calvo flower vase and stand, *Flexi* (1992–93)

Alison Filippo samovar, *Vesevo* (1984), manufactured by Sabattini Argenteria

Alison Filippo coffeepot, *Filumena 2* (1984), manufactured by Sabattini Argenteria

Carlo Forcolini light, *Polifemo* (1983), manufactured by Artemide

Carlo Forcolini light, *Nestore* (1988), manufactured by Artemide

Carlo Forcolini chairs, *Miro* (1989), manufactured by Alias

Carlo Forcolini table, *Onlyou*, manufactured by Alias

Rund Jan Kokke *Museum Wander Stool TC* (1990), manufactured by Vormegeversassociatie

Cheryl Riley two *Tudor Coin Encrusted Tables* (1992), manufactured by Right Angle Interiors

Stiletto Studios armchair, *Consumer's Rest* (c. 1991)

Norman Vincent Sukkar side chair, *Square* (1992–93)

### Denver Art Museum

Achille Castiglioni lamp, *Snoopy* (1967), manufactured by Flos

Gerard Dalmon side chair, *YM* (1988), manufactured by Néotù

Marcello Fantoni bowl (c. 1960)

Elsa Freund bracelet and earrings (1965)

Kristian Gavoille side chair, *Atheo* (1991), manufactured by Néotù

Keith Evan Hayes section and elevations for the Seattle Art Museum, Seattle, Washington (1990)

Arne Jacobsen teapot, *Cylinda* (1967), manufactured by Stelton

Arne Jacobsen coffee pot, *Cylinda* (1967), manufactured by Stelton

Henner Kuckuck armchair, *K3* (1922–93)

George Ranalli door handle (1991), manufactured by Union Company Ltd

Jørgen Rasmussen side chair, *Kevi* (no. 1904), (1970), manufactured by Knoll International

David Rowland side chair, *10/1* (1964), manufactured by GF Business Furniture

David Rowland side chair, *40/4* (1964), manufactured by GF Business Furniture

Richard Sapper minitimer (1960s), manufactured by Terraillon

Richard Schultz coffee table, *#3421* (1966), manufactured by Knoll Associates Inc.

**Kevin D. Scott** perspective, site plan and elevation of visionary project, *Redon Bay Complex* (1992)

**Ettore Sottsass** telephone (c. 1986) manufactured by Enorme Corporation

**Ettore Sottsass** plate, *Renaissance* (1986), manufactured by Swid Powell

**George James Sowden** cabinet, *d'Antibe* (1981), manufactured by Memphis

**Kazuhide Takahama** lounge chair, *Suzanne* (1969), manufactured by Knoll International

**Robert Venturi** cold meat fork and pierced tablespoon (1992), manufactured by Reed & Barton Silversmiths for Swid Powell

## Metropolitan Museum of Art, New York

**Morison Cousins** bowl, *Soup to Nuts* (prototype) (1991)

**Hans Hollein** wristwatch, *Parentesi* (1991), manufactured by Cleto Munari

**John Horn** carving set (1986)

**Mary Merkel-Hess** basket, *Brown Reed* (1989)

**Ettore Sottsass** fruit bowl, *Murmansk* (1982), manufactured by Memphis

**Philippe Starck** flatware (prototype) (1987), manufactured by Sasaki

**Gino Valle** clock, *Cifra 3* (1965), manufactured by Solari

**Richard Yelle** *Elegant Vase* (1991)

## Museum of Modern Art, New York

**Junichi Arai** scarf (1989), manufactured by NUNO Corporation

**Frank Gehry** dining table, *Easy Edges* (1982)

**Frank Gehry** six side chairs, *Easy Edges* (1982)

**Frank Gehry** armchair, *Cross Check* (1991)

**Frank Gehry** armchair, *Power Play* (1991)

**Ari 'T Hart** fishing reed (1990), manufactured by ATH Design International

**Peter Karpf** side chair (1991), manufactured by Swedese Möbler AB

**Ruud Jan Kokke** stacking stools, *Wander* (1990), manufactured by Designum

**Rolf Kothrade and Kurt Zimmereli** water flask (1992), manufactured by SIGG

**Kyoko Kumai** wall hanging, *Wind from the Cloud* (1992)

**David Lewis** subwoofer loudspeaker, *Beovox Cona* (1988), manufactured by Bang & Olufsen of America

**David Lewis** loudspeakers, *Beolab 6000* (1992), manufactured by Bang & Olufsen of America

**Mallory Industries** nine three-dimensional cams, manufactured by Mallory Industries

**Reiko Sudo** fabric (1990), manufactured by NUNO Corporation

## Philadelphia Museum of Art

**Carol Cassidy** hand-woven hanging (1992), manufactured by LAO Textiles

**Carol Cassidy** silk tapestry and compound weave (1993)

**Chungi Choo** decanter (1980)

**Wharton Esherick** music stand (1960)

**Thomas A. Hoadley** Nerikomi vessel (1992)

**James Krenov** cabinet (1992)

**Shiro Kuramata** chair, *How High the Moon* (1986), manufactured by Vitra GmbH

**Dona Look** basket with lid

**Sam Maloof** rocking chair (1977)

**Ingo Maurer** lamp, *Bibibibi* (1982), manufactured by Design M Ingo Maurer GmbH

**Judy McKie** panther bench (1982)

**Faith Ringgold** quilt, *Tar Beach II/24* (c. 1990)

**Richard Sapper** tea kettle (1983), manufactured by Alessi SpA

**David Shaner** bowl

**Toshiko Takaezu** form (1990)

**Beatrice Wood** chalice

**Beatrice Wood** bowl

**Toots (Mary Ann) Zynsky** untitled landscape (1992)